Fodo
Florence,
Tuscany &
Umbria

D0377901

Reprinted from *Fodor's Italy*
Fodor's Travel Publications, Inc.
New York • Toronto • London • Sydney • Auckland

Fodor's Florence, Tuscany & Umbria

Editors: Joan Fisher Carroll, Robert I. C. Fisher, Kristin Moehlmann, Alison Stern
Editorial Contributors: Robert Andrews, Barbara Walsh Angelillo, Echo Garrett, Holly Hughes, Laura M. Kidder, Dawn Lawson, Bevin McLaughlin, Melanie Roth, Mary Ellen Schultz, George Sullivan, Nancy van Itallie
Creative Director: Fabrizio La Rocca
Cartographer: David Lindroth
Illustrator: Karl Tanner
Cover Photograph: Antonio Sferlazzo

Design: Vignelli Associates

Special Sales

Contents

Maps

Foreword

We would like to express our gratitude to Barbara Walsh Angelillo and Rob Andrews for their patience, enthusiasm, and hard work.

While every care has been taken to ensure the accuracy of the information in this guide, the passage of time will always bring change, and consequently, the publisher cannot accept responsibility for errors that may occur.

All prices and opening times quoted here are based on information supplied to us at press time. Hours and admission fees may change, however, and the prudent traveler will avoid inconvenience by calling ahead.

Fodor's wants to hear about your travel experiences, both pleasant and unpleasant. When a hotel or restaurant fails to live up to its billing, let us know and we will investigate the complaint and revise our entries where the facts warrant it.

Send your letters to the editors of Fodor's Travel Publications, 201 E. 50th Street, New York, NY 10022.

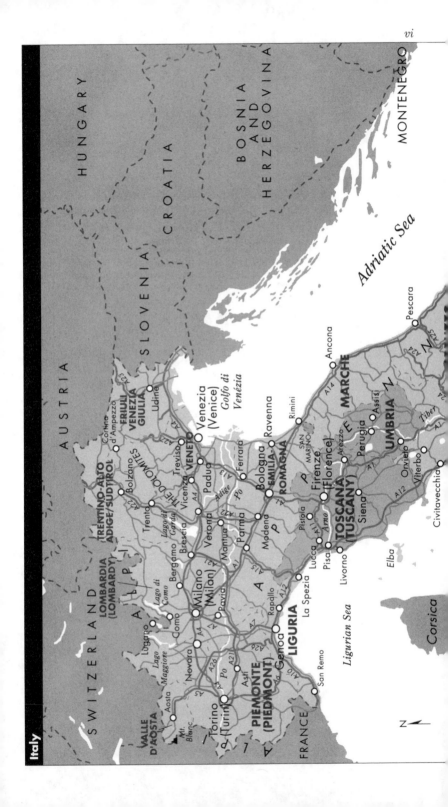

Italy

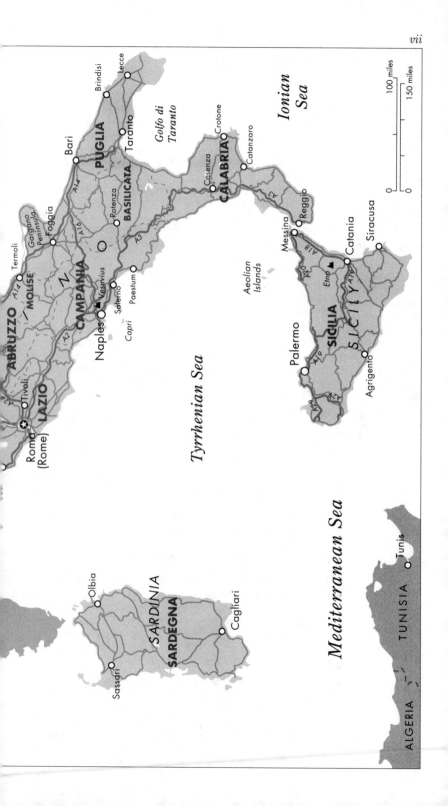

Introduction

By Robert Andrews

Born and educated in England, writer/ journalist Robert Andrews inherited his interest in Italy from his Italian mother. He contributes to Harpers & Queen, Time Out, *and other magazines as well as to travel books.*

Just as Tuscany and Umbria straddle the boot, so their contribution to the Italian jigsaw is massive and inescapable. Their influence pervades Italian culture and percolates far beyond, to the extent that their impact has been felt throughout European and even world history. Tuscany—and to a lesser extent Umbria—saw the birth of humanism, that classically leaning, secular-tending current that effloresced in the Renaissance and to which the West owes its cultural complexion. In the graphic arts, architecture, astronomy, sculpture, engineering, art history, poetry, political theory, biography . . . in every field of human endeavor the people of these regions have loomed large. The Italian language itself is Tuscan, due largely to Dante's use of his local dialect to compose his *Divine Comedy*. When Italy became a modern state in 1865, Florence was the natural choice for the national capital until Rome's entry six years later.

It is hard to think of any other area that has seen such a dense concentration of human achievement as Tuscany and Umbria, but it is equally difficult to find anywhere so riven by conflict and factions. The strange thing is how neatly the periods of maximum creativity and bellicosity coincided. Was the restless, innovative impulse a consequence of the social turmoil, or the principal cause of it? It is surely no accident that Tuscany and Umbria in general and Florence in particular contain the most quarrelsome elements ever thrown together, as a cursory flip through some of the names in the local annals can testify: the Florentine Niccolò Machiavelli, who became a very synonym for the Devil (Old Nick); Savonarola, whose energetic career pitched church and state into headlong confrontation, igniting the famous "Bonfire of Vanities" in Florence's main square, site of the Dominican friar's own incineration not long afterwards; the town of Pistoia, from which the word "pistol" is derived; Perugia, populated, according to the historian Sigismondo, by "the most warlike people in Italy, who always preferred Mars to the Muse" . . . the very street-names of Florence and Siena recall the clash of medieval factions. Outside the towns, there is hardly a hill, stream, or mountain pass whose name does not evoke some siege, battle, or act of treachery. The historic rivalry of Guelph and Ghibelline never reached such intense acrimony as in these seemingly tranquil hills, and nowhere was allegiance worn so lightly, with communes and families swapping sides whenever their rivals changed theirs.

The sense of opposition is alive in Tuscany and Umbria today just as strongly as it ever was. Visitors can witness it on every two-toned marble church front. Blacks and whites imperial, feudal and commercial, Renaissance and Gothic—the antagonism is embedded in art history, revived in every discussion of the background of every great work. It is a fixed feature of the local scene: the Sienese are still suspicious of the Florentines, the

Florentines disdainful of the Sienese, while Siena itself seems to live in a permanent state of warfare within its own city walls, as any spectator of the Palio and the months of preparation that precede it can testify. Outsiders contribute to the debate: for Mary McCarthy, Florence was manly, Siena feminine, and tourists take sides whenever they lay down their reasons for preferring Florence to Siena or vice versa, as if there had to be a dualistic appreciation of the two.

Walking through the city streets of present-day Florence, you can't fail to be struck by the contrast between the austere and unwelcoming external appearance of the palaces and the sumptuous comforts within, or by the 1990s elegance and modernity of the Florentines in the midst of the thoroughly medieval churches and piazzas. Florence is a modern industrial city, and the Florentines themselves perennial modernists, their eyes fixed firmly in front. This helps to explain both their past inventiveness and the ambivalent attitude they hold toward that same past, composed of roughly equal parts of ennui and fierce pride. To its inhabitants, that the city of Florence stands on a par with Athens and Rome is self-evident: To them tourism, which feeds on the past, is reactionary, decadent, and often intrusive, making a burden of the historical heritage. It is tolerated as a business, in a city that has a high regard for business . . . but it is only one of many. In Italy, Florentines are reckoned the most impenetrable, cautious, and circumspect of Italians, a reputation they have held since the days of the Medicis. Nevertheless, Italians have coined a word—*fiorentinità*—to refer to the good taste and fine workmanship that are flaunted here, in a city renowned for its leather goods, handbags, shoes, jewelry, and a host of famous brand-names. Pucci, Gucci, Ferragamo, Cellerini are just four of the high-profile craft-turned-fashion designers that exude *fiorentinitá*. Neither are the region's cuisine and fine wines to be taken lightly. Talk to any Florentines about these present-day aspects of their civilization, and they will perk up and debate enthusiastically; mention their past glories and they will stifle a yawn.

Other Tuscan cities possess the same compelling mix of elements: What Tuscany's older centers share is an immaculate medieval setting, modern life taking place within the shell of the past; what divides them is a complex mental set. Needless to say, all of them were rivals at one time or another, and each prevailed in distinct spheres. Pisa, for example, was one of Italy's four great maritime republics, its architectural style visible wherever its ships touched port. Once the most powerful force in the Tyrrhenian, it lost its hegemony on the sea to its trading rival, Genoa, and, land, to Florence. Pisa owed its prestige to a university that bequeathed a scholarly, scientific, and legal tradition to the town, and to its location on the River Arno, though this position much later was responsible for its being one of the most devastated cities in World War II. Skillful rebuilding has ensured a relatively harmonious appearance, however, and the city would still hold plenty of interest if the Leaning Tower had never been built.

Livorno, on the other hand, the main Tuscan port of today, is the Pisa that never was. By Tuscan standards it is a recent affair, developed as a sea outlet for Florence after Pisa's port had silted up. Livorno reveals a highly un-Tuscan cosmopolitan character, a result of 16th-century growth that brought immigration. Livorno's most famous son, the sculptor Amedeo Modigliani, for example, was brought up speaking French, Italian, English, and Hebrew, though in other ways this hard-drinking Bohemian did not typify the soberly respectable citizens for whom Livorno is best known. Also heavily bombed in the war, the port was not restored as tastefully as Pisa, though it can at least boast a vigorous culinary tradition, with its range of fresh seafood.

South from Livorno stretches a riviera of varying degrees of summer saturation, including numerous select spots where sun- and sea-bathing can be enjoyed in relative peace. The island of Elba—scene of Napoléon's nine-month incarceration—is today more likely to be somewhere to escape to rather than from, and together with the islands of Giglio and Capraia offers everything from absurd overdevelopment to true isolation.

Lucca, the principal enemy of Pisa during the Middle Ages, has been called "the most enchanting walled town in the world." The city's formidable girdle of walls has resisted the intrusions of modern life better than any other Tuscan center and contains within a wealth of palaces and churches wildly out of proportion to the size of what is, after all, a small provincial town. Much of Lucca's present-day success is based on, of all things, the manufacture of lingerie.

A much weightier substance—gold—forms, together with antique furniture, the basis of the wealth of the less imposing town of Arezzo. Such worldly items again form a counterpoint to the fact that this town has produced more than its fair share of pioneers in literature (Petrarch, Pietro Aretino), art (Vasari), and music (Guido d'Arezzo, also called Guido Monaco, inventor of notation and the musical scale).

Arezzo shares a university with Siena, another Tuscan town preserved in the aspic of its medieval past. It is said that there are three subjects you should avoid if you're in a hurry while in Siena: wild pigs (a prized quarry for hunters), the Palio (an object of fanatical zeal), and the battle of Montanerti (Siena's moment of military glory—a perennial obsession). To the rest of Italy, Siena is best known for its banks and its mystics—a characteristically incompatible duo—though foreign visitors are more enchanted by the city's artworks, its easy pace of life, and the pleasing hue of its rose-colored buildings.

Prato and Pistoia, a short roll up the *autostrada* (toll highway) from Florence, have traditionally fallen within the sphere of that city's influence. Prato combines some choice examples of Renaissance art and architecture with a strong industrial identity, mainly based on its wool exports; Pistoia, on the other hand, was renowned for its ironwork, and its citizens for their murderous propensities.

Across the regional boundary in Umbria, the hilltop town of Perugia is dominated by the cold gothic stone of its major monuments, its secretive alleys and steps, yet its animating spirit is among the most progressive and trend-setting in Italy. Within its medieval walls the town hosts one of Europe's prime jazz festivals, a modern tradition that has taken its lead from the international Two Worlds festival at nearby Spoleto. As in Tuscany, modernity lives alongside medievalism in Umbria, a case not so much of collision as coexistence. In the same spirit, the imposing monuments of its towns were built by a new wealthy mercantile class in the teeth of almost uninterrupted warfare throughout the Middle Ages. Spoleto, Gubbio, and Orvieto owed their influence not so much to their continual brawling as to their interchange of goods and ideas. A university was founded in Perugia as early as 1308, and it was the small Umbrian town of Foligno that published the first edition of Dante's *Divine Comedy*. The belligerence of the age paralleled an intense spiritual activity, championed by such towering religious figures as St. Francis, St. Clare, St. Benedict, and the locally venerated St. Rita (as well as the more worldly St. Valentine)—a legacy nowhere so apparent as in the town of Assisi.

Although many of the urban centers of Tuscany and Umbria have cleanly defined boundaries beyond which the countryside abruptly begins, the towns harmonize with the surrounding landscape more closely than anywhere else in Italy. Even if devoid of museums or souvenir shops, the hinterland holds as much of the region's quintessential character as the cities of Tuscany and Umbria, and such unsung treasures as San Gimignano, Todi, and Bevagna are as revealing as anything seen in the galleries. This is your chance to immerse yourself in the region's less tangible pleasures, to rest your eyes on the gentle ochre stone of villages artfully situated above vine-strung, neatly terraced slopes. From the wine-producing hills of Chianti to the Carrara mountains where Michelangelo quarried to the soft contours of the Vale of Spoleto, the tidy cypress-speared landscape displays a weird inertia like some illustration from a fable. It has a geometric precision that underlines the strict rural economy practiced by the Tuscan and Umbrian peasants, for whom every tree has its purpose. The Tuscans in particular have long been considered the most skilled and intelligent of Italian farmers, having created for themselves a region that is largely self-sufficient, producing a little of everything, and excelling in certain areas, not least in wine-production, for which the Tuscans have nurtured one of the most dynamic wine regions of Italy.

Like the great examples of urban architecture, the country in Tuscany and Umbria presents, for the most part, an ordered, rational, controlled appearance. It is the crust of civilization concealing the greatest paradox of all in this heartland of reason and classical elegance. For buried underneath lies a much older, earthier civilization of which most visitors to the region are oblivious. In every respect the ancient Etruscan civilization that flourished here was opposed to the values of the Renaissance, its vital, animistic spirit murky, dark, and mysterious to us, mainly known from subterranean tombs and wall-paintings. Almost erased from the face of the earth by the Romans, the Etruscan culture—its centers scattered throughout Tuscany and Umbria (Perugia, Orvieto, Chiusi, Roselle, Vetulonia, Volterra, Cortona, Arezzo, Fiesole were the main ones)—was central to the history of Tuscany and Umbria. Like the Hermes Trimegistus incongruously placed on the marble pavement of Siena's cathedral, the Etruscans are a mischievous element amid the harmony of Renaissance Tuscany and Umbria. Their precise influence is unclear, but it may well turn out to have been the contentious and destructive spirit ever-present in the golden age of these regions, harassing, hindering, entangling. Alternatively, it may have been the restless worm of invention, the defiant individuality that brought about the triumph of art in the face of adversity—which is, after all, the greatest achievement of Tuscany and Umbria.

1 Essential Information

Before You Go

Government Tourist Offices

In the U.S. Contact the Italian Government Travel Office at 630 5th Avenue, Suite 1565, New York, NY 10111, tel. 212/245–4822, fax 212/586–9249; 500 N. Michigan Avenue, Chicago, IL 60611, tel. 312/644–0990, fax 312/644–3019; 12400 Wilshire Blvd., Suite 550, Los Angeles, CA 90025, tel. 310/820–0098, fax 310/820–6357.

U.S. Government Travel Briefings The U.S. Department of State's **Overseas Citizens Emergency Center** (Room 4811, Washington, DC 20520; enclose S.A.S.E.) issues Consular Information Sheets, which cover crime, security, political climate, and health risks, as well as embassy locations, entry requirements, currency regulations, and other routine matters. For the latest information, stop in at any U.S. passport office, consulate, or embassy; call the interactive hot line (tel. 202/647–5225; fax 202/647–3000); or, with your PC's modem, tap into the Bureau of Consular Affairs' computer bulletin board (tel. 202/647–9225).

In Canada 1 Place Ville Marie, Montréal, Québec H3B 3M9, tel. 514/866–7667.

In the U.K. 1 Princes Street, London W1R 8AY England, tel. 0171/408–1254.

Tours and Packages

Should you buy your travel arrangements to Florence, Tuscany, and Umbria already packaged or should you do it yourself? There are advantages either way. You can save money by buying a package, particularly if you find one that includes exactly what you want, and you will have a pretty good idea what your trip will cost from the outset. As to most destinations, packages to Italy come in two forms: fully escorted tours and independent packages. Escorted tours are generally the most hassle-free way to see a city or region, as well as generally the least expensive. Taking a tour means traveling with strangers, most often via motor coach, with a tour director in charge. Your baggage is handled, your time rigorously scheduled, and most meals are planned. Independent packages allow flexibility. They generally include airline travel and hotels, with other options available, such as sightseeing, car rental, and excursions. They are usually more expensive than escorted tours, but your time is your own.

Travel agents are the best source of information for both tours and independent packages. They should have a large selection available, and the cost to you is the same as buying direct. Whatever program you ultimately choose, be sure to find out exactly what is included: taxes, tips, transfers, meals, baggage handling, ground transportation, entertainment, excursions, sports, or recreation (and rental equipment if necessary). Ask about the level of hotel used, its location, the size of its rooms, the kind of beds, and amenities such as pools, room service, or programs for children, if they're important to you. Find out the operator's cancellation penalties. Nearly everyone charges them, and the only way to avoid them is to buy trip-cancellation insurance (*see* Trip Insurance, *below*). Also ask about the single supplement, a surcharge assessed to solo travelers. Some operators do not make you pay it if you agree to be matched with a roommate of the same sex, even if one is not found by departure time. Remember that a program that has features you won't use, whether for rental sporting equipment or discounted museum admissions, may not be the most cost-wise choice for you. Don't buy a Rolls-Royce, even at a reduced price, if all you want is a Chevy!

Fully Escorted Tours Escorted tours are usually sold in three categories: deluxe, first-class, and tourist or budget class. The most important differences are the price, of course, and the level of accommodations. Some operators specialize in one category, while others offer a range. The following companies offer tours that include destinations in Tuscany and Umbria.

In the deluxe category, try **Maupintour** (Box 807, Lawrence, KS 66044, tel. 800/255–4266 or 913/843–1211) or **Tauck Tours** (11 Wilton Rd., Westport, CT 06881, tel. 203/226–6911 or 800/468–2825). In the first-class category, which has the broadest selection of tours, offerings include **Brendan Tours** (15137 Califa St., Van Nuys, CA 91411, tel. 818/785–9696 or 800/421–8446), **Caravan** (401 N. Michigan Ave., Chicago, IL 60611, tel. 800/227–2826), **Central Holiday Tours** (206 Central Ave., Jersey City, NJ 07307, tel.201/798–5777 or 800/935–5000), **Certified Vacations** (Box 1525, Ft. Lauderdale, FL 33302, tel. 305/522–1414 or 800/233–7260), **CIT Tours Corp.** (342 Madison Ave., Suite 207, New York, NY 10173, tel. 212/697–2100 or 800/248–8687; 310/670–4269 or 800/248–7245 in western U.S.), **Donna Franca Tours** (470 Commonwealth Ave., Boston, MA 02215, tel. 617/227–3111 or 800/225–6290), **Globus** (5301 S. Federal Cir., Littleton, CO 80123, tel. 303/797–2800 or 800/221–0090), **Trafalgar Tours** (21 E. 26th St., New York, NY 10010, tel. 212/689–8977 or 800/854–0103), and **Travcoa** (Box 2630, Newport Beach, CA 92658, tel. 714/476–2800 or 800/992–2003). Escorted programs from **Perillo Tours** (577 Chestnut Ridge Rd., Woodcliff Lake, NJ 07675, tel. 201/307–1234 or 800/431–1515), particularly those that feature as many as four nights in one city, have some flexibility. Budget offerings include programs from **AESU Travel** (2 Hamill Rd., Suite 248, Baltimore, MD 21210, tel. 410/323–4416 or 800/638–7640), **Cosmos Tourama,** a sister company of **Globus** (*see above*), and the "Cost Savers" of **Trafalgar Tours** (*see above*).

Most itineraries are jam-packed with sightseeing, so you see a lot in a short amount of time (usually one place per day). To judge just how fast-paced the tour is, review the itinerary carefully. If you are in a different hotel each night, you will be getting up early each day to head out, travel to your next destination, do some sightseeing, have dinner, and go to bed, then you'll start all over again. If you want some free time, make sure it's mentioned in the tour brochure; if you want to be escorted to every meal, confirm that any tour you consider does that. Also, when comparing programs, be sure to find out if the motor coach is air-conditioned and has a rest room on board. Make your choice based on price and stops on the itinerary.

Independent Packages Independent packages, which travel agents call FITS (for foreign independent travel), are offered by airlines, tour operators who may also do escorted programs, and any number of other companies from large, established firms to small, new entrepreneurs. Among the many programs with a wide choice of hotels and sightseeing options, some with car rentals, are **Abercrombie & Kent** (1520 Kensington Rd., Oak Brook, IL 60521, tel. 708/954–2944 or 800/323–7308), **American Airlines Fly AAway Vacations** (tel. 800/321–2121), **Certified Vacations** (*see above*), **CIT Tours** (*see above*), **Continental's Grand Destinations** (tel. 800/634–5555), **DER Tours** (11933 Wilshire Blvd., Los Angeles, CA 90025, tel. 310/479–4140 or 800/782–2424), **Italiatour** (tel. 800/237–0517), **TWA Getaway Vacations** (tel. 800/438–2929), **United Airlines' Vacation Planning Center** (tel. 800/328–6877), and **V E Tours** (1150 N.W. 72nd Ave., Suite 450, Miami, FL 33126, tel. 800/222–8383).

These programs come in a wide range of prices based on levels of luxury and options—in addition to hotel and airfare, sightseeing, car rental, transfers, admission to local attractions, and other extras may be offered. Again, base your choice on what's available in your budget for the destinations you want to visit.

Special-Interest Travel Italy caters to the special-interest traveler, particularly if your special interest is eating well. But everything from ballooning to biking is also available. Special-interest programs may be fully escorted or independent. Some require a certain amount of expertise, but most are for the average traveler with an interest in the subject, and they are usually hosted by experts. When the program is escorted, it enjoys the advantages and disadvantages of all escorted programs; because your fellow travelers are apt to be passionate or knowledgeable about the subject, they can prove as enjoyable a part of your travel experience as the destination itself. The price range is wide, but the cost is usually higher—sometimes a lot higher—than for ordinary escorted tours and packages, because of the expert guidance and special activities.

Adventure **Mountain Travel Sobek** (6420 Fairmount Ave., El Cerrito, CA 94530, tel. 510/527–8100 or 800/227–2384) and **Wilderness Travel** (801 Allston Way, Berkeley, CA 94710, tel. 510/548–0420 or 800/368–2794) can take you on hiking tours through the medieval hill towns of Tuscany.

Art and Architecture Major American museums sponsor escorted art and architecture tours to Italy, often led by art historians. For instance, New York City's Metropolitan Museum of Art (tel. 212/879–5500, Development Office) offers a "Genius of Italy" tour, with stops in Lucca and Pisa. **Esplanade Tours** (581 Boylston St., Boston, MA 02116, tel. 617/266–7465 or 800/426–5492) has art-treasure tours and cruises with guest lecturers.

Ballooning **Buddy Bombard Balloon Adventures** (6727 Curran St., McLean, VA 22101–3804, tel. 703/448–9407 or 800/862–8537) takes groups of a dozen or fewer for gentle floats above Siena, San Gimignano, and the rolling hills of the Tuscan countryside. Fine dining back on the ground complements the program.

Biking **Backroads** (1516 5th St., Suite Q333, Berkeley, CA 94710–1740, tel. 510/527–1555 or 800/245–3874) has trips for all levels of ability, with inn accommodations and a sag wagon just in case the hills are too much for you.

Food **Lorenza de'Medici's Villa Table** (Badia a Coltibuono, 53013, Gaiole in Chianti, SI, tel. 0577/749498, fax 0577/749235; U.S. address: Judy Ferrell Ebrey, The Villa Table, 7707 Willow Vine Ct., Dallas, TX 75230, tel. 214/373–1161) offers weeklong courses for English-speaking visitors at a restored 17th-century monastery and winery, taught by the renowned author of 20 cookbooks, including *Italy: The Beautiful Cookbook* (Harper/Collins) and *The Renaissance of Italian Cooking* (Fawcett/Columbine). The school is within an hour's drive from Siena and Florence. **Giuliano Bugialli's Cooking in Florence** (Via dei Pilastri 52, 50121 Florence, tel. 055/242128, fax 055/245356; U.S. address: Box 1650, Canal St. Station, New York, NY 10013, tel. 212/966–5325) is another famous cooking school. Bugialli, a native of Florence and author of the best-selling *Foods of Italy* (Stewart, Tabori & Chang), conducts classes at a centuries-old farmhouse located just outside Florence; he also organizes cooking tours through regions of Italy.

Gardens **Endless Beginnings** (9825 Dowdy Dr., Suite 105, San Diego, CA 92126, tel. 619/566–4166 or 800/822–7855) visits Tuscan gardens and villas.

Horseback Riding **FITS Equestrian** (685 Lateen Rd., Solvang, CA 93463, tel. 805/688–9494 or 800/666–3487) has a trio of "City Slickers Go Italian" tours.

Music **Dailey-Thorp Travel** (330 W. 58th St., New York, NY 10019, tel. 212/307–1555), a performing arts specialist, offers music and opera tours to Italy. **Smolka Tours** (Box 856, Frederick, MD 21705, tel. 301/695–3661 or 800/722–0057) can arrange custom summer Italian opera, concert, and music festival tours.

Nature In the United Kingdom, **Ramblers Holidays Ltd.** (Longcroft House, Fretherne Rd., Welwyn Garden City, Hertfordshire AL8 6PQ, tel 01707/331133) has a one- to two-week walking tour package in Siena.

When to Go

The main tourist season runs from mid-April to the end of September. The best months for sightseeing are April, May, June, September, and October, when the weather is generally pleasant and not too hot. The hottest months are July and August, when brief afternoon thunderstorms are common in inland areas. Winters are relatively mild but always include some rainy spells.

Foreign tourists crowd the major art cities at Easter, when Italians flock to resorts and to the country. From March through May, bus loads of eager schoolchildren on excursions take cities of artistic and historical interest by storm.

If you can avoid it, don't travel at all in Italy in August, when much of the population is on the move. The heat can be oppressive, and vacationing Italians cram roads, trains, and planes on their way to shore and mountain resorts. All this is especially true around Ferragosto, the August 15 national holiday.

Florence has no off-season as far as hotel rates go, though some hotels will reduce rates during the slack season upon request.

You may want to plan your trip to take in some spectacular local *festa* (festival) or to satisfy a special interest—in opera, food, or wine, for instance. From May through September the calendar is dotted with local folkloric festivals and other special events; outdoor music and opera festivals are held mainly in July and August (*see* Festivals and Seasonal Events, *below*).

Climate The following are average daily maximum and minimum temperatures for Florence and Assisi.

Florence								
Jan.	48F	9C	**May**	73F	23C	**Sept.**	79F	26C
	36	2		54	12		59	15
Feb.	52F	11C	**June**	81F	27C	**Oct.**	68F	20C
	37	3		59	15		52	11
Mar.	57F	14C	**July**	86F	30C	**Nov.**	57F	14C
	41	5		64	18		45	7
Apr.	66F	19C	**Aug.**	86F	30C	**Dec.**	52F	11C
	46	8		63	17		39	10

Assisi	Jan.	45F	7C	May	70F	21C	Sept.	75F	24C
		36	2		52	11		59	15
	Feb.	48F	9C	June	77F	25C	Oct.	64F	18C
		36	2		59	15		52	11
	Mar.	54F	12C	July	82F	28C	Nov.	55F	13C
		41	5		64	18		45	7
	Apr.	61F	16C	Aug.	82F	28C	Dec.	48F	9C
		46	8		63	17		39	4

Information Sources For current weather conditions and forecasts for cities abroad, plus the local time and helpful travel tips, call the **Weather Channel Connection** (tel. 900/932–8437; 95¢ per minute) from a Touch-Tone phone.

Festivals and Seasonal Events

Top seasonal events in Florence, Tuscany, and Umbria include carnival celebrations in January and February; Epiphany celebrations in January; Easter celebrations in Florence; the Florence May Music Festival; and Siena's Palio horse race in July and August. Contact the **Italian Government Travel Office** for exact dates and further information.

January 5–6 **Epiphany Celebrations.** Roman Catholic Epiphany celebrations and decorations are evident throughout Tuscany and Umbria.

February **Carnival in Viareggio.** Masked pageants, fireworks, a flower show, and parades are among the festivities along the Tuscan Riviera.

Easter Sunday (April 16, 1995) (April 14, 1996) The **Scoppio del Carro,** or "Explosion of the Cart," in Florence, is a cartful of fireworks in the Cathedral Square, set off by a mechanical dove released from the altar during High Mass.

Late April– Early July The **Florence May Music Festival** is the oldest and most prestigious Italian festival of the performing arts.

Mid-May **Race of the Candles.** This procession, in local costume, leads to the top of Mount Ingino in Gubbio.

Late May The **Palio of the Archers** is a medieval crossbow contest in Gubbio.

Early June The **Battle of the Bridge,** in Pisa, is a medieval parade and contest. The **Regatta of the Great Maritime Republics** sees keen competition among the four former maritime republics—Amalfi, Genoa, Pisa, and Venice.

Mid-June– Mid-July The **Festival of Two Worlds,** in Spoleto, is a famous performing-arts festival.

Late June **Soccer Games in 16th-Century Costume,** in Florence, commemorate a match played in 1530. Festivities include fireworks displays.

Early July and Mid-August The **Palio Horse Race,** in Siena, is a colorful bareback horse race with participants competing for the *palio* (banner).

Early August The **Joust of the Quintana** is a historical pageant in Ascoli Piceno.

Late August– Early Sept. The **Siena Music Week** features opera, concerts, and chamber music.

Early Sept. The **Joust of the Saracen** is a tilting contest with knights in 13th-century armor in Arezzo.

Mid-Sept. The **Joust of the Quintana** is a 17th-century-style joust and historical procession in Foligno.

October 4 The **Feast of St. Francis** is celebrated in Assisi, his birthplace.

What to Pack

Clothing   The weather is considerably milder in Tuscany and Umbria all year round than it is in the north and central United States or Great Britain. In summer, stick with clothing that's as light as possible, although a sweater or woolen stole may be necessary in the cool of the evening, even during the hot months. Brief summer afternoon thunderstorms are common in inland cities, so carry an umbrella. And if you go into the mountains, you will find the evenings there quite chilly. During the winter a medium-weight coat and a raincoat will stand you in good stead. Central heating may not be up to your standards and interiors can be cold and damp; take wools rather than sheer fabrics, flannel rather than flimsy nightwear, and boots or shoes that can accommodate socks rather than dainty pumps. As a matter of fact, pack sturdy walking shoes, preferably with crepe or rubber soles, at any time of the year, because cobblestone streets and gravel paths are common and can be murder on both feet and footwear.

In general, Italians dress well and are not sloppy. They do not usually wear shorts in the city, unless longish bermudas happen to be in fashion. Even when dressed casually or informally, they are careful about the way they look, which is why so few restaurants establish dress codes. Men aren't required to wear ties or jackets anywhere, except in some of the grander hotel dining rooms and top-level restaurants. Formal wear is the exception rather than the rule at the opera nowadays, though people in expensive seats usually do get dressed up.

Dress codes are strict for visits to churches. Women must cover bare shoulders and arms—a shawl will do—but no longer need cover their heads. Shorts are taboo for both men and women.

Miscellaneous   To protect yourself against purse snatchers and pickpockets, take a handbag with long straps that you can sling across your body bandolier-style and with a zippered compartment for your money and other valuables. Better yet, wear a money belt. Take your own soap if you stay in budget hotels. Many do not provide soap or else give guests only one tiny bar per room. Also, travel with a washcloth, or face flannel, if you use one; Italian hotels generally supply only towels. Bring an extra pair of eyeglasses or contact lenses in your carry-on luggage. If you have a health problem that requires a prescription drug, pack enough to last the duration of the trip or have your doctor write a prescription using the drug's generic name, because brand names vary from country to country. Always carry prescription drugs in their original packaging to avoid problems with customs officials. Don't pack them in luggage that you plan to check, in case your bags go astray. Pack a list of the offices that supply refunds for lost or stolen traveler's checks.

Electricity   The electrical current in most of Italy is 220 volts, 50 cycles alternating current (AC); the United States runs on 110-volt, 60-cycle AC current. Unlike wall outlets in the United States, which accept plugs that have two flat prongs, Italian outlets take Continental-type plugs, with two round prongs.

Adapters,   To use U.S.-made electric appliances abroad, you'll need an adapter
Converters,   plug. Unless the appliance is dual-voltage and made for travel, you'll
Transformers   also need a converter. Hotels sometimes have 110-volt outlets for low-wattage appliances (marked "For Shavers Only") near the sink; don't use them for a high-wattage appliance like a blow-dryer. If you're traveling with an older laptop computer, carry a transform-

er. New laptop computers are auto-sensing, operating equally well on 110 and 220 volts, so you need only the appropriate adapter plug. For a copy of the free brochure "Foreign Electricity is No Deep Dark Secret," send a stamped, self-addressed envelope to adapter-converter manufacturer Franzus Company (Customer Service, Dept. B50, Murtha Industrial Park, Box 142, Beacon Falls, CT 06403, tel. 203/723–6664).

Luggage Free airline baggage allowances depend on the airline, the route,
Regulations and the class of your ticket; ask in advance. In general, on domestic flights and on international flights between the United States and foreign destinations, you are entitled to check two bags—neither exceeding 62 inches, or 158 centimeters (length + width + height), or weighing more than 70 pounds (32 kilograms). A third piece may be brought aboard as a carryon; its total dimensions are generally limited to less than 45 inches (114 centimeters) so that it will fit easily under the seat in front of you or in the overhead compartment. In the United States, the Federal Aviation Administration (FAA) gives airlines broad latitude to limit carry-on allowances and tailor them to different aircraft and operational conditions. Charges for excess, oversize, or overweight pieces vary, so inquire before you pack.

If you are flying between two foreign destinations, note that baggage allowances may be determined not by the piece method but by the weight method, which generally allows 88 pounds (40 kilograms) of luggage in first class, 66 pounds (30 kilograms) in business class, and 44 pounds (20 kilograms) in economy. If your flight between two cities abroad *connects* with your transatlantic flight, the piece method still applies.

Safeguarding Before leaving home, itemize your bags' contents and their worth in
Your Luggage case they go astray. To minimize that risk, tag them inside and out with your name, address, and phone number. (If you use your home address, cover it so that potential thieves can't see it.) Put a copy of your itinerary inside each bag, so that you can easily be tracked. At check-in, make sure that the tag attached by baggage handlers bears the correct three-letter code for your destination. If your bags do not arrive with you, or if you detect damage, file a written report with the airline before you leave the airport.

Taking Money Abroad

Traveler's Traveler's checks are preferable in metropolitan centers, although
Checks you'll need cash in rural areas and small towns. The most widely recognized are **American Express, Citicorp, Diners Club, Thomas Cook,** and **Visa,** which are sold by major commercial banks. Both American Express and Thomas Cook issue checks that can be countersigned and used by you or your traveling companion. Typically the issuing company or the bank at which you make your purchase charges 1% to 3% of the checks' face value as a fee. Some foreign banks charge as much as 20% of the face value as the fee for cashing traveler's checks in a foreign currency. Buy a few checks in small denominations to cash toward the end of your trip, so you won't be left with excess foreign currency. Record the numbers of checks as you spend them, and keep this list separate from the checks.

Currency Banks offer the most favorable exchange rates. If you use currency-
Exchange exchange booths at airports, rail and bus stations, hotels, stores, and privately run exchange firms, you'll typically get less favorable rates, but you may find the hours more convenient.

You can get good rates and avoid long lines at airport currency exchange booths by getting a small amount of currency at **Thomas Cook Currency Services** (630 5th Ave., New York, NY 10111, tel. 212/757–6915 or 800/223–7373 for locations in major metropolitan areas throughout the U.S.) or **Ruesch International** (tel. 800/424–2923 for locations) before you depart.

Getting Money from Home

Cash Machines Many automated-teller machines (ATMs) are tied to international networks such as **Cirrus** and **Plus.** You can use your bank card at ATMs away from home to withdraw money from an account and get cash advances on a credit-card account if your card has been programmed with a personal identification number, or PIN. Check in advance on limits on withdrawals and cash advances within specified periods. Ask whether your bank-card or credit-card PIN will need to be reprogrammed for use in the area you'll be visiting. Four digits are commonly used overseas. Note that Discover is accepted only in the United States. On cash advances you are charged interest from the day you receive the money from ATMs as well as from tellers. Although transaction fees for ATM withdrawals abroad may be higher than fees for withdrawals at home, Cirrus and Plus exchange rates are excellent, because they are based on wholesale rates only offered by major banks.

Plan ahead: Obtain ATM locations and the names of affiliated cash-machine networks before departure. For specific foreign Cirrus locations, call 800/424–7787; for foreign Plus locations, consult the Plus directory at your local bank.

Wiring Money You don't have to be a cardholder to send or receive a **MoneyGram from American Express** for up to $10,000. Go to a MoneyGram agent in retail and convenience stores and American Express travel offices, pay up to $1,000 with a credit card and anything over that in cash. You are allowed a free long-distance call to give the transaction code to your intended recipient, who needs only present identification and the reference number to the nearest MoneyGram agent to pick up the cash. MoneyGram agents are in more than 70 countries (call 800/926–9400 for locations). Fees range from 3% to 10%, depending on the amount and how you pay.

You can also use **Western Union.** To wire money, take either cash or a cashier's check to the nearest office or call and use your MasterCard or Visa. Money sent from the United States or Canada will be available for pick up at agent locations in Italy within minutes. Once the money is in the system it can be picked up at *any* one of 22,000 locations (call 800/325–6000 for the one nearest you).

Currency

The unit of currency in Italy is the lira. There are bills of 100,000, 10,000, 5,000, 2,000, and 1,000 lire. Coins are 500, 200, 100, 50, 20, and 10, but the last two are rarely found, and prices are often rounded out to the nearest 50 lire. At press time (September 1994) the exchange rate was about 1,480 lire to the U.S. dollar, 1,157 lire to the Canadian dollar, and 2,449 lire to the pound sterling.

What It Will Cost

Italy's prices are in line with those in the rest of Europe, with costs in its main cities comparable to those in other major capitals, such as

Paris and London. The days when the country's high-quality attractions came with a comparatively low Mediterranean price tag are long gone. With the cost of labor and social benefits rising and an economy struggling to emerge from recession, Italy is therefore not a bargain, but there is an effort to hold the line on hotel and restaurant prices that had become inordinately expensive by U.S. standards. Depending on season and occupancy, you may be able to obtain unadvertised lower rates in hotels; always inquire.

When you make hotel reservations, ask explicitly whether breakfast is included in the rate. By law, breakfast is optional, but some hotels pressure guests to eat breakfast on the premises—and then charge a whopping amount for it. Find out what breakfast will cost at the time you book, or at least when you check in, and if it seems high, avoid misunderstanding by clearly stating that you want a room without breakfast.

Taxes Both U.S. and Italian airport departure taxes are charged on a U.S.–Italy round-trip by air; these and other fees, such as a U.S. Customs users fee, are added to the total you pay when you buy the ticket. The Value-Added Tax (VAT, or IVA in Italy) is a sales tax levied in European Union countries; the amount varies from country to country, and also within a country depending on the nature of the goods or services. In Italy the amount is 12% on clothing and shoes, 19% on luxuries. On most consumer goods, it is already included in the amount shown on the price tag, whereas on services, it may not be. The 9% IVA is generally included in the price quoted for hotel rooms, but some five-star hotels quote rates that are *not* inclusive of the 13% IVA applicable to the luxury category; the 19% IVA on car rentals is also usually an extra charge, added when you settle the bill. The IVA paid on consumer goods can be refunded to travelers in some cases (*see* Shopping in Staying in Florence, Tuscany, and Umbria, *below*).

A service charge of approximately 15% is added to all restaurant bills; in some cases the menu may state that the service charge is already included in the menu prices. A similar service charge applies to hotels and is included in the rates quoted.

Sample Prices These sample prices are meant only as a general guide.

Admission to the Uffizi Gallery: 10,000 lire

Inexpensive hotel room for two, including breakfast, in Florence: 140,000 lire (Bellettini)

Inexpensive Siena dinner: 35,000 lire

Coca-Cola (standing) at a café: 2,200 lire

Cup of coffee: 1,100 to 1,400 lire

Bowl of pasta: 11,000 lire

Cover charge in an inexpensive restaurant: 2,000 lire

½ liter carafe of house wine: 4,000 lire

Movie ticket: 10,000 lire

Daily English-language newspaper: 2,400 lire

Pint of beer in a pub: 7,000 lire

Rosticceria lunch: 14,000 lire

Round-trip train (IC) from Rome to Florence: 62,600 lire

Long-Distance Calling

AT&T, MCI, and Sprint have several services that make calling home or the office more affordable and convenient when you're on the road. Use one of them to avoid pricey hotel surcharges. **AT&T Calling Card** (tel. 800/225–5288) and the **AT&T Universal Card** (tel. 800/662–7759) give you access to the service. With **AT&T's USADirect** (tel. 800/874–4000 for codes in the countries you'll be visiting) you can reach an AT&T operator with a local or toll-free call. **MCI's Call USA** (MCI Customer Service, tel. 800/444–4444) allows that service from 85 countries or from country to country via MCI WorldReach. **Sprint Express** (tel. 800/793–1153) has a toll-free number travelers abroad can dial to reach a Sprint operator in the United States.

Passports and Visas

If your passport is lost or stolen abroad, report the loss immediately to the nearest embassy or consulate and to the local police. If you can provide the consular officer with the information contained in the passport, he or she will usually be able to issue you a new passport promptly. For this reason, keep a photocopy of the data page of your passport separate from your money and traveler's checks. Also leave a photocopy with a relative or friend at home.

U.S. Citizens All U.S. citizens, even infants, need a valid passport to enter Italy for stays of up to three months. You can pick up new and renewal application forms at any of the 13 U.S. Passport Agency offices and at some post offices and courthouses. Although passports are usually mailed within four weeks of your application's receipt, allow five weeks or more from April through summer. Call the Department of State Office of Passport Services' information line (tel. 202/647–0518) for fees, documentation requirements, and other details.

Canadian Citizens Canadian citizens need a valid passport to enter Italy for stays of up to three months; check with the nearest Italian consulate regarding longer stays. Application forms are available at 23 regional passport offices as well as post offices and travel agencies. Whether for a first or subsequent passport, you must apply in person. Children under 16 may be included on a parent's passport but must have their own to travel alone. Passports are valid for five years and are usually mailed within two weeks of an application's receipt. For more information in English or French, call the passport office (tel. 514/283–2152 or 800/567–6868).

U.K. Citizens Citizens of the United Kingdom need a valid passport to enter Italy for purposes of tourism. Applications for new and renewal passports are available from main post offices as well as at the six passport offices, in Belfast, Glasgow, Liverpool, London, Newport, and Peterborough. You may apply in person at all passport offices, or by mail to all except the London office. Children under 16 may travel on an accompanying parent's passport. All passports are valid for 10 years. Allow a month for processing.

A British Visitor's Passport is valid for holidays and some business trips of up to three months to Italy. It can include both partners of a married couple. Valid for one year, it will be issued on the same day that you apply. You must apply in person at a main post office.

Customs and Duties

On Arrival There are two levels of duty-free allowances for visitors to Italy.

For goods obtained anywhere outside the EU or for goods purchased in a duty-free shop within an EU country, the allowances are: (1) 200 cigarettes or 100 cigarillos or 50 cigars or 250 grams of tobacco; (2) 2 liters of still table wine plus (3) 1 liter of spirits over 22% volume or 2 liters of spirits under 22% volume (fortified and sparkling wines); and (4) 60 milliliters of perfume and 250 milliliters of toilet water.

For goods obtained (duty and tax paid) within another EU country, the allowances are: (1) 300 cigarettes or 150 cigarillos or 75 cigars or 400 grams of tobacco; (2) 5 liters of still table wine plus (3) 1.5 liters of spirits over 22% volume or 5 liters of spirits under 22% volume (fortified or sparkling wines) or 3 more liters of table wine; and (4) 75 milliliters of perfume and 375 milliliters of toilet water.

Other items including cameras and films can be brought in duty-free up to a value of £136 for non-EU citizens, £71 for EU citizens. Officially, two still cameras with 10 rolls of film each and one movie camera with 10 rolls of film may be brought in duty-free. Other items intended for personal use are generally admitted, as long as the quantities are reasonable.

Returning Home
U.S. Customs Provided you've been out of the U.S. for at least 48 hours and haven't already used the exemption, or any part of it, in the past 30 days, you may bring home $400 worth of foreign goods duty-free. So can each member of your family, regardless of age; and your exemptions may be pooled, so that one of you can bring in more if another brings in less. A flat 10% duty applies to the next $1,000 of goods; above $1,400, the rate varies with the merchandise. (If the 48-hour or 30-day limits apply, your duty-free allowance drops to $25, which may *not* be pooled.)

Travelers 21 or older may bring back 1 liter of alcohol duty-free, provided the beverage laws of the state through which they reenter the United States allow it. In addition, 100 non-Cuban cigars and 200 cigarettes are allowed, regardless of age. Antiques and works of art over 100 years old are duty-free.

Gifts valued at less than $50 may be mailed to the United States duty-free, with a limit of one package per day per addressee, and do not count as part of your exemption (do not send alcohol or tobacco products or perfume valued at more than $5); mark the package "Unsolicited Gift" and write the nature of the gift and its retail value on the outside. Most reputable stores will handle the mailing for you.

For a copy of "Know Before You Go," a free brochure detailing what you may and may not bring back to the United States, rates of duty, and other pointers, contact the **U.S. Customs Service** (Box 7407, Washington, DC 20044, tel. 202/927–6724).

Canadian Customs Once per calendar year, when you've been out of Canada for at least seven days, you may bring in C$300 worth of goods duty-free. If you've been away less than seven days but more than 48 hours, the duty-free exemption drops to C$100 but can be claimed any number of times (as can a C$20 duty-free exemption for absences of 24 hours or more). You cannot combine the yearly and 48-hour exemptions, use the C$300 exemption only partially (to save the balance for a later trip), or pool exemptions with family members. Goods claimed under the C$300 exemption may follow you by mail; those claimed under the lesser exemptions must accompany you on your return.

Alcohol and tobacco products may be included in the yearly and 48-hour exemptions but not in the 24-hour exemption. If you meet the age requirements of the province through which you reenter Canada, you may bring in, duty-free, 1.14 liters (40 imperial ounces) of wine or liquor *or* two dozen 12-ounce cans or bottles of beer or ale. If you are 16 or older, you may bring in, duty-free, 200 cigarettes, 50 cigars or cigarillos, and 400 tobacco sticks or 400 grams of manufactured tobacco. Alcohol and tobacco must accompany you on your return.

An unlimited number of gifts valued up to C$60 each may be mailed to Canada duty-free. These do not count as part of your exemption. Label the package "Unsolicited Gift—Value under $60." Alcohol and tobacco are excluded.

For more information, including details of duties on items that exceed your duty-free limit, ask the Revenue Canada Customs and Excise Department (2265 St. Laurent Blvd. S, Ottawa, Ontario, K1G 4K3, tel. 613/957–0275) for a copy of the free brochure "I Declare/Je Déclare."

U.K. Customs If your journey was wholly within EU countries, you no longer need to pass through customs when you return to the United Kingdom. According to EU guidelines, you may bring in 800 cigarettes, 400 cigarillos, 200 cigars, and 1 kilogram of smoking tobacco, plus 10 liters of spirits, 20 liters of fortified wine, 90 liters of wine, and 110 liters of beer. If you exceed these limits, you may be required to prove that the goods are for your personal use or are gifts.

No animals or pets of any kind can be brought into the United Kingdom without a lengthy quarantine. The law is strictly enforced with severe penalties.

For further information or a copy of "A Guide for Travellers," which details standard customs procedures as well as what you may bring into the United Kingdom from abroad, contact HM Customs and Excise (Dorset House, Stamford St., London SE1 9PY, tel. 0171/928–3344).

Traveling with Cameras, Camcorders, and Laptops

Film and Cameras If your camera is new or if you haven't used it for a while, shoot and develop a few rolls of film before leaving home. Store film in a cool, dry place—never in the car's glove compartment or on the shelf under the rear window.

Airport security X-rays generally aren't harmful to film with ISO below 400. To protect your film, carry it with you in a clear plastic bag and ask for a hand inspection. Such requests are honored at U.S. airports; abroad, it's up to the inspector. Don't depend on a lead-lined bag to protect film in checked luggage—the airline may increase the radiation to see what's inside. Call the Kodak Information Center (tel. 800/242–2424) for details.

Camcorders Before your trip, put camcorders through their paces, invest in a skylight filter to protect the lens, and check all the batteries. Most newer camcorders are equipped with batteries that can be recharged with a universal or worldwide AC adapter charger (or multivoltage converter) usable whether the voltage is 110 or 220. All that's needed is the appropriate plug.

Videotape Videotape is not damaged by X-rays, but it may be harmed by the magnetic field of a walk-through metal detector, so ask for a hand-check. Airport security personnel may ask you to turn on the camcorder to prove that it's what it appears to be, so make sure the battery is charged. Note that rather than the National Television System Committee (NTSC) video standard used in the United States and Canada, Italy uses PAL technology. You will not be able to view your tapes through the local TV set or view movies bought there in your home VCR. Blank tapes bought in Italy can be used for NTSC camcorder taping, but they are pricey.

Laptops Security X-rays do not harm hard-disk or floppy-disk storage, but you may request a hand-check, at which point you may be asked to turn on the computer to prove that it is what it appears to be. (Check your battery before departure.) Most airlines allow you to use your laptop aloft except during takeoff and landing (so as not to interfere with navigation equipment). For international travel, register your foreign-made laptop with U.S. Customs as you leave the country. If your laptop is U.S.-made, call the consulate of the country you'll be visiting to find out whether it should be registered with customs upon arrival. Before departure, find out about repair facilities at your destination, and don't forget any transformer or adapter plug you may need (*see* Electricity, *above*).

Language

In the main tourist cities, language is no problem. You can always find someone who speaks at least a little English, albeit with a heavy accent; remember that the Italian language is pronounced exactly as it is written (many Italians try to speak English as it is written, with disconcerting results). You may run into a language barrier in the countryside, but a phrase book and close attention to the Italians' astonishing use of pantomime and expressive gestures will go a long way.

Staying Healthy

There are no serious health risks associated with travel to Italy and no inoculations are needed to enter the country. However, the Centers for Disease Control (CDC) in Atlanta caution that most of Southern Europe is in the "intermediate" range for risk of contacting traveler's diarrhea. Part of this risk may be attributed to an increased consumption of olive oil and wine, which can have a laxative effect on stomachs used to a different diet. (Pepto Bismol is recommended for minor cases of traveler's diarrhea.) The CDC also advises all international travelers to swim only in chlorinated swimming pools, unless they are absolutely certain the local beaches and fresh-water lakes are not contaminated.

Finding a The **International Association for Medical Assistance to Travellers**
Doctor (IAMAT, 417 Center St., Lewiston, NY 14092, tel. 716/754–4883; 40 Regal Rd., Guelph, Ontario N1K 1B5; 57 Voirets, 1212 Grand-Lancy, Geneva, Switzerland) publishes a worldwide directory of English-speaking physicians whose qualifications meet IAMAT standards and who have agreed to treat members for a set fee. Membership is free.

Assistance Pretrip medical referrals, emergency evacuation or repatriation,
Companies 24-hour telephone hot lines for medical consultation, dispatch of medical personnel, relay of medical records, up-front cash for emergencies, and other personal and legal assistance are among the services provided by several membership organizations specializing in medical assistance to travelers. Among them are **International SOS Assistance** (Box 11568, Philadelphia, PA 19116, tel. 215/244–1500 or

800/523–8930; Box 466, pl. Bonaventure, Montréal, Québec H5A 1C1, tel. 514/874–7674 or 800/363–0263), **Medex Assistance Corporation** (Box 10623, Baltimore, MD 21285, tel. 410/296–2530 or 800/874–9125), **Near Services** (450 Prairie Ave., Suite 101, Calumet City, IL 60409, tel. 708/868–6700 or 800/654–6700), and **Travel Assistance International** (1133 15th St. NW, Suite 400, Washington, DC 20005, tel. 202/331–1609 or 800/821–2828), part of Europ Assistance Worldwide Services, Inc. Because these companies will also sell you death-and-dismemberment, trip-cancellation, and other insurance coverage, there is some overlap with the travel-insurance policies discussed under Insurance, *below*.

Insurance

U.S. Residents
Most tour operators, travel agents, and insurance agents sell specialized health-and-accident, flight, trip-cancellation, and luggage insurance as well as comprehensive policies with some or all of these features. But before you make any purchase, review your existing health and home-owner policies to find out whether they cover expenses incurred while traveling.

Health-and-Accident Insurance
Specific policy provisions of supplemental health-and-accident insurance for travelers include reimbursement for up to $150,000 worth of medical and/or dental expenses caused by an accident or illness during a trip. The personal-accident, or death-and-dismemberment provision pays a lump sum to your beneficiaries if you die or to you if you lose a limb or your eyesight; the lump sum awarded ranges from $15,000 to $500,000. The medical-assistance provision may reimburse you for the cost of referrals, evacuation, or repatriation and other services, or it may automatically enroll you as a member of a particular medical-assistance company (*see* Assistance Companies, *above*).

Flight Insurance
Often bought as a last-minute impulse at the airport, flight insurance pays a lump sum when a plane crashes—either to a beneficiary if the insured dies or sometimes to a surviving passenger who loses eyesight or a limb. Like most impulse buys, flight insurance is expensive and basically unnecessary. It supplements the airlines' coverage described in the limits-of-liability paragraphs on your ticket. Charging an airline ticket to a major credit card often automatically entitles you to coverage and may also embrace travel by bus, train, and ship.

Baggage Insurance
In the event of loss, damage, or theft on international flights, airlines' liability is $20 per kilogram for checked baggage (roughly about $640 per 70-pound bag) and $400 per passenger for unchecked baggage. On domestic flights, the ceiling is $1,250 per passenger. Excess-valuation insurance can be bought directly from the airline at check-in for about $10 per $1,000 worth of coverage. However, you cannot buy it at any price for the rather extensive list of excluded items shown on your airline ticket.

Trip Insurance
Trip-cancellation-and-interruption insurance protects you in the event you are unable to undertake or finish your trip, especially if your airline ticket, cruise, or package tour does not allow changes or cancellations. The amount of coverage you purchase should equal the cost of your trip should you, a traveling companion, or a family member fall ill, forcing you to stay home, plus the nondiscounted one-way airline ticket you would need to buy if you had to return home early. Read the fine print carefully, especially sections defining "family member" and "preexisting medical conditions." Default or bankruptcy insurance protects you against a supplier's failure to

deliver. Such policies often do not cover default by a travel agency, tour operator, airline, or cruise line if you bought your tour and the coverage directly from the firm in question. Tours packaged by one of the 33 members of the United States Tour Operators Association (USTOA, 211 E. 51 St., Suite 12B, New York, NY 10022; tel. 212/750–7371), which requires members to maintain $1 million each in an account to reimburse clients in case of default, are likely to present the fewest difficulties. Even better, pay for travel arrangements with a major credit card, so that you can refuse to pay the bill if services have not been rendered—and let the card company fight your battles.

Comprehensive Policies Companies supplying comprehensive policies with some or all of the above features include **Access America, Inc.** (Box 90315, Richmond, VA 23230, tel. 800/284–8300); **Carefree Travel Insurance,** (Box 310, 120 Mineola Blvd., Mineola, NY 11501, tel. 516/294–0220 or 800/323–3149); **Tele-Trip** (Mutual of Omaha Plaza, Box 31762, Omaha, NE 68131, tel. 800/228–9792); **The Travelers Companies** (1 Tower Sq., Hartford, CT 06183, tel. 203/277–0111 or 800/243–3174); **Travel Guard International,** (1145 Clark St., Stevens Point, WI 54481, tel. 715/345–0505 or 800/782–5151); and **Wallach and Company, Inc.** (107 W. Federal St., Box 480, Middleburg, VA 22117, tel. 703/687–3166 or 800/237–6615).

U.K. Residents Most tour operators, travel agents, and insurance agents sell specialized policies covering accident, medical expenses, personal liability, trip cancellation, and loss or theft of personal property. You can also buy an annual travel-insurance policy valid for every trip (usually of less than 90 days) you make during the year in which it's purchased. Make sure you will be covered if you have a preexisting medical condition or are pregnant.

For advice by phone or a free booklet, "Holiday Insurance," that sets out what to expect from holiday-insurance policies and gives price guidelines, contact the Association of British Insurers, a trade association representing 450 insurance companies (51 Gresham St., London EC2V 7HQ, tel. 0171/600–3333; 30 Gordon St., Glasgow G1 3PU, tel. 0141/226–3905; Scottish Providence Bldg., Donegall Sq. W, Belfast BT1 6JE, tel. 01232/249176; call for other locations).

Car Rentals

Most major car-rental companies are represented in Italy, including **Avis** (tel. 800/331–1212, 800/879–2847 in Canada); **Budget** (tel. 800/527–0700); **Eurodollar Rent A Car Ltd.** (tel. 800/800–6000); **Hertz** (tel. 800/654–3131, 800/263-0600 in Canada); and **National** (tel. 800/227–7368), known internationally as InterRent and Europcar. In cities, weekly unlimited-mileage rates range from about $250 to $400. This does not include VAT tax, which in Italy is 19% on car rentals. Many rental companies impose mandatory theft coverage on all rentals; this amounts to about $10–$15 per day.

Requirements Your own driver's license is acceptable, although an International Driver's Permit, available from the American or Canadian Automobile Association, is a good idea.

Extra Charges Picking up the car in one city and leaving it in another may entail substantial drop-off charges or one-way service fees. The cost of a collision or loss-damage waiver (*see below*) can be high, also. Some rental agencies will charge you extra if you return the car *before* the time specified on your contract. Ask before making unscheduled drop-offs. Fill the tank before you turn in the vehicle to avoid being charged for refueling at what you'll swear is the most expensive pump in town. In Europe manual transmissions are standard, and air-conditioning is a rarity and often unnecessary. Asking for an automatic transmission or air-conditioning can significantly increase the cost of your rental.

Cutting Costs Major international companies have programs that discount their standard rates by 15% to 30% if you make the reservation before departure (anywhere from 24 hours to 14 days), rent for a minimum number of days (typically three or four), and prepay the rental. More economical rentals may come as part of fly/drive or other packages, even bare-bones deals that only combine the rental and an airline ticket (*see* Tours and Packages, *above*).

Several companies operate as wholesalers—they do not own their own fleets but rent in bulk from those that do and are thus able to pass on advantageous rates to their retail customers. Rentals through such companies must be arranged and paid for before you leave the United States. Among them are **Auto Europe** (Box 1097, Camden, ME 04843, tel. 207/236–8235 or 800/223–5555; 800/458–9503 in Canada); **Europe by Car** (mailing address, 1 Rockefeller Plaza, New York, NY 10020; walk-in address, 14 W. 49th St., New York, NY 10020, tel. 212/581–3040 or 212/245–1713; 9000 Sunset Blvd., Los Angeles, CA 90069, tel. 213/252–9401; 800/223–1516 in CA); **Foremost Euro-Car** (5430 Van Nuys Blvd., Suite 306, Van Nuys, CA 91401, tel. 818/786–1960 or 800/272–3299); and **The Kemwel Group** (106 Calvert St., Harrison, NY 10528, tel. 914/835–5555 or 800/678–0678). You won't see these wholesalers' deals advertised; they're even better in summer, when business travel is down. Always ask whether the prices are guaranteed in U.S. dollars or foreign currency and if unlimited mileage is available. Find out about any required deposits, cancellation penalties, and drop-off charges, and confirm the cost of any required insurance coverage.

Insurance and Before you rent a car, find out exactly what coverage, if any, is
Collision provided by your personal auto insurer and the rental company.
Damage Don't assume that you are covered. If you do want insurance from
Waiver the rental company, secondary coverage may be the only type offered. You may already have secondary coverage if you charge the rental to a credit card. Note that some credit-card companies do not cover cars rented in Italy.

In general, if you have an accident, you are responsible for the automobile. Car rental companies may offer a collision damage waiver (CDW), which ranges in cost from $4 to $14 a day. You should decline the CDW only if you are certain you are covered through your personal insurer or credit-card company.

Rail Passes

For those planning on doing a lot of traveling by train, rail passes can be a bargain. They allow unlimited travel within a given period of time, and they usually come in versions for first- and second-class travel. They are generally available only to foreign travelers visiting a country and sometimes must be bought before you leave the United States. Their validity begins on the first day of their use, which must be validated by a station official. A further advantage of rail passes is that they spare you time spent waiting in line to buy tickets, and holders are often exempt from paying supplements for seat reservations and for riding special trains (although if seat reservations are necessary, you will still be obliged to make them).

Italy has three rail passes, which can be bought at main train stations in Italy or in the United States through travel agents or the official representative for **Italian State Railways, CIT Tours Corp.** (342 Madison Ave., Room 207, New York, NY 10173, tel. 212/697–2100 or 800/223–7987; tel. 310/670–4269 or 800/248–7245 in western United States). **DER Tours** (Box 1606, Des Plaines, IL 60017, tel. 800/782–2424) is another source for all except the Italian Kilometric ticket. In the past, you saved money buying the passes in the United States, but check if an improved rate of exchange for the dollar will make it more economical to purchase the passes in Italy.

The **Italian Tourist Ticket (BTLC)**—the country's basic unlimited-travel rail pass—is an excellent value because it covers the entire system, including Sicily. The pass is available in a first-class version for periods of eight days ($236 in United States/269,000 lire in Italy), 15 days ($294), 21 days ($340), and 30 days ($406). For second-class travel, the prices for the same periods are $162, $200, $230, and $274.

A variation on the BTLC is the **Italy Flexi Railcard,** which entitles purchasers to four days of travel within nine days of validity; eight days of travel within 21 days; and 12 days of travel within 30 days. Rates for the three types for first-class travel are $180 in the United States, $260, and $324; for second-class travel, $126, $174, and $220.

The third Italian rail pass is the **Italian Kilometric Ticket,** which is a good bet for families. It is valid for 20 train trips, up to a total of 3,000 kilometers (1,875 miles) of train travel, within a two-month period, and it can be used by up to five people (related or not). Children under 12 are counted for only half the distance, those under four travel free. A first-class ticket costs $274 and a second-class ticket $166 if bought in the United States.

The **EurailPass,** valid for unlimited first-class train travel through 17 countries, including Italy, is an excellent value if you plan on traveling around the Continent. Standard passes are available for 15 days ($498), 21 days ($648), one month ($728), two months ($1,098), and three months ($1,398). **Eurail Saverpasses,** valid for 15 days, cost $430 per person, 21 days for $550, one month for $678 per person; you must do all your traveling with at least one companion (two companions from April through September). **Eurail Youthpasses,** which cover second-class travel, cost $578 for one month, $768 for two; you must be under 26 on the first day you travel. **Eurail Flexipasses** allow you to travel first class for five ($348), 10 ($560), or 15 ($740) days within any two-month period. **Eurail Youth Flexipasses,** available to those under 26 on their first travel day, allow you to travel second class for five ($255), 10 ($398), or 15 ($540) days within any two-month period. Apply through your travel agent or **Rail Europe** (226–230 Westchester Ave., White Plains, NY 10604, tel. 914/682–5172 or 800/848–7245; or 2087 Dundas East, Suite 105, Mississauga, Ontario L4X 1M2, tel. 416/602–4195), **DER Tours** (Box 1606, Des Plaines, IL 60017, tel. 800/782–2424), or **CIT Tours Corp.** (*see above*).

Once in Italy, travelers under 26 who have not invested in any of the above passes should inquire about the **Carta Verde,** or Green Card (40,000 lire for one year), which entitles the holder to a 20% discount on all first- and second-class tickets. Travelers over 60 are entitled to similar discounts with the **Carta d'Argento** (*see* Hints for Older Travelers, *below*). Those under 26 should also inquire about discount travel fares under the Billet International Jeune (BIJ) scheme. The special one-trip tickets are sold by **EuroTrain Interna-**

tional (no connection with EurailPass) at its offices in various European cities, including Rome, and by travel agents, mainline rail stations, and youth travel specialists (*see* Centro Turistico Studentesco, *below*).

Student and Youth Travel

Travel Agencies The **Centro Turistico Studentesco** (CTS) is a student and youth travel agency with offices in major Italian cities; CTS helps its clients find low-cost accommodations and bargain fares for travel in Italy and elsewhere and also serves as a meeting place for young people of all nations. The Florence office is at Via di Ginori 25 (tel. 55/289721). CTS is also the representative for **EuroTrain International.**

Council Travel Services (CTS), a subsidiary of the nonprofit Council on International Educational Exchange (CIEE), specializes in low-cost travel arrangements abroad for students and is the exclusive U.S. agent for several discount cards. Also newly available from CTS are domestic air passes for bargain travel within the United States. CIEE's twice-yearly *Student Travels* magazine is available at the CTS office at CIEE headquarters (205 E. 42nd St., 16th Floor, New York, NY 10017, tel. 212/661–1450) and in Boston (tel. 617/266–1926), Miami (tel. 305/670–9261), Los Angeles (tel. 310/208–3551), and at 43 branches in college towns nationwide (free in person, $1 by mail). **Campus Connections** (1100 E. Marlton Pike, Cherry Hill, NJ 08034, tel. 800/428–3235) specializes in discounted accommodations and airfares for students. The **Educational Travel Centre** (438 N. Frances St., Madison, WI 53703, tel. 608/256–5551) offers low-cost domestic and international airline tickets, mostly for flights departing from Chicago, and rail passes. Other travel agencies catering to students include **TMI Student Travel** (1146 Pleasant St., Watertown, MA 02172, tel. 617/661–8187 or 800/245–3672) and **Travel CUTS** (187 College St., Toronto, Ontario M5T 1P7, tel. 416/979–2406).

Discount Cards For discounts on transportation and on museum and attractions admissions, buy the **International Student Identity Card** (ISIC) if you're a bona fide student, or the **International Youth Card** (IYC) if you're under 26. In the United States the ISIC and IYC cards cost $16 each and include basic travel accident and sickness coverage. Apply to **CIEE** (*see above*, tel. 212/661–1414; the application is in *Student Travels*). In Canada the cards are available for $15 each from **Travel CUTS** (*see above*). In the United Kingdom they cost £5 and £4 respectively at student unions and student travel companies, including Council Travel's London office (28A Poland St., London W1V 3DB, tel. 0171/437–7767).

Hosteling A **Hostelling International** (HI) membership card is the key to more than 6,000 hostels in 70 countries; the sex-segregated, dormitory-style sleeping quarters, including some for families, go for $7 to $20 a night per person. Membership is available in the United States through **Hostelling International/American Youth Hostels** (HI/AYH, 733 15th St. NW, Suite 840, Washington, DC 20005, tel. 202/783–6161), the United States link in the worldwide chain, and costs $25 for adults 18 to 54, $10 for those under 18, $15 for those 55 and over, and $35 for families. Volume 1 of the *AYH Guide to Budget Accommodation* lists hostels in Europe and the Mediterranean ($13.95, including shipping). HI membership is available in Canada through **Hostelling International-Canada** (205 Catherine St., Suite 400, Ottawa, Ontario K2P 1C3, tel. 613/748–5638) for $26.75, and in the United Kingdom through the **Youth Hostel Association of England**

and Wales (Trevelyan House, 8 St. Stephen's Hill, St. Albans, Hertfordshire AL1 2DY, tel. 01727/855215) for £9.

Traveling with Children

Although Italians love children and are generally very tolerant and patient with them, they provide few amenities for them. In restaurants and trattorias you may find a high chair or a cushion for the child to sit on, but there is no such thing as a children's menu. Order a half-portion (*mezza porzione*) of any dish, or ask the waiter for a child's portion (*porzione da bambino*).

Discounts do exist. Always ask about a *sconto-bambino* before purchasing tickets. Children under six or under a certain height ride free on municipal buses and trams. Children under 18 are admitted free to state-run museums and galleries, and there are similar privileges in many municipal or private museums.

Publications
Newsletter — *Family Travel Times*, published 10 times a year by Travel With Your Children (TWYCH, 45 W. 18th St., 7th Floor Tower, New York, NY 10011, tel. 212/206–0688; annual subscription $55), covers destinations, types of vacations, and modes of travel.

Books — *Traveling with Children—And Enjoying It*, by Arlene K. Butler ($11.95 plus $3 shipping; Globe Pequot Press, Box 833, Old Saybrook, CT 06475, tel. 800/243–0495 or 800/962–0973 in CT), helps you plan your trip with children, from toddlers to teens. *Innocents Abroad: Traveling with Kids in Europe*, by Valerie Wolf Deutsch and Laura Sutherland ($15.95 or $4.95 paperback; Penguin USA, 120 Woodbine St., Bergenfield, NJ 07621, tel. 800/253–6476), covers child- and teen-friendly activities, food, and transportation.

Tour Operators — **Grandtravel** (6900 Wisconsin Ave., Suite 706, Chevy Chase, MD 20815, tel. 301/986–0790 or 800/247–7651) offers international and domestic tours for people traveling with their grandchildren. The catalogue, as charmingly written and illustrated as a children's book, positively invites armchair traveling with lap-sitters aboard. **Families Welcome!** (21 W. Colony Pl., Suite 140, Durham, NC 27705, tel. 919/489–2555 or 800/326–0724) packages and sells family tours to Europe.

Getting There
Airfares — On international flights, the fare for infants under age two not occupying a seat is generally either free or 10% of the accompanying adult's fare; children ages two through 11 usually pay half to two-thirds of the adult fare. On domestic flights, children under two not occupying a seat travel free, and older children currently travel on the "lowest applicable" adult fare.

Baggage — In general, infants paying 10% of the adult fare are allowed one carry-on bag, not to exceed 70 pounds or 45 inches (length + width + height) and a collapsible stroller; check with the airline before departure, because you may be allowed less if the flight is full. The adult baggage allowance applies for children paying half or more of the adult fare.

Safety Seats — A certain amount of confusion surrounds children's car seats aloft. The FAA recommends their use and details approved models in the free leaflet "**Child/Infant Safety Seats Recommended for Use in Aircraft**" (available from the FAA, APA–200, 800 Independence Ave. SW, Washington, DC 20591, tel. 202/267–3479). Airline policy varies. U.S. carriers allow FAA-approved models bearing a sticker declaring their FAA approval. Because these seats are strapped into a regular passenger seat they may require that parents buy a ticket even for an infant under two who would otherwise ride free. Foreign carriers may not allow infant seats, may charge the child's rather than the infant's fare for their use, or may require you to hold your baby during takeoff and landing, thus defeating the seat's purpose.

Facilities Aloft Some airlines provide other services for children, such as children's meals and freestanding bassinets (only to those with seats at the bulkhead, where there's enough legroom). Make your request when reserving. The annual February/March issue of *Family Travel Times* gives details of the children's services of dozens of airlines. "Kids and Teens in Flight" (free from the U.S. Department of Transportation, tel. 202/366–2220) offers tips for children flying alone.

Lodging Children are generally welcome in Italian hotels, which will set up extra beds in the parents' room or give families adjoining rooms. The charge for an extra bed should be no more than 35% of the double room rate. If you are traveling with an infant, it is best to bring along your own folding crib.

CIGA Hotels (reservations: tel. 800/221–2340) has two hotels in Florence, the Excelsior and the Grand, both of which welcome families. (For information on alternative lodgings, *see* Home Exchange and Apartment and Villa Rentals in Staying in Florence, Tuscany, and Umbria, *below*).

Hints for Travelers with Disabilities

Italy has only recently begun to provide facilities such as ramps, telephones, and toilets for people with disabilities; such things are still the exception, not the rule. ENIT (Italian Government Travel Office) can provide travelers with a list of accessible hotels and with the addresses of Italian associations for people with disabilities. Travelers' wheelchairs must be transported free of charge, according to Italian law, but the logistics of getting a wheelchair on and off trains and buses can make this requirement irrelevant. Seats are reserved for people with disabilities on public transportation, but buses have no lifts for wheelchairs. High, narrow steps for boarding trains create additional problems. In many monuments and museums, even in some hotels and restaurants, architectural barriers make it difficult, if not impossible, for those with disabilities to gain access.

To bring a Seeing Eye dog into Italy requires an import license, a current certificate detailing the dog's inoculations, and a letter from your veterinarian certifying the dog's health. Contact the nearest Italian consulate for particulars.

Organizations Several organizations provide travel information for people with disabilities, usually for a membership fee, and some publish newsletters and bulletins. Among these are the **Information Center for Individuals with Disabilities** (Fort Point Pl., 27–43 Wormwood St., Boston, MA 02210, tel. 617/727–5540 or 800/462–5015 in MA between 11 and 4, or leave message; TDD 617/345–9743); **Mobility International USA** (Box 10767, Eugene, OR 97440, tel. and TDD 503/343–1284, fax 503/343–6812), the U.S. branch of an international organization based in Britain and present in 30 countries; **MossRehab Hospital Travel Information Service** (1200 W. Tabor Rd., Philadelphia, PA 19141, tel. 215/456–9603, TDD 215/456–9602); **Travel Industry and Disabled Exchange** (TIDE, 5435 Donna Ave., Tarzana, CA 91356, tel. 818/368–5648, fax 818/344–0078); and **Travelin' Talk** (Box 3534, Clarksville, TN 37043, tel. 615/552–6670, fax 615/552–1182).

Travel Agency **Flying Wheels Travel** (143 W. Bridge St., Box 382, Owatonna, MN 55060, tel. 507/451–5005 or 800/535–6790) is a travel agency specializing in domestic and worldwide cruises, tours, and independent travel itineraries for people with mobility impairments.

In the United Main sources include the **Royal Association for Disability and Reha-**
Kingdom **bilitation** (RADAR, 12 City Forum, 250 City Rd., London ECIV 8AF, tel. 0171/250–322), which publishes travel information for people with disabilities in Britain, and **Mobility International** (228 Borough High St., London SE1 1JX, tel. 0171/403–5688), the headquarters of an international membership organization that serves as a clearinghouse of travel information for people with disabilities. **Holiday Care Service** (2 Old Bank Chambers, Station Rd., Horley, Surrey RH6 9HW, tel. 01293/774535) is a charity that provides guides, accommodation listings, and general information for tourists with special needs.

Publications Two free publications are available from the Consumer Information Center (Pueblo, CO 81009): "New Horizons for the Air Traveler with a Disability," a U.S. Department of Transportation booklet describing changes resulting from the 1986 Air Carrier Access Act and those still to come from the 1990 Americans with Disabilities Act (include Department 608Y in the address), and the Airport Operators Council's *Access Travel: Airports* (Dept. 5804), which describes facilities and services for people with disabilities at more than 500 airports worldwide.

Travelin' Talk Directory (*see* Organizations, *above*) was published in 1993. This 500-page resource book ($35) is packed with information for travelers with disabilities. Twin Peaks Press (Box 129, Vancouver, WA 98666, tel. 206/694–2462 or 800/637–2256) publishes the *Directory of Travel Agencies for the Disabled* ($19.95), listing more than 370 agencies worldwide and *Wheelchair Vagabond* ($14.95), a collection of personal travel tips. Add $2 per book for shipping.

Hints for Older Travelers

In Italy, travelers over 60 can purchase the **Carta d' Argento**, a rail pass good for a 30% discount on the Italian State railway system. It costs 40,000 lire and is valid for one year, except for June 26–August 14 and December 18–28. Travelers over 60 are also entitled to free admission to state museums, as well as to many other museums—always ask at the ticket office. Older travelers planning to visit Italy during the hottest months should be aware that few public buildings, restaurants, and shops are air-conditioned. Public toilets are few and far between, other than those in coffee bars, restaurants, and hotels. Older travelers may find it difficult to board trains and some buses and trams with very high steps and narrow treads.

Organizations The **American Association of Retired Persons** (AARP, 601 E St. NW, Washington, DC 20049, tel. 202/434–2277) offers independent travelers who are members of the AARP (open to those age 50 or older; $8 per person or couple annually) the Purchase Privilege Program, which provides discounts on hotels, car rentals, and sightseeing. AARP also arranges group tours, cruises, and apartment living through AARP Travel Experience from American Express (400 Pinnacle Way, Suite 450, Norcross, GA 30071, tel. 800/927–0111 or 800/745–4567).

Two other organizations offer discounts on lodgings, car rentals, and other travel products, along with such nontravel perks as magazines and newsletters: the **National Council of Senior Citizens** (1331

F St. NW, Washington, DC 20004, tel. 202/347–8800; membership $12 annually) and **Mature Outlook** (6001 N. Clark St., Chicago, IL 60660, tel. 800/336–6330; $9.95 annually).

Note: Mention your senior-citizen identification card when booking hotel reservations for reduced rates, not when checking out. At restaurants, show your card before you're seated; discounts may be limited to certain menus, days, or hours. If you are renting a car, ask about promotional rates that might improve on your senior-citizen discount.

Educational Travel The nonprofit **Elderhostel** (75 Federal St., 3rd Floor, Boston, MA 02110, tel. 617/426–7788) has offered inexpensive study programs for people 60 and older since 1975. Held at more than 1,800 educational institutions, courses cover everything from marine science to Greek myths and cowboy poetry. Participants usually attend lectures in the morning and spend the afternoon sightseeing or on field trips; they live in dorms on the host campuses. Fees for two- to three-week international trips—including room, board, and transportation from the United States—range from $1,800 to $4,500.

Interhostel (University of New Hampshire, 6 Garrison Ave., Durham, NH 03824, tel. 800/733–9753), a slightly newer enterprise than Elderhostel, caters to a slightly younger clientele—50 and over—and runs programs overseas in some 25 countries. The idea is similar: Lectures and field trips mix with sightseeing, and participants stay in dormitories at cooperating educational institutions or in modest hotels. Programs are usually two weeks in length and cost $1,500–$2,100, excluding airfare.

Tour Operators The following tour operators specialize in older travelers: **Evergreen Travel Service** (4114 198th St. SW, Suite 3, Lynnwood, WA 98036, tel. 206/776–1184 or 800/435–2288), has introduced the "Lazy Bones" tours for those who like a slower pace. If you want to take your grandchildren, look into **Grandtravel** (*see* Traveling with Children, *above*); **Saga International Holidays** (222 Berkeley St., Boston, MA 02116, tel. 800/343–0273) caters to those over age 60 who like to travel in groups.

Publications *The 50+ Traveler's Guidebook: Where to Go, Where to Stay, What to Do,* by Anita Williams and Merrimac Dillon ($12.95; St. Martin's Press, 175 5th Ave., New York, NY 10010), is available in bookstores and offers many useful tips. "The Mature Traveler" (Box 50820, Reno, NV 89513, tel. 702/786–7419; $29.95), a monthly newsletter, contains many travel deals for older travelers.

Hints for Gay and Lesbian Travelers

Organizations The **International Gay Travel Association** (Box 4974, Key West, FL 33041, tel. 800/448–8550), which has 700 members, will provide you with names of travel agents and tour operators who specialize in gay travel. The **Gay & Lesbian Visitors Center of New York Inc.** (135 W. 20th St., 3rd Floor, New York, NY 10011, tel. 212/463–9030 or 800/395–2315; $100 annually) mails a monthly newsletter, valuable coupons, and more to its members.

Tour Operators and Travel Agencies The dominant travel agency in the market is **Above and Beyond** (3568 Sacramento St., San Francisco, CA 94118, tel. 415/922–2683 or 800/397–2681). Tour operator **Olympus Vacations** (8424 Santa Monica Blvd., Suite 721, West Hollywood, CA 90069; tel. 310/657–2220) offers all-gay-and-lesbian resort holidays. **Skylink Women's Travel** (746 Ashland Ave., Santa Monica, CA 90405, tel. 310/452–0506 or 800/225–5759) handles individual travel for lesbians all over the

world and conducts two international and five domestic group trips
annually.

Publications The premiere international travel magazine for gays and lesbians is
Our World (1104 N. Nova Rd., Suite 251, Daytona Beach, FL 32117,
tel. 904/441–5367; $35 for 10 issues). **"Out & About"** (tel. 203/789–
8518 or 800/929–2268; $49 for 10 issues) is a 16-page monthly news-
letter with extensive information on resorts, hotels, and airlines
that are gay-friendly.

Further Reading

The Italians, by Luigi Barzini, is a comprehensive and lively analy-
sis of the Italian national character, still worthy reading although
published in 1964 (Atheneum). More recent musings on Italian life
include *Italian Days*, by Barbara Grizzuti Harrison (Ticknor &
Fields), and *That Fine Italian Hand*, by Paul Hofmann (Henry
Holt), for many years *New York Times* bureau chief in Rome. Mat-
thew Spender's *Within Tuscany* (Viking) is an account of life in rural
Tuscany by a British expatriate.

A classic of the travel essay genre is Mary McCarthy's *The Stones of
Florence* (Harcourt Brace). For historical background, Edward
Gibbon's *Decline and Fall of the Roman Empire* is available in three
volumes (Modern Library). Consult Giorgio Vasari's *Lives of the
Artists*, *The Autobiography of Benvenuto Cellini*, and Machiavelli's
The Prince (all available in Penguin Classics) for eyewitness ac-
counts of the 16th century. Otherwise, many still consider *The Civilization of the Renaissance in Italy*, by 19th-century Swiss
historian Jacob Burckhardt (Modern Library), must reading. Chris-
topher Hibbert's *The House of Medici* (Quill/William Morrow) details the family's rise and fall.

To catch a glimpse of the Tuscan landscape pick up Ethne Clarke's
The Gardens of Tuscany (Weidenfeld & Nicolson), Harold Acton's
Great Houses of Italy: The Tuscan Villas (Viking), or Carey More's
Views from a Tuscan Vineyard (Pavillion). *A Tuscan in the Kitch-
en: Recipes and Tales from My Home* by Pino Luongo with Barbara
Raives & Angela Hederman (C.N. Potter/Crown) is a mix of Tuscan
cookery and customs. Florence is the setting for two of Magdalen
Nabb's entertaining thrillers, *Death in Autumn* and *Death of a
Dutchman*. For a recent look at Umbrian life, try Lisa St. Aubin de
Terán's *A Valley in Italy: The Many Seasons of a Villa in Umbria*
(HarperCollins).

Waverley Root's *The Food of Italy* (Vintage), published in 1977, is
not a cookbook but an unsurpassed region-by-region exploration of
the subject. Marcella Hazan's new *Essentials of Classic Italian
Cooking* (Knopf) is an update, with modern sensibilities and lowfat
diets in mind, of her earlier cookbooks. It goes well with *Italian
Wine* (Knopf), by her husband, Victor Hazan, or with *Vino*, by Bur-
ton Anderson (Little Brown). For cookbooks on classic Tuscan
cuisine, see the many volumes by Lorenza de'Medici and Giuliano
Bugialli. *Made in Italy*, a shopper's guide by Annie Brody and Pa-
tricia Schultz (1988, Workman) is unrevised but still valuable for its
knowledge of Italian products and producers.

What about a video? Merchant/Ivory's *Room with a View* (1986), a
period piece based on the E.M. Forster novel of the same name, is
good cinema with good views of Florence. Also available is a video of
John Mortimer's *Summer Lease*, a popular television mystery about
an English family's summer rental of a Tuscan farmhouse.

A magazine for Italophiles, *Italy Italy*, published in Italy in English, is available in the United States (Italian American Multimedia Corporation, 138 Wooster St., New York, NY 10012, tel. 212/674–4132, fax 212/674–4933; $30 for 6 yearly issues). Italian travel magazines, such as *Bell'Italia, Dove,* and *Gulliver,* often give pointers to new, exotic, and overlooked destinations.

Arriving and Departing

From North America by Plane

Flights are either nonstop, direct, or connecting. A nonstop flight requires no change of plane and makes no stops. A direct flight stops at least once and can involve a change of plane, although the flight number remains the same; if the first leg is late, the second waits. This is not the case with a connecting flight, which involves a different plane and a different flight number.

Airports and Airlines Airlines serving Italy nonstop from the United States are **Alitalia** (tel. 800/223–5730), **Delta** (tel. 800/241–4141), and **TWA** (tel. 800/892–4141), which all fly to Rome and Milan, and **American** (800/624–6262), which flies to Milan only. These flights land at Rome's **Leonardo da Vinci Airport,** better known as Fiumicino (from its location outside the city) and at Milan's **Malpensa Airport.** For details on getting to Florence or other cities in Tuscany using domestic carriers such as ATI and Merediana, *see* "Arriving and Departing by Plane" in individual chapters *below.*

Flying Time The flying time to Rome from New York is 8½ hours; from Chicago, 10–11 hours; from Los Angeles, 12–13 hours.

Cutting Flight Costs The Sunday travel section of most newspapers is a good source of deals. When booking, particularly through an unfamiliar company, call the Better Business Bureau and your local or state Consumer Protection Bureau to find out whether any complaints have been registered against the company, pay with a credit card if you can, and consider trip-cancellation and default insurance (*see* Insurance, *above*).

Promotional Airfares Less expensive fares, called promotional or discount fares, are round-trip and involve restrictions, which vary according to the route and season. You must usually buy the ticket—commonly called an APEX (advance purchase excursion) when it's for international travel—in advance (seven, 14, or 21 days are usual), although some of the major airlines have added cheap, no-frills flights to compete with new bargain airlines on certain routes.

With the major airlines the cheaper fares generally require minimum and maximum stays (for instance, over a Saturday night or at least seven and no more than 30 days). Airlines generally allow some return date changes for a $25 to $50 fee, but most low-fare tickets are nonrefundable. Only a death in the family would prompt the airline to return any of your money if you cancel a nonrefundable ticket. However, you can apply an unused nonrefundable ticket toward a new ticket, again with a small fee. The lowest fare is subject to availability, and only a small percentage of the plane's total seats will be sold at that price. Contact the U.S. Department of Transportation's Office of Consumer Affairs (I–25, Washington, DC 20590, tel. 202/366–2220) for a copy of "Fly-Rights: A Guide to Air Travel in the U.S." *The Official Frequent Flyer Guidebook*, by Randy Petersen ($14.99 plus $3 shipping; 4715-C Town Center Dr., Colorado

Springs, CO 80916, tel. 719/597–8899, 800/487–8893, or 800/485–8893), yields valuable hints on getting the most for your air-travel dollars.

Consolidators Consolidators or bulk-fare operators—"bucket shops"—buy blocks of seats on scheduled flights that airlines anticipate they won't be able to sell. They pay wholesale prices, add a markup, and resell the seats to travel agents or directly to the public at prices that still undercut the airline's promotional or discount fares (higher than a charter ticket but lower than an APEX ticket, and usually without the advance-purchase restriction). Moreover, some consolidators sometimes give you your money back. Carefully read the fine print detailing penalties for changes and cancellations. If you doubt the reliability of a company, call the airline once you've made your booking and confirm that you do, indeed, have a reservation on the flight.

The biggest U.S. consolidator, C.L. Thomson Express, sells only to travel agents. Well-established consolidators selling to the public include **UniTravel** (Box 12485, St. Louis, MO 63132, tel. 314/569–0900 or 800/325–2222), **Council Charter** (205 E. 42nd St., New York, NY 10017, tel. 212/661–0311 or 800/800–8222), and **Travac** (989 6th Ave., New York, NY 10018, tel. 212/563–3303 or 800/872–8800).

Charter Flights Charters usually have the lowest fares and the most restrictions. Departures are limited and seldom on time, and you can lose all or most of your money if you cancel. (The closer to departure you cancel, the more you lose, although sometimes you will be charged only a small fee if you supply a substitute passenger.) The charterer, on the other hand, may legally cancel the flight for any reason up to 10 days before departure; within 10 days of departure, the flight may be canceled only if it becomes physically impossible to operate it. The charterer may also revise the itinerary or increase the price after you have bought the ticket, but if the new arrangement constitutes a "major change," you have the right to a refund. Before buying a charter ticket, read the fine print for the company's refund policy and details on major changes. Money for charter flights is usually paid into a bank escrow account, the name of which should be on the contract. If you don't pay by credit card, make your check payable to the escrow account (unless you're dealing with a travel agent, in which case, his or her check should be payable to the escrow account). The U.S. Department of Transportation's Office of Consumer Affairs (I–25, Washington, DC 20590, tel. 202/366–2220) can answer questions on charters and send you its "Plane Talk: Public Charter Flights" information sheet.

Charter operators may offer flights alone or with ground arrangements that constitute a charter package. You typically must book charters through your travel agent. One good source is **Charterlink** (988 Sing Sing Rd., Horseheads, NY 14845, tel. 607/739–7148 or 800/221–1802), a no-fee charter broker that operates 24 hours a day.

Discount Travel clubs offer members unsold space on airplanes, cruise ships, *Travel Clubs* and package tours at as much as 50% below regular prices. Membership may include a regular bulletin or access to a toll-free hot line giving details of available trips departing from three or four days to several months in the future. Most also offer 50% discounts off hotel rack rates, but double-check with the hotel to make sure it isn't offering a better promotional rate independent of the club. Clubs include **Discount Travel International** (114 Forrest Ave., Suite 203, Narberth, PA 19072, tel. 215/668–7184; $45 annually, single or family), **Entertainment Travel Editions** (Box 1014, Trumbull, CT 06611, tel. 800/445–4137; $28–$48 annually), **Great American Traveler** (Box

27965, Salt Lake City, UT 84127, tel. 800/548–2812; $29.95 annually), **Moment's Notice Discount Travel Club** (425 Madison Ave., New York, NY 10017, tel. 212/486–0503; $45 annually, single or family), **Privilege Card** (3391 Peachtree Rd. NE, Suite 110, Atlanta, GA 30326, tel. 404/262–0222 or 800/236–9732; domestic annual membership $49.95, international, $74.95), **Travelers Advantage** (CUC Travel Service, 49 Music Sq. W, Nashville, TN 37203, tel. 800/548–1116; $49 annually, single or family), and **Worldwide Discount Travel Club** (1674 Meridian Ave., Miami Beach, FL 33139, tel. 305/534–2082; $50 annually for family, $40 single).

Enjoying the Flight
Fly at night if you're able to sleep on a plane. Because the air aloft is dry, drink plenty of beverages while on board; remember that drinking alcohol contributes to jet lag, as do heavy meals. Sleepers usually prefer window seats to curl up against; restless passengers ask to be on the aisle. Bulkhead seats, in the front row of each cabin, have more legroom, but since there's no seat ahead, trays attach awkwardly to the arms of your seat, and you must stow all possessions overhead. Bulkhead seats are usually reserved for people with disabilities, the elderly, and people traveling with babies.

Smoking
Since February 1990, smoking has been banned on all domestic flights of less than six hours' duration; the ban also applies to domestic segments of international flights aboard U.S. and foreign carriers. On U.S. carriers flying overseas, a seat in a no-smoking section must be provided for every passenger who requests one, and the section must be enlarged to accommodate such passengers if necessary, as long as they have complied with the airline's deadline for check-in and seat assignment. Foreign airlines are exempt from these rules but do provide no-smoking sections, and some nations, including Canada, have gone as far as to ban smoking on all domestic flights; other countries may ban smoking on flights of less than a specified duration. The International Civil Aviation Organization has set July 1, 1996, as the date to ban smoking aboard airlines worldwide, but the body has no power to enforce its decisions.

From North America by Ship

Cunard Line (555 5th Ave., New York, NY 10017, tel. 212/880–7500 or 800/528–6273) operates the *Queen Elizabeth II (QE2)*, the only ocean liner that makes regular transatlantic crossings (Apr.–Dec., between New York City and Southampton, England).

Other cruise lines whose ships are in Europe for the summer and the Caribbean for the winter make repositioning crossings: eastbound in spring and westbound in fall. Check the travel pages of your Sunday newspaper or contact a travel agent for lines and sailing dates.

From the United Kingdom by Plane, Car, Train, and Bus

By Plane
Alitalia (tel. 0171/602–7111) and **British Airways** (tel. 0181/897–4000) operate direct flights from London (Heathrow) to Pisa and Florence. Flying time is 2½ to three hours. Standard fares are extremely high. Both airlines offer less expensive APEX tickets (usual booking restrictions apply) and PEX and Super-PEX tickets (which don't have to be bought in advance). The Eurobudget ticket (no length-of-stay or advance-purchase restrictions) is another option.

Less expensive flights are available: It pays to look around in the classified advertisements of reputable newspapers and magazines such as *Time Out*. But remember to check the *full* price, inclusive of airport taxes and surcharges. Some of the bargains are not as inexpensive as they seem at first glance.

By Car The distance from London to Florence is about 500 kilometers (900 miles) via Calais/Boulogne/Dunkirk and 1,435 kilometers (860 miles) via Oostende/Zeebrugge (excluding sea crossings). The drive from the Continental ports takes about 20 hours; the trip in total takes about three days. The shortest and quickest channel crossings are via Dover or Folkestone to one of the French ports (Calais or Boulogne); the ferry takes around 75 minutes and the Hovercraft just 35 minutes. Crossings from Dover to the Belgian ports take about four hours, but Oostende and Zeebrugge have good road connections. The longer crossing from Hull to Zeebrugge is useful for travelers from the north of England. The Sheerness–Vlissingen (Holland) route makes a comfortable overnight crossing; it takes about nine hours.

Fares on the cross-channel ferries vary considerably from season to season. Until the end of June and from early September onward, savings can be made by traveling midweek. Don't forget to budget for the cost of gas and road tolls, plus a couple of nights' accommodations.

The Channel Tunnel opened officially in May 1994, providing the fastest route across the Channel—35 minutes from Folkestone to Calais, or 60 minutes from motorway to motorway. It consists of two large 50-kilometer (31-mile)-long tunnels for trains, one in each direction, linked by a smaller service tunnel running between them. Le Shuttle (tel. 01345/353535 in the U.K., 800/388–3876 in the U.S.), a special car, bus, and truck train, which was scheduled to begin service in June 1994, operates a continuous loop, with trains departing every 15 minutes at peak times and at least once an hour through the night. No reservations are necessary, although tickets may be purchased in advance from travel agents. Most passengers stay in their own car throughout the "crossing"; progress updates are provided on display screens and radio. Motorcyclists park their bikes in a separate section with its own passenger compartment, while foot passengers must book passage by coach.

The tunnel is reached from exit 11a of the M20/A20. Drivers purchase tickets from toll booths, then pass through frontier control before loading onto the next available service. Unloading at Calais takes eight minutes. Ticket prices start at £130 for a low-season five-day round trip in a small car and are based on season, time of day, length of stay, and car size regardless of the number of passengers. Peak-season fares are not always competitive with ferry prices.

Roads from the channel ports to Italy are mostly toll-free. The exceptions are French autoroutes, the road crossing the Ardennes, the Swiss superhighway network (for which a special tax sticker must be bought at the frontier or in advance), the St. Gotthard Tunnel, and the road between the tunnel and the Italian superhighway system. The reduced-price petrol coupons once offered by the Italian government have been discontinued, but it won't hurt to check with the AA or RAC before departure to be sure they haven't become available again.

If these distances seem too great to drive, there's always the Motorail from the channel ports. However, no car/sleeper expresses run beyond Milan, 575 kilometers (360 miles) north of Rome.

By Train Traveling to Florence by train from London entails an overnight trip with several transfers. Daily service from Victoria Station departs in the morning and travels by way of Calais and Metz, reaching Florence the next morning. Train schedules are subject to change, so consult with **French Railways** (tel. 0171/493–9731) and **British Rail** (tel. 0171/834–2345) before you leave.

By Bus **Eurolines** (13 Lower Regent St., London SW1Y 4LR, tel 0171/730–0202 or any National Express agent) runs twice-weekly bus service to Florence that increases to three times a week between June and September. Buses leave on Monday, Wednesday, and Friday in summer, and on Monday and Friday the rest of the year.

Staying in Florence, Tuscany, and Umbria

Getting Around

By Plane **Alitalia** and its domestic affiliate **ATI,** in addition to smaller, privately run companies such as **Meridiana,** complete an extensive network of internal flights in Italy. Apart from the major international airports, you can find frequent flights between smaller cities. Flight times are never much more than an hour, and most of these smaller airports are close to the cities and linked by good bus services. Italian travel agents will inform you of the discounts available, which include a 50% family reduction for a spouse and/or children traveling with you, or up to 30% for certain night flights.

By Train There is frequent train service among the towns of Tuscany and Umbria. The fastest trains on the **FS,** the state-owned railroad, are *intercity* and *rapido* trains, for which you pay a supplement and for which seat reservations may be required and are always advisable. *Espresso* trains usually make more stops and are a little slower. *Diretto* and *locale* are the slowest.

To avoid long lines at station windows, buy tickets and make seat reservations at least a day in advance at travel agencies displaying the FS emblem. If you have to reserve at the last minute, reservation offices at the station accept reservations up to three hours before departure. You can also get a seat assignment just before boarding the train; look for the conductor on the platform. Trains can be very crowded on weekends and during holiday and vacation seasons; we strongly advise reserving seats in advance or, if the train originates where you get on, getting to the station early to find a seat. A card just outside the compartment or over the seat indicates whether it has been reserved. Carry compact bags for easy overhead storage. You can buy train tickets for destinations close to main cities at tobacconists and at ticket machines in stations; they must be stamped in the little machines near the track before you board the train.

There is refreshment service on all long-distance trains, with mobile carts and a cafeteria or dining car. Tap water on trains is not drinkable.

Rail Passes For those planning on doing a lot of traveling by train, the **Italian Tourist Ticket (BTLC)** is an excellent value. (*See* Rail Passes in Before You Go, *above.*)

By Bus Italy's bus network is extensive, although not as attractive as those in other European countries, partly because of the low cost of train travel. Schedules are often drawn up with commuters and students in mind and may be sketchy on weekends. Regional bus companies often provide the only means of getting to out-of-the-way places. Even when this is not the case, buses can be faster and more direct than local trains, so it's a good idea to compare bus and train schedules. Among the major Italian long-distance bus companies are **SITA** (Viale Cadorna 105, Florence, tel. 055/278611), which operates throughout Italy; **Autostradale** (Piazzale Castello 1, Milan, tel. 02/801161), serving much of northern Italy; and **Lazzi** (Via Mercadante 2, Florence, tel. 055/363041), operating in Tuscany and central Italy. Bus information is available at local tourist offices and travel agencies.

Local bus companies operate in many regions (*see* Getting Around By Bus in most chapters). In the hillier parts of Italy, they take over when the gradients become too steep for train travel. A village shop or café will sometimes double as the ticket office and bus stop for these. You should have your ticket before you board.

Most of the major cities have urban bus services, usually operating on a system involving the prepurchase of tickets (from a machine, a newsstand, or a tobacco store). These buses are inexpensive, but they can become unbearably jammed at rush hours. Remember that there are also lunchtime rush hours in the hotter periods, when people go home for a siesta.

By Car There is an extensive network of *autostrade* (toll highways), complemented by equally well-maintained but free *superstrade* (expressways). All are clearly signposted and numbered. The ticket you are issued upon entering an autostrada must be returned when you exit and pay the toll; on some shorter autostrade, mainly connecting highways, the toll is paid upon entering. Viacard cards, on sale at many autostrada locations, make paying tolls easier and faster. A *raccordo* is a connecting expressway. *Strade statali* (state highways, denoted by S or SS numbers) may be single-lane roads, as are all secondary roads; directions and turnoffs are not always clearly marked. Information is obtainable from **ACI** (Automobile Club of Italy, Via Marsala 8, 00185 Rome, tel. 06/499–8389) and from ACI offices throughout Italy.

Rules of the Road Driving is on the right, as in the United States. Regulations are largely as in Britain and the United States, except that the police have the power to levy on-the-spot fines. In most Italian towns the use of the horn is forbidden in certain, if not all, areas; a large sign, ZONA DI SILENZIO, indicates where. Speed limits are 130 kph (80 mph) on autostrade and 110 kmh (70 mph) on state and provincial roads, unless otherwise marked. Fines for driving after drinking are heavy, with the additional possibility of six months' imprisonment, but there is no fixed blood-alcohol regulation and no official test.

Parking In most cities, parking space is at a premium; historic town centers are closed to most traffic, and peripheral parking areas are usually full. Parking in a *zona disco* is allowed for limited periods (30 minutes to two hours or more—the limit is posted); if you don't have the cardboard disk to show what time you parked, you can use a piece of paper. It's advisable to leave your car only in guarded parking areas; many are run by ACI. Unofficial parking attendants can help you find a space but offer no guarantees. In major cities your car may be towed away if illegally parked.

Gas Gas ranges from 1,550 lire to 1,600 lire per liter, the equivalent of about $4 a U.S. gallon. Only a few gas stations are open on Sunday, and most close for a couple of hours at lunchtime and at 7 PM for the night. Self-service pumps may be few and far between outside major cities. Gas stations on autostrade are open 24 hours.

Breakdowns **ACI Emergency Service** (Servizio Soccorso Stradale, Via Solferino 32, 00185 Rome, tel. 06/44595) offers 24-hour road service. Dial 116 to reach the nearest ACI service station.

Telephones

Local Calls Pay phones take either a 200-lire coin, two 100-lire coins, a *gettone* (token), or a *scheda* (prepaid calling card). The gettone-only phones are being phased out; if you happen upon one, buy tokens from the nearest cashier or the token machine near the phone. Insert the token (which doesn't drop right away), dial your number, wait for an answer, then complete the connection by pushing the knob at the token slot. When the token drops, the other party is able to hear you. Scheda phones are becoming common everywhere. You buy the card (values vary—2,000 lire, 5,000 lire, etc.) at Telefoni offices and tobacconists. Insert the card as indicated by the arrow, and its value will be visible in the window. After you hang up, the card is returned so you can use it until its value runs out. Don't forget it. The card makes long-distance direct dialing (*teleselezione*) much easier than it used to be. Without it, insert at least five coins and have more handy; unused coins will be returned.

International Since hotels tend to overcharge, sometimes exorbitantly, for long-
Calls distance and international calls, it is best to make such calls from Telefoni offices, where operators will assign you a booth, help you place your call, and collect payment when you have finished, at no extra charge. There are Telefoni offices, designated SIP (sometimes also ASST), in all cities and towns. You can make collect calls from any phone by dialing 170, which will get you an English-speaking operator. Rates to the United States are lowest round the clock on Sunday and 11 PM–8 AM, Italian time, on weekdays.

See also Long-Distance Calling in Before You Go, *above.*

Operators and For general information in English on calling in Europe and the
Information Mediterranean area, dial 176. For operator-assisted service in those areas, dial 15. For operator-assisted service and information regarding intercontinental calls, dial 170.

Mail

Postal Rates Airmail letters (lightweight stationery) to the United States and Canada cost 1,100 lire for the first 19 grams and an additional 1,700 lire for up to 50 grams. Airmail postcards cost 950 lire if the message is limited to a few words and a signature; otherwise, you pay the letter rate. Airmail letters to the United Kingdom cost 750 lire; postcards, 650 lire. You can buy stamps at tobacconists.

Receiving Mail service is generally slow; allow up to 14 days for mail from Brit-
Mail ain, 21 days from North America. Correspondence can be addressed to you care of the Italian post office. Letters should be addressed to your name, "c/o Ufficio Postale Centrale," followed by "FERMO POSTA" on the next line, and the name of the city (preceded by its postal code) on the next. You can collect it at the central post office by showing your passport or photo-bearing ID and paying a small fee. American Express also has a general-delivery service. There's no charge for cardholders, holders of American Express Traveler's checks, or anyone who booked a vacation with American Express.

Tipping

Tipping practices vary, depending on where you are. The following guidelines apply in major cities, but Italians tip smaller amounts in smaller cities and towns. Tips may not be expected in cafés and taxis north of Rome.

In restaurants a service charge of about 15% usually appears as a separate item on your check. A few restaurants state on the menu that cover and service charge are included. Either way, it's customary to leave an additional 5%–10% tip for the waiter, depending on the service. Checkroom attendants expect 500 lire per person. Restroom attendants are given from 200 lire in public restrooms, and more in expensive hotels and restaurants. Tip 100 lire for whatever you drink standing up at a coffee bar, 500 lire or more for table service in a smart café, and less in neighborhood cafés. At a hotel bar tip 1,000 lire for a round or two of cocktails.

Taxi drivers are usually happy with 5%–10% of the meter amount. Railway and airport porters charge a fixed rate per bag. Tip an additional 500 lire per person, but more if the porter is very helpful. Theater ushers expect 500 lire per person, but more for very expensive seats. Give a barber 2,000–3,000 lire and a hairdresser's assistant 3,000–8,000 lire for a shampoo or cut, depending on the type of establishment.

On sightseeing tours, tip guides about 2,000 lire per person for a half-day group tour, more if they are very good. In museums and other places of interest where admission is free, an offering is expected; give anything from 500 to 1,000 lire for one or two persons, more if the guardian has been especially helpful. Service station attendants are tipped only for special services.

In hotels, give the *portiere* about 15% of his bill for services, or 5,000–10,000 lire if he has been generally helpful. For two people in a double room, leave the chambermaid about 1,000 lire per day, or about 4,000–5,000 a week, in a Moderate ($$) hotel (*see* Dining and Lodging in individual chapters for a definition of price categories); tip a minimum of 1,000 lire for valet or room service. Increase these amounts by one-half in an Expensive ($$$) hotel, and double them in a Very Expensive ($$$$) hotel. Tip doormen in a Very Expensive hotel 1,000 lire for calling a cab and 2,000 lire for carrying bags to the check-in desk. In a Very Expensive hotel tip a bellhop 2,000–5,000 lire for carrying your bags to the room and 2,000–3,000 lire for room service. In a Moderate hotel tip a bellhop 1,000–2,000 lire for carrying your bags and 1,000–2,000 for room service.

Opening and Closing Times

Banks Branches are open weekdays 8:30–1:30 and 2:45–3:45.

Churches Most are open from early morning until noon or 12:30, when they close for two hours or more; they open again in the afternoon, closing about 7 PM or later. Major cathedrals and basilicas, such as Florence's Duomo, are open all day. Sightseeing in churches during religious rites is usually discouraged. Be sure to have a fistful of 100-lire coins handy for the *luce* (light) machines that illuminate the works of art in the perpetual dusk of ecclesiastical interiors. A pair of binoculars will help you get a good look at painted ceilings and domes.

Museums Hours vary and may change with the seasons. Many important national museums have short hours and are closed one day a week, often on Monday. They are open on some holidays, closed on others.

Check individual listings in the individual chapters and always check locally. Remember that ticket offices close from 30 minutes to one hour before official closing time.

Shops There are individual variations, depending on climate and season, but most are open 9:30 to 1 and 3:30 or 4 to 7 or 7:30. Food shops open earlier in the morning and later in the afternoon. In all but resorts and small towns, shops close on Sunday and one half-day during the week. Some tourist-oriented shops in places such as Florence and Pisa are open all day, as are some department stores and supermarkets. Post offices are open 8–2; central and main district post offices stay open until 8 or 9 PM for some operations. Barbers and hairdressers, with some exceptions, are closed Sunday and Monday.

National Holidays January 1 (New Year's Day); January 6 (Epiphany); April 16, 17, 1995 and April 14, 15, 1996 (Easter Sunday and Monday); April 25 (Liberation Day); May 1 (Labor Day or May Day); August 15 (Assumption of Mary, also known as Ferragosto); November 1 (All Saints Day); December 8 (Immaculate Conception); December 25, 26 (Christmas Day and Boxing Day).

The feast days of patron saints are also holidays, observed locally. Many businesses and shops may be closed in Florence on June 24 (St. John the Baptist).

Shopping

The best buys in Italy are leather goods of all kinds—from gloves to bags to jackets—in addition to silk goods, knitwear, gold jewelry, ceramics, and local handicrafts. Every region has its specialties. Florence is known for straw goods, gold jewelry, leather, and paper products; Assisi for embroidery; and Deruta and Gubbio for ceramics.

Unless your purchases are too bulky, avoid having them shipped home; if the shop seems extremely reliable about shipping, get a written statement of what will be sent, when, and how. (*See* Shopping in individual chapters for details.)

IVA (VAT) Refunds Under Italy's IVA-refund system, a non-EU resident can obtain a refund of tax paid after spending a total of 300,000 lire in one store (before tax—and note that price tags and prices quoted, unless otherwise stated, include IVA). Shop with your passport and ask the store for an invoice itemizing the article(s), price(s), and the amount of tax. At departure, take the still-unused goods and the invoice to the customs office at the airport or other point of departure and have the invoice stamped. (If you return to the United States or Canada directly from Italy, go through the procedure at Italian customs; if your return is, say, via Britain, take the Italian goods and invoice to British customs.) Once back home—and within 90 days of the date of purchase—mail the stamped invoice to the store, which will forward the IVA rebate to you. A growing number of stores in Italy (and Europe) are members of the Tax-Free Shopping System, which expedites things by providing an invoice that is actually a Tax-Free Cheque in the amount of the refund. Once stamped, it can be cashed at the Tax-Free Cash refund window at major airports and border crossings.

Bargaining The notice *prezzi fissi* (fixed prices) means just that; in shops displaying this sign it's a waste of time to bargain unless you're buying a sizable quantity of goods or a particularly costly object. Always bargain, instead, at outdoor markets and when buying from street vendors.

Participant Sports

Italians are sports lovers, and there are several daily newspapers devoted solely to sports. The climate makes it almost impossible to resist the temptation to try a cannonball serve on the red-clay tennis courts, sink a birdie putt on a scenic green, or just hike up a hill to savor the fresh air and views. Winters see ski enthusiasts trying their luck on the slopes of the Apennines.

Golf Relatively new to Italy, golf is catching on, and more courses are being laid out near major cities. For information, contact the **Federazione Italiana Golf** (Viale Tiziano 74, 00196 Rome, tel. 06/36851).

Horseback Riding An excursion on horseback is a pleasant way to see the countryside, and many types of tours are offered. Some include overnight stays in country estates in Tuscany. For information, contact the **Associazione Nazionale per il Turismo Equestre** (Via A. Borelli 5, 00161 Rome, tel. 06/444–1179).

Sailing It is especially popular off the coast of Tuscany. For information, contact the **Federazione Italiana Vela** (Viale Brigata Bisagno 2, 16129 Genoa, tel. 010/589431).

Tennis Tennis is one of Italy's most popular sports, and most towns have public courts available for a booking fee. Many hotels have courts that are open to the public; some private clubs offer temporary visitors' memberships to travelers. Contact local tourist information offices for information.

Spectator Sports

Basketball Many Americans play on Italian pro teams, and basketball is gaining a big following around the country. For information, contact the **Federazione Italiana Pallacanestro** (Via Fogliano 15, 00199 Rome, tel. 06/886–3071).

Soccer *Calcio* (soccer) is the most popular spectator sport in Italy. All major cities, and most smaller ones, have teams playing in one league or another. Big-league games are played on Sunday afternoons from September through May. Inquire locally or write to the **Federazione Italiana Giuoco Calcio** (Via Gregorio Allegri 14, 00198 Rome, tel. 06/84911).

Beaches

Italy isn't the place for an exclusively "beach" holiday. With rare exceptions, you'll find cleaner water and better beaches at lower prices in other parts of the world. Topless bathing is widespread, except for a few staid family-type beaches near large cities. Singles will enjoy resorts on the coast of Tuscany.

Dining

Dining in Italy is a pleasant part of the total Italian experience, a chance to enjoy authentic Italian specialties and ingredients. Visitors have a choice of eating places, ranging from a *ristorante* (restaurant) to a *trattoria, tavola calda,* or *rosticceria.* A trattoria is usually a family-run place, simpler in decor, menu, and service than a ristorante, and slightly less expensive. Some rustic-looking spots call themselves *osterie* but are really restaurants. (A true *osteria* is a wineshop, a very basic and down-to-earth tavern.) The countless fast-food places opening up everywhere are variations of the older Italian institutions of the tavola calda or rosticceria, which offer a selection of hot and cold dishes to be taken out or eaten on the premises. At either a tavola calda or rosticceria, some items are priced by the portion, others by weight. You usually select your food, find out how much it costs, and then pay the cashier, who will give you a stub to be given to the counterman when you pick up the food.

None of the above eateries serves breakfast; in the morning you go to a coffee bar, which is where, later in the day, you will also find sandwiches, pastries, and snacks. Tell the cashier what you want, pay for it, and then take the stub to the counter, where you order. Remember that table service is extra, and you are expected not to occupy tables unless you are being served; on the other hand, you can linger as long as you like at a table without being pressed to move on.

In eating places of all kinds, the menu is posted in the window or just inside the door so you can see what you're getting into (in a snack bar or tavola calda the price list is usually displayed near the cashier). In all but the simplest places there's a *coperto* (cover charge) and usually also a *servizio* (service charge) of 10%–15%, only part of which goes to the waiter. A *menù turistico* (tourist menu) includes taxes and service, but beverages are usually extra.

Generally speaking, a typical Italian meal in a restaurant or trattoria consists of at least two courses: a first course of pasta, risotto, or soup, and a second course of meat and fish. Side dishes, such as vegetables and salads cost extra, as do desserts. There is no such thing as a side dish of pasta; pasta is a course in itself and Italians would never think of serving a salad with it; the salad comes later. Years ago, pasta dishes were inexpensive because restaurateurs made their profit on the total of first and second course. Now, tourists and even some diet-conscious Italians, tend to order only one course—usually a pasta, perhaps followed by a salad or vegetables—so hosts have jacked up the price of first courses. Now, about antipasto: Many a misunderstanding arises over a lavish offering of antipasto. The term *antipasto* means, literally, "before the meal." No matter how generous and varied the antipasto, the host expects those who have one to order at least one other course. Pizza is in a category by itself and is a one-dish meal, even for the Italians. But some like to have a small pizza as a starter, as an alternative to a pasta course.

Beware of menu items marked "SQ" (according to quantity), which means you will be charged according to the weight of the item, or "L. 18,000 hg," which means the charge will be 18,000 lire per hectogram (3½ ounces). Pricing by weight usually refers to items such as fresh fish or Florentine steaks.

Mealtimes Lunch is served in Florence from 12:30 to 2:30, dinner from 7:30 to 9:30, or later in some restaurants. Service begins and ends a half-hour earlier in smaller towns. Almost all eating places close one day a week and for vacations in summer and/or winter.

Precautions Tap water is safe almost everywhere unless labeled *"Non Potabile."* Most people order bottled *acqua minerale* (mineral water), either *gassata* (carbonated) or *naturale*, or *non gassata* (without bubbles). In a restaurant you order it by the *litro* (liter) or *mezzo litro* (half-liter); often the waiter will bring it without being asked, so if you don't like it, or want to keep your check down, make a point of ordering *acqua semplice* (tap water). You can also order *un bicchiere di acqua minerale* (a glass of mineral water) at any bar. If you are on a low-sodium diet, ask for everything (within reason) *senza sale* (without salt).

Ratings   Restaurants in our listings are divided by price into four categories: Very Expensive ($$$$), Expensive ($$$), Moderate ($$), and Inexpensive ($). (*See* Dining in individual chapters for specific prices, which vary from region to region.) Prices quoted are for a three-course meal with house wine, including all service and taxes; particularly recommended establishments are indicated by a star ★.

Lodging

Tuscany and Umbria offer a good choice of accommodations. However, it is becoming more difficult to find satisfactory accommodations in the lower price categories, as more and more hotels are being refurbished and upgraded. Throughout Tuscany and Umbria you will find everything from deluxe five-star hotels to charming country inns, villas for rent, campgrounds, and hostels, in addition to well-equipped vacation villages in resort areas.

Hotels   Italian hotels are classified from five-star (deluxe) to one-star (guest houses and small inns). Stars are assigned according to standards set by regional boards (Italy has 20 regions), but rates are set by each hotel. In the major cities, room rates are on a par with other European capitals: Deluxe and four-star rates can be downright extravagant. In those categories, ask for one of the better rooms, since less desirable rooms—and there usually are some—don't give you what you're paying for. Hotels are justifying higher rates by refurbishing rooms and bathrooms and installing such accessories as blow-dryers and personal safes. During slack periods, or when a hotel is not full, it is often possible to negotiate a discounted rate.

In all hotels you will find a rate card inside the door of your room or inside the closet door; it tells you exactly what you will pay for that particular room (rates in the same hotel may vary according to the location and type of room). On this card, breakfast and any other optionals must be listed separately. Any discrepancy between the basic room rate and that charged on your bill is cause for complaint to the manager and to the local tourist office. The service charge and the 9% IVA, or VAT tax, are included in the rate except in five-star deluxe hotels, where the IVA (13% on luxury hotels) may be a separate item added to the bill at departure.

Although, by law, breakfast is supposed to be optional, most hotels quote room rates including breakfast. When you book a room, ask specifically whether the rate includes breakfast (*colazione*). You are under no obligation to take breakfast at your hotel, but in practice most hotels expect you to do so. Considering that Italian hotel breakfasts usually are very simple, even skimpy, this is not good value for the money; you can eat better for less at the nearest coffee bar.

Hotels that we list as $$ and $ may charge extra for optional air-conditioning. In older hotels the quality of rooms may be very uneven; if you don't like the room you're given, ask for another. This applies to noise, too. Front rooms may be larger and have a view, but they also may get a lot of street noise. Specify if you care about having either a bath or shower, since not all rooms have both. In the $$ and $ categories, showers may be the drain-in-the-floor type, guaranteed to flood the bathroom. Such amenities as porters, room service, and in-house cleaning and laundering are disappearing in hotels of these same categories, which, in general, are not up to U.S. standards of comfort and facilities.

Among the best-known chains operating in Italy are **CIGA** (745 5th Ave., New York, NY 10151, tel. 800/221–2340, fax 212/421–5929), which has more than 20 Italian properties, almost all five-star deluxe; **Jolly** (800/247–1277 in New York State, 800/221–2626 elsewhere, 800/237–0319 in Canada), with 32 four-star hotels in Italy; **Atahotels** (Via Lampedusa 11/A, 20141 Milano, tel. 02/895261, fax 02/8465568, or toll-free in Italy 1678/23013; some bookable through E & M Associates, 212/599–8280 or 800/223–9832), with 20 mostly five- and four-star hotels; and **Starhotels** (Via Belfiore 27, 50144 Florence, tel. 055/36921, fax 055/36924, or book through 800/44–UTELL), with 14 mainly four-star hotels. **Space Hotels** (toll-free in Italy 1678/13013; or book through Supranational, 416/927–1133 or 800/843–3311) has about 50 independently owned five- and four-star (some three-star) hotels. **Italhotels** (toll-free in Italy 1678/01004) also has about 50 independently owned five- and four-star hotels.

AGIP Motels (reservations in Italy: 06/444–0183) is a chain of about 50 motels on main highways, mostly four-star (these are commercial, functional digs for traveling salesmen and tourists needing forty winks, but they—and the Jolly hotels—can be the best choice in many out-of-the-way places). The **Forte** group has taken over some top-of-the-line AGIP properties. **Best Western,** an international association of independently owned hotels, has some 75 mainly four- and three-star hotels in Italy (tel. 800/528–1234 for reservations or to request the *Europe and Middle East Atlas* that lists them).

Family Hotels (Via Faenza 77, 50123 Florence, tel. 055/217975, fax 055/238–1905), grouping about 75 independently owned, family-run three- and two-star hotels (some one-star), offers good value. For information in Italy, contact the address above (not a central booking service, however).

Major cities have hotel-reservation service booths in train stations.

Home Exchange
You can find a house, apartment, or other vacation property to exchange for your own by becoming a member of a home-exchange organization, which then sends you its annual directories listing available exchanges and includes your own listing in at least one of them. Arrangements for the actual exchange are made by the two parties to it, not by the organization. For more information contact the **International Home Exchange Association** (IHEA, 41 Sutter St., Suite 1090, San Francisco, CA 94104, tel. 415/673–0347 or 800/788–2489). Principal clearinghouses include **HomeLink International** (Box 650, Key West, FL 33041, tel. 800/638–3841), with thousands of foreign and domestic listings, which publishes four annual directories plus updates; the $50 membership includes your listing in one book. **Intervac International** (Box 590504, San Francisco, CA 94159, tel. 415/435–3497) publishes three annual directories; membership is $62, or $72 if you want to receive the directories but remain unlisted. **Loan-a-Home** (2 Park La., Apt. 6E, Mount Vernon, NY 10552, tel. 914/664–7640) specializes in long-term exchanges; there is no charge to list your home, but the directories cost $35 or $45 depending on the number you receive. **Villa Leisure** (Box 30188, Palm Beach, FL 33420, tel. 800/526–4244) facilitates swaps.

Apartment and Villa Rentals
If you want a home base that's roomy enough for a family and comes with cooking facilities, a furnished rental may be the solution. It's generally cost-wise, too, although not always—some rentals are luxury properties (economical only when your party is large). Home-exchange directories do list rentals—often second homes owned by prospective house swappers—and there are services that not only look for a house or apartment for you, but also handle the

paperwork. Some send an illustrated catalogue and others send photographs of specific properties, sometimes at a charge; up-front registration fees may apply. In Italy, the possibilities include rustic, converted stone farmhouses, seaside villas, city apartments, and even quarters in a 16th-century Renaissance palace or two.

Among the companies are **At Home Abroad** (405 E. 56th St., Suite 6H, New York, NY 10022, tel. 212/421–9165); **Interhome Inc.** (124 Little Falls Rd., Fairfield, NJ 07004, tel. 201/882–6864); **Europa-Let** (92 N. Main St., Ashland, OR 97520, tel. 503/482–5806 or 800/462–4486); **Overseas Connection** (31 North Harbor Dr., Sag Harbor, NY 11963, tel. 516/725–9308); **Property Rentals International** (1 Park West Cir., Suite 108, Midlothian, VA 23113, tel. 804/378–6054 or 800/220–3332); **Rent a Home International** (7200 34th Ave. NW, Seattle, WA 98117, tel. 206/789–9377 or 800/488–7368); **Vacation Home Rentals Worldwide** (235 Kensington Ave., Norwood, NJ 07648, tel. 201/767–9393 or 800/633–3284); **Villas and Apartments Abroad** (420 Madison Ave., Suite 1105, New York, NY 10017, tel. 212/759–1025 or 800/433–3020); and **Villas International** (605 Market St., Suite 510, San Francisco, CA 94105, tel. 415/281–0910 or 800/221–2260). **Hideaways International** (15 Goldsmith St., Box 1270, Littleton, MA 01460, tel. 508/486–8955 or 800/843–4433) functions as a travel club. Membership ($99 yearly per person or family at the same address) includes receipt of two annual guides plus quarterly newsletters; rentals are arranged directly between members, not by the club staff.

All of the above represent properties in Italy along with other locations worldwide. Two companies that focus on Italy nearly exclusively are **Cuendet USA** (165 Chestnut St., Allendale, NJ 07401, tel. 201/327–2333), the U.S. representative of Cuendet of Italy, and **Vacanze in Italia** (22 Railroad St., Great Barrington, MA 01230, tel. 413/528–6610 or 800/533–5405).

Also of interest is **Italy Farm Holidays** (547 Martling Ave., Tarrytown, NY 10591, tel. 914/631–7880, fax 914/631–8831), which specializes in *agriturismo* properties. These are working farms that supplement their income by renting out furnished bed-and-breakfast rooms or apartments or separate houses with kitchens. The accommodations, which range from $366 to $630 per couple per week in a B&B (more for larger quarters holding more people), can be too rustic for some or unreliable in quality, but IFH personally inspects all of its properties in Umbria and Tuscany.

Two companies in England with a good selection of rentals on their books are **Villas Italia Ltd.** (Astral Towers, Betts Way, Crawley, West Sussex RH10 2GX, tel. 01293/599988) and **CV Travel** (43 Cadogan St., London SW3 2PR, tel. 0171/581–0851).

Camping Camping is becoming a popular choice for Italians themselves, who can avail themselves of some 1,700 official campsites. Apart from cost considerations, camping is a good way to find accommodations in otherwise overcrowded resorts. Make sure you stay only on authorized campsites (camping on private land is frowned upon). You must also have an international camping *carnet* (permit), which you can obtain from your local camping association before you leave home. You can obtain a directory of campgrounds in Italy by writing to the **Federazione Italiana del Campeggio e del Caravanning** (Federcampeggio, Casella Postale 23, 50041 Calenzano, Florence, fax 055/882–5918) and requesting *Campeggiare in Italia;* send three international reply coupons to cover mailing. (This directory is also available through the Italian Government Travel Office in the United

States or at tourist information offices in Italy, until supplies run out.) The Touring Club Italiano publishes a multilingual *Guida Camping d'Italia* (campsite directory), available in bookstores in Italy for about 30,000 lire, with more detailed information on the sites. Rates for two persons, with tent, average about 30,000 lire a day. **Camper rental agencies** operate throughout Italy; contact your travel agency for details.

Hostels The Italian Youth Hostels Association operates about 50 hostels in Italy. Rates are about 18,000 lire per person per night, including breakfast, but it's not easy to find accommodations, especially in tourist centers, unless you have reservations. Access to international hostels comes with membership in the International Youth Hostel Federation, which, in turn, is provided by membership in any national association; guidebooks listing the hostels worldwide are available through these same associations. (*See* Hosteling in Student and Youth Travel, *above*, for particulars.) In Italy, contact the **Associazione Italiana Alberghi per la Gioventù**, c/o **Ostello della Gioventù** (Viale a Righi ¾, Florence, tel. 55/600315), the Italian member of the International Youth Hostel Federation.

Ratings Hotels in our listings are divided by price into four categories: Very Expensive ($$$$), Expensive ($$$), Moderate ($$), and Inexpensive ($). (*See* Lodging sections in individual chapters for specific prices, which differ according to region.) Hotels in some regions offer attractive half- and full-board packages (in which some or all meals are included in the price) and usually require that you stay a number of days. These deals can often "lower" an establishment into a less expensive classification in real terms because the inclusive deal is a bargain. Particularly recommended places are indicated by a star ★.

Credit Cards

The following credit card abbreviations are used throughout this guide: AE, American Express; DC, Diners Club; MC, MasterCard; V, Visa.

2 Portrait of Florence, Tuscany, and Umbria

Florence, Tuscany, and Umbria at a Glance: A Chronology

c. 1000 BC   Etruscans arrive in central Italy.

c. 800   Rise of Etruscan city-states.

510   Foundation of the Roman republic; expulsion of Etruscans from Roman territory.

c. 350   Rome extends rule to Tuscia (Tuscany), the land of the Etruscans.

c. 220   Umbria, the land of the Umbri and later Etruscans, come under Roman sway.

133   Rome rules entire Mediterranean Basin except Egypt.

49   Julius Caesar conquers Gaul.

46   Julian calendar introduced; it remains in use until AD 1582.

44   Julius Caesar is assassinated.

27   Rome's Imperial Age begins; Octavian (now named Augustus) becomes the first emperor and is later deified. The Augustan Age is celebrated in the works of Virgil (70 BC–AD 19), Ovid (43 BC–AD 17), Livy (59 BC–AD 17), and Horace (65 BC–AD 27).

AD 14   Augustus dies.

65   Emperor Nero begins the persecution of Christians in the empire; Saints Peter and Paul are executed.

117   The Roman Empire reaches its apogee.

165   A smallpox epidemic ravages the Empire.

c. 150–200   Christianity gains a foothold within the Empire, with the theological writings of Clement, Tertullian, and Origen.

212   Roman citizenship is conferred on all nonslaves in the Empire.

238   The first wave of Germanic invasions penetrates Italy.

293   Diocletian reorganizes the Empire into West and East.

313   The Edict of Milan grants toleration of Christianity within the Empire.

410   Rome is sacked by Visigoths.

476   The last Roman Emperor, Romulus Augustus, is deposed.

552   Eastern Emperor Justinian (527–565) recovers control of Italy.

570   Lombards gain control of much of Italy, including Rome.

590   Papal power expands under Gregory the Great.

c. 600–750   Lucca is chief city of Tuscany.

774   Frankish ruler Charlemagne invades Italy under papal authority and is crowned Holy Roman Emperor by Pope Leo III (800).

c. 800–900   The breakup of Charlemagne's (Carolingian) realm leads to the rise of Italian city-states.

1077   Pope Gregory VII leads the Holy See into conflict with the Germanic Holy Roman Empire.

1152–1190   Frederick I (Barbarossa) is crowned Holy Roman Emperor (1155); punitive expeditions by his forces (Ghibellines) are countered by the Guelphs, creators of the powerful Papal States in central Italy. Guelph–Ghibelline conflict becomes a feature of medieval life.

c. 1200   Lucca appears strongest of Tuscan cities. Religious revival in Umbria centers around activities of St. Francis of Assisi and the foundation of the Franciscan order. Umbria takes the lead in art and architecture attracting Pisano, Cimabue, Giotto, Simone Martini, and Lorenzetti.

c. 1250   Florence takes the cultural and financial lead.

1262   Florentine bankers issue Europe's first bills of exchange.

1264   Charles I of Anjou invades Italy, intervening in the continuing Guelph–Ghibelline conflict.

1290–1375   Tuscan literary giants Dante Alighieri (1265–1321), Francesco Petrarch (1304–74), and Giovanni Boccaccio (1313–75) form the basis of literature in the modern Italian language.

1309   The pope moves to Avignon in France, under the protection of French kings.

1376   The pope returns to Rome, but rival Avignonese popes stand in opposition, creating the Great Schism until 1417.

c. 1380–1420   Umbrian cities ruled by *condottieri*.

1402   The last German intervention into Italy is repulsed by the Lombards.

1443   Brunelleschi's dome is completed on Florence's Duomo (Cathedral).

1469–92   Lorenzo "Il Magnifico," the Medici patron of the arts, rules in Florence.

1498   Girolamo Savonarola, the austere Dominican friar, is executed for heresy after leading Florence into a drive for moral purification, typified by his burning of books and decorations in the "Bonfire of Vanities" the year before.

1504   Michelangelo's *David* is unveiled in Florence's Piazza della Signoria.

1513   Machiavelli's *The Prince* is published.

1521   The Pope excommunicates Martin Luther of Germany, precipitating the Protestant Reformation.

1540   Pope Paul III consolidates rule of Umbria with other Papal states.

1545–63   The Council of Trent formulates the Catholic response to the Reformation.

1573–1610   Caravaggio pioneers a painting style using violently contrasting light and dark themes.

1720–90   The Great Age of the Grand Tour. Northern Europeans visit Italy and start the vogue for classical studies. Among the famous visitors are Edward Gibbon (1758), Jacques-Louis David (1775), and Johann Wolfgang von Goethe (1786).

1796   Napoléon begins his Italian campaigns, annexing Rome and imprisoning Pope Pius VI four years later.

1801   Tuscany is made kingdom of Etruria within French domain.

1807–1809	Tuscany is a French département.
1808	Umbria annexed to French empire as département of Trasimeno.
1815	Austria controls much of Italy after Napoléon's downfall.
1848	Revolutionary troops under Risorgimento (Unification) leaders Giuseppe Mazzini (1805–72) and Giuseppe Garibaldi (1807–82) establish a republic in Rome.
1849	French troops crush rebellion and restore Pope Pius IX.
1860	Garibaldi and his "Thousand" defeat the Bourbon rulers in Sicily and Naples.
1861	Tuscany and Umbria join Kingdom of Sardinia, which becomes Kingdom of Italy.
1870	Rome finally captured by Risorgimento troops and declared capital of Italy by King Victor Emmanuel II.
1900	King Umberto I is assassinated by an anarchist; he is succeeded by King Victor Emmanuel III.
1915	Italy enters World War I on the side of the Allies.
1922	Fascist "black shirts" under Benito Mussolini march on Rome; Mussolini becomes prime minister and later "Duce" (head of Italy).
1929	The Lateran Treaty: Mussolini recognizes Vatican City as a sovereign state, and the Church recognizes Rome as the capital of Italy.
1940–44	In World War II, Italy fights with the Axis powers until its capitulation (1943), when Mussolini flees Rome.
1957	The Treaty of Rome is signed, and Italy becomes a founding member of the European Economic Community.
1966	November flood damages many of Florence's artistic treasures.
1968–79	The growth of left-wing activities leads to the formation of the Red Brigades and provokes right-wing reactions. Bombings and kidnappings culminate in the abduction and murder of Prime Minister Aldo Moro in 1980.
1992	The Christian Democrat Party, in power throughout the postwar period, loses its hold on a relative majority in Parliament.
1993	Italians vote for sweeping reforms after the Tangentopoli (Bribe City) scandal exposes widespread political corruption, including politicians' collusion with organized crime. A bomb outside the Uffizi Gallery in Florence kills five, but spares the museum's most precious artworks; authorities blame the Mafia, flexing its muscles in the face of a crackdown.
1994	A center-right coalition wins the spring elections, and media magnate Silvio Berlusconi becomes premier. Italian politics seem to be evolving into the equivalent of a two party system.

3 Florence

By George Sullivan

Florence is one of the preeminent treasures of Europe, and it is a time-honored mecca for sightseers from all over the world. But as a city, it can be surprisingly forbidding to the first-time visitor. Its architecture is predominantly Early Renaissance and retains many of the harsh, implacable, fortresslike features of pre-Renaissance palazzi, whose facades were mostly meant to keep intruders out rather than to invite sightseers in. With the exception of a very few buildings, the stately dignity of the High Renaissance and the exuberant invention of the Baroque are not to be found here. The typical Florentine exterior gives nothing away, as if obsessively guarding secret treasures within.

The treasures, of course, are very real. And far from being a secret, they are famous the world over. The city is an artistic treasure house of unique and incomparable proportions. A single historical fact explains the phenomenon: Florence gave birth to the Renaissance. In the early 15th century the study of antiquity—of the glory that was Greece and the grandeur that was Rome—became a Florentine passion, and with it came a new respect for learning and a new creativity in art and architecture. In Florence, that remarkable creativity is everywhere in evidence.

Prior to the 15th century, Florence was a medieval city not much different from its Tuscan neighbors. It began as a Roman settlement, laid out in the first century BC, and served as a provincial capital when the Roman Empire was at its height. Its rise to real power, however, did not begin until the era of the medieval Italian city-states, beginning in the 11th century.

From the 11th to the 14th centuries, northern Italy was ruled by feudal lords, and by the 13th century Florence was a leading contender in the complicated struggle between the Guelphs and the Ghibellines. Florence was mostly Guelph, and its Ghibelline contingent ruled the city only sporadically (which did not, however, keep the Florentine Guelphs from squabbling among themselves). In those bloody days Florence was filled with tall defensive towers built by the city's leading families on a competitive anything-you-can-build-I-can-build-bigger basis; the towers (and the houses below them) were connected by overhead bridges and catwalks, constructed to allow the members of allied families access to each other's houses without venturing into the dangerous streets below. The era gave rise, possibly for the first time in history, to the concept of turf, and its urban conflicts were at times just as vicious and irrational as the gang warfare within cities today.

The Guelph–Ghibelline conflict ended, finally, with the victory of the Guelphs and the rise of the Medici in the 15th century. The famous dynasty that ruled Florence, and later all Tuscany, for more than three centuries began with Giovanni di Bicci de' Medici and his son Cosimo, who transformed themselves from bankers into rulers. The dynasty reached its zenith with Cosimo's grandson Lorenzo the Magnificent (1449–92), patron and friend of some of Florence's most famous Renaissance artists. The towers were torn down, and the city assumed a slightly softer aspect. It still looks today much as it did then.

The history of modern Florence was shaped by its six years as the capital of the Kingdom of Italy. In 1861 Tuscany united with most of the other states on the Italian peninsula, and in 1865 Florence became the new nation's capital. In 1871 Florence relinquished the honor, when the final unification of Italy was effected by the capitulation of Rome.

But the city's history was equally influenced by the flood of November 4, 1966. The citizens of Florence went to bed the night before in a heavy downpour after three days of rain and a particularly wet autumn; they awoke the next morning to confront the worst disaster in the city's history. Florence was entirely under water. Piazza del Duomo became a rushing river; the church of Santa Croce was battered by a torrent more than 20 feet deep; the Ponte Vecchio disappeared completely as the Arno broke into the walls of its shops and flowed through. Only toward midnight did the flood begin to recede.

The Ponte Vecchio—amazingly—survived. But the damage to the rest of the city, including some of its greatest artistic treasures, was horrific. Technologically and financially ill-equipped to cope with such a disaster, Florence asked for, and received, advice and help from an army of international experts. Today, most of the damage has been repaired, although little has been done to keep this kind of ruin from happening again. A more recent near disaster was the terrorist bomb that exploded near the Uffizi Gallery in 1993, killing five people, destroying a medieval tower, shattering the museum's skylights, and shredding some paintings. Fortunately, no major works were irreparably damaged.

Essential Information

Important Addresses and Numbers

Tourist Information The city information office is at Via Cavour 1/r (next to Palazzo Medici–Riccardi, tel. 055/276–0382; open 8:30–7). Another municipal information office is next to the train station (tel. 055/212245; closed after 2 PM in winter).

The **APT** (tourist office) is just off Piazza Beccaria, at Via Manzoni 16 tel. 055/234–6284; open Mon.–Sat. 8:30–1:30). There is another information office near Piazza della Signoria, at Chiasso dei Baroncelli 17/r (tel. 055/230–2124).

Consulates **U.S.** Lungarno Vespucci 38, tel. 055/239–8276; open weekdays 8:30–noon and 2–4.
British. Lungarno Corsini 2, tel. 055/284133; open weekdays 9:30–12:30 and 2:30–4:30.
Canadians should contact their embassy in Rome.

Emergencies **Police.** Tel. 113. The main police station is located at Via Zara 2, near Piazza della Libertà.

Doctors and Dentists For English-speaking doctors and dentists, get a list from the U.S. consulate, or contact **Tourist Medical Service** (Viale Lorenzo Il Magnifico, tel. 055/475411).

Ambulance. Call 118 or Misericordia (Piazza del Duomo 20, tel. 055/212222). If you need hospital treatment—and an interpreter—you can call AVO, a group of volunteer interpreters who offer their services free (tel. 055/403126, or Mon., Wed., Fri. from 4–6 PM, 055/234–4567).

Late-Night Pharmacies. The following are open 24 hours a day, seven days a week. For others, call 055/110.

Comunale No. 13 (train station, tel. 055/289435).

Molteni (Via Calzaiuoli 7/r, tel. 055/289490).

Taverna (Piazza San Giovanni 20/r, tel. 055/284013).

English-Language Bookstores **Paperback Exchange** (Via Fiesolana 31/r, tel. 055/247–8154) will do just that, besides selling books outright. **BM Bookshop** (Borgo Ognissanti 4/r, tel. 055/294575) has a fine selection of books on Florence. **Seeber** (Via Tornabuoni 68, tel. 055/215697) has English-language books alongside the other titles. All are open 9–1 and 3:30–7:30, closed Sunday and Monday morning.

Travel Agencies **American Express** (Via Guicciardini 49/r, near Piazza Pitti, tel. 055/288751) is also represented by **Universalturismo** (Via Speziali 7/r, off Piazza della Repubblica, tel. 055/217241). **CIT** has a main office (Via Cavour 56, tel. 055/294306) and also a branch near the train station (Piazza Stazione 51, tel. 055/239–6963). **Thomas Cook** is represented by **World Vision** (Via Cavour 154/r, tel. 055/579294). All agencies are open weekdays 9–12:30 and 3:30–7:30, Saturday 9–noon.

Arriving and Departing by Plane

Airports and Airlines The A. Vespucci Airport, called **Peretola** (tel. 055/373498), is 10 kilometers (6 miles) northwest of Florence. Although it accommodates flights from Milan, Rome, and some European cities, it is still a relatively minor airport. **Galileo Galilei Airport** in Pisa (tel. 050/44325) is 80 kilometers (50 miles) west of Florence and is used by most international carriers; for flight information, call the Florence Air Terminal at Santa Maria Novella train station or Galilei airport information (tel. 055/500707).

International travelers flying on Alitalia to Rome's **Leonardo da Vinci Airport** can go directly nonstop to Florence's Santa Maria Novella Station via Alitalia's twice-daily airport train. Luggage is checked through to Florence, and meals and extras are available on the train. Airport train arrangements must be made when you buy your plane ticket. The service also operates in the other direction, returning from Florence to the da Vinci airport.

Between the Airports and Downtown **By Car:** From Peretola take autostrada A11 directly into the city. Driving from the airport in Pisa, take S67, a direct route to Florence.

By Train: A scheduled service connects the station at Pisa's Galileo Galilei Airport with Santa Maria Novella Station in Florence, roughly a one-hour trip. Trains start running about 7 AM from the airport, 6 AM from Florence, and continue service every hour until about 11:30 PM from the airport, 8 PM from Florence. You can check in for departing flights at the air terminal at Track 5 of the train station (tel. 055/216073).

By Bus: There is no direct bus service from Pisa's airport to Florence. Buses do go to Pisa itself, but then you have to change to a slow train service. There is a local bus service from Peretola to Florence. (*See also* Getting Around By Bus, *below.*)

Arriving and Departing by Car, Train, and Bus

By Car Florence is connected to the north and south of Italy by the Autostrada del Sole (A1). It is about an hour's scenic drive from Bologna (although heavy truck traffic over the Apennines often makes for slower going) and about three hours from Rome. The Tyrrhenian coast is an hour away on A11 west. In the city, abandon all hope of using a car, since most of the downtown area is a pedestrian zone. For traffic information in Florence, call 055/577777.

By Train Florence is on the principal Italian train route between most European capitals and Rome and within Italy is served quite frequently from Milan, Venice, and Rome by nonstop Intercity (IC) trains. The **Santa Maria Novella** Station is near the downtown area; avoid trains that stop only at the Campo di Marte Station in an inconvenient location on the east side of the city. For train information in Florence, call 055/288785.

By Bus Long-distance buses run by **SITA** (Via Santa Caterina da Siena 15/r, tel. 055/483651 weekdays, 211487 on weekends) and **Lazzi Eurolines** (Via Mercadante 2, tel. 055/215154) offer inexpensive if somewhat claustrophobic service between Florence and other cities in Italy and Europe.

Getting Around

By Bus Maps and timetables are available for a small fee at the ATAF booth next to the train station or at the office at Piazza del Duomo 57/r, or for free at tourist information offices (*see* Important Addresses and Numbers, *above*). Tickets must be bought in advance and can be purchased at tobacco stores, newsstands, from automatic ticket machines near main stops, or at ATAF booths (next to the station and at strategic locations throughout the city). The ticket must be canceled in the small validation machine immediately upon boarding. Two types of tickets are available, both valid for one or more rides on all lines. One costs 1,200 lire and is valid for 60 minutes from the time it is first canceled; the other costs 1,500 lire and is valid for 120 minutes. A multiple ticket—eight tickets each valid for 60 minutes—costs 9,000 lire. A 24-hour tourist ticket costs 5,000 lire. Long-term visitors or frequent users of the bus should consider a monthly pass, which is sold at the ATAF office.

By Taxi Taxis usually wait at stands throughout the city (such as in front of the train station and in Piazza della Repubblica), or they can be called by dialing 055/4390 or 055/4798. The meter starts at 3,200 lire.

By Moped Those who want to go native and rent a noisy Vespa (Italian for wasp) or other make of motorcycle or moped may do so at **Motorent** (Via San Zanobi 9/r, tel. 055/490113) or **Alinari** (Via Guelfa 85/r, tel. 055/280500). Helmets are mandatory and can be rented here.

By Bicycle Brave souls many also rent bicycles at easy-to-spot locations at Fortezza da Basso, Santa Maria Novella train station, and Piazza Pitti, from **Alinari** or **Motorent** (*see above*), or from **Ciao e Basta** (Lungarno Pecori Girardi 1, tel. 055/234–2726).

By Foot This is definitely the best way to see the major sights of Florence, since practically everything of interest is within walking distance along the city's crowded, narrow streets or is otherwise accessible by bus.

Guided Tours

Orientation Visitors who have a limited amount of time in Florence may find guided tours an efficient way of covering the city's major sights. The major bus operators (*see* Arriving and Departing by Car, Train, and Bus, *above*) offer half-day itineraries, all of which generally follow the same plan, using comfortable buses staffed with English-speaking guides. Morning tours begin at 9, when buses pick visitors up at the main hotels. Stops include the cathedral complex, with its baptistery and bell tower, the Accademia to see Michelangelo's famous statue of David, Piazzale Michelangelo for a fine view of Florence, and the Pitti Palace (or the Museo dell'Opera del Duomo on Monday when the Pitti is closed) for a guided tour. Afternoon tours stop at the main hotels at 2 PM and take in Piazza della Signoria, the Uffizi Gallery (or the Palazzo Vecchio on Monday, when the Uffizi is closed), the nearby town of Fiesole, and, on the return, the church of Santa Croce. A half-day tour costs about 45,000 lire, including museum admissions.

Excursions   Contact the above operators a day in advance, if possible, because excursions are popular. Comfortable buses with English-speaking guides make full-day trips from Florence to Siena and San Gimignano (departure 9 AM, return 6 PM, lunch not included) and afternoon excursions to Pisa (departure 2 PM, return 7 PM), with pickup and return from the main hotels. The Siena excursion costs about 58,000 lire, the Pisa excursion about 38,000 lire. Good bus and train connections make it easy for you to do these on your own, however.

Exploring Florence

No city in Italy can match Florence's astounding artistic wealth. Important paintings and sculptures are everywhere, and art scholars and connoisseurs have been investigating the subtleties and complexities of these works for hundreds of years. But what makes the art of Florence a revelation to the ordinary sightseer is a simple fact that scholarship often ignores: An astonishing percentage of Florence's art is just plain beautiful. Nowhere in Italy—perhaps in all Europe—is the act of looking at art more rewarding.

But a word of warning is in order here. For some years now, Florentine psychiatrists have recognized a peculiar local malady to which foreign tourists are particularly susceptible. It's called "Stendhal's syndrome," after the 19th-century French novelist, who was the first to describe it in print. The symptoms can be severe: confusion, dizziness, disorientation, depression, and sometimes persecution anxiety and loss of identity. Some victims immediately suspect food poisoning, but the true diagnosis is far more outlandish. They are suffering from art poisoning, brought on by overexposure to so-called Important Works of High Culture. Consciously or unconsciously, they seem to view Florentine art as an exam (Aesthetics 101, 10 hours per day, self-taught, pass/fail), and they are terrified of flunking.

Obviously, the art of Florence should not be a test. So if you are not an inveterate museum goer or church collector with established habits and methods, take it easy. Don't try to absorb every painting or fresco that comes into view. There is second-rate art even in the Uffizi and the Pitti (*especially* the Pitti), so find some favorites and enjoy them at your leisure. Getting to know a few paintings well will be far more enjoyable than seeing a vast number badly.

And when fatigue begins to set in, stop. Take time off, and pay some attention to the city itself. Too many first-time visitors trudge dutifully from one museum to the next without really seeing what is in between. They fail to notice that Florence the city (as opposed to Florence the museum) is a remarkable phenomenon: a bustling metropolis that has managed to preserve its predominantly medieval street plan and predominantly Renaissance infrastructure while successfully adapting to the insistent demands of 20th-century life. The resulting marriage between the very old and the very new is not always tranquil, but it is always fascinating. Florence the city can be chaotic, frenetic, and full of uniquely Italian noise, but it is alive in a way that Florence the museum, however beautiful, is not. Do not miss the forest for the trees.

The three walking tours outlined in the following pages are best taken a day at a time. Attempts to complete them in fewer than three days will prove frustrating, for many (if not most) Florentine museums and churches close sometime between noon and 2, and only the churches reopen in the late afternoon.

A special museum ticket valid for six months at seven city museums, including the Palazzo Vecchio, the Museum of Firenze Com'Era (Museum of Florentine History), and the Museum of Santa Maria Novella, costs 10,000 lire and is a good buy if you're planning on doing some of these museums. Inquire at any city museum.

Highlights for First-Time Visitors

Duomo (Cathedral of Santa Maria del Fiore; *see* Tour 1: From the Duomo to the Boboli Gardens).

Battistero (Baptistery; *see* Tour 1: From the Duomo to the Boboli Gardens).

Museo dell'Opera del Duomo (*see* Tour 1: From the Duomo to the Boboli Gardens).

Bargello (Museo Nazionale; *see* Tour 1: From the Duomo to the Boboli Gardens).

Piazza della Signoria (*see* Tour 1: From the Duomo to the Boboli Gardens).

Galleria degli Uffizi (*see* Tour 1: From the Duomo to the Boboli Gardens).

Ponte Vecchio (*see* Tour 1: From the Duomo to the Boboli Gardens).

Galleria dell'Accademia (*see* Tour 3: From the Duomo to Santa Croce and Beyond).

Santa Croce (*see* Tour 3: From the Duomo to Santa Croce and Beyond).

Tour 1: From the Duomo to the Boboli Gardens

Numbers in the margin correspond to points of interest on the Florence map.

The first tour begins with the Cathedral of Santa Maria del Fiore, more familiarly known as the **Duomo,** located in Piazza del Duomo, with its adjacent **Battistero** (Baptistery), the octagonal building that faces the Duomo facade. The Baptistery is one of the oldest buildings in Florence, and local legend has it that it was once a Roman temple of Mars; modern excavations, however, suggest its foundation was laid in the sixth or seventh century AD, well after the collapse of the Roman Empire. The round-arched Romanesque decoration on the exterior probably dates from the 11th or 12th century. The interior ceiling mosaics (finished in 1297) are justly famous, but—glitteringly beautiful as they are—they could never outshine the building's most renowned feature: its bronze Renaissance doors decorated with panels crafted by Lorenzo Ghiberti (1378–1455). The doors, on which Ghiberti spent most of his adult life (from 1403 to 1452), are on the north and east sides of the baptistery—at least copies of them are—while the south door panels, in the Gothic style, were designed by Andrea Pisano in 1330. The originals of the Ghiberti doors were removed to protect them from the effects of pollution and acid rain and have been beautifully restored; some of the panels are now on display in the Cathedral Museum (*see*

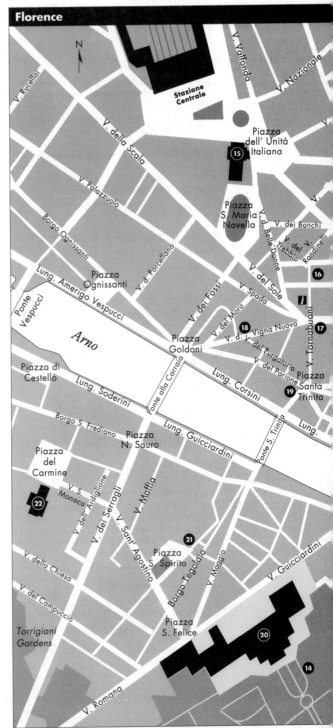

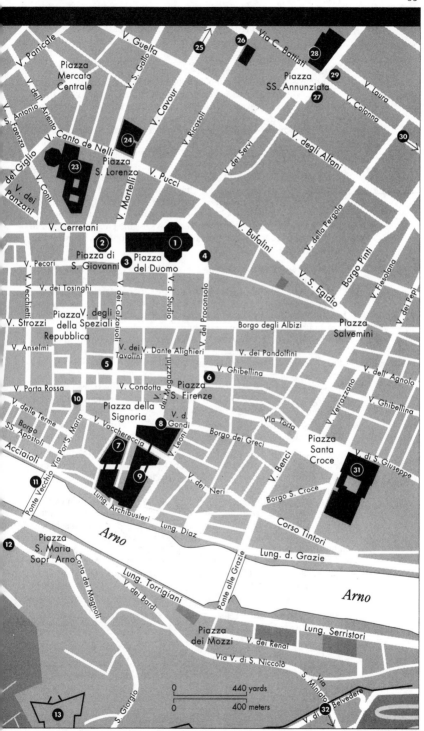

Museo dell'Opera del Duomo, *below*). The copy of the east doors now installed on the Baptistery does not do Ghiberti's work justice. *Admission free to Baptistery interior. Open Mon.–Sat. 1:30–6, Sun. 9–1.*

Ghiberti's north doors depict scenes from the life of Christ; his later east doors, facing the Duomo facade, depict scenes from the Old Testament. They are worth a close examination, for they are very different in style and illustrate with great clarity the artistic changes that marked the beginning of the Renaissance. Look, for instance, at the far right panel of the middle row on the earlier north doors *(Jesus Calming the Waters)*. Ghiberti here captured the chaos of a storm at sea with great skill and economy, but the artistic conventions he used are basically pre-Renaissance: Jesus is the most important figure, so he is the largest; the disciples are next in size, being next in importance; the ship on which they founder is a mere toy. But you can sense Ghiberti's impatience with these artificial spatial conventions. The Cathedral Works Committee made him retain the decorative quatrefoil borders of the south doors for his panels here, and in this scene Ghiberti's storm seems to want to burst the bounds of its frame.

On the east doors, the decorative borders are gone. The panels are larger, more expansive, more sweeping, and more convincing. Look, for example, at the middle panel on the left-hand door. It tells the story of Jacob and Esau, and the various episodes of the story (the selling of the birthright, Isaac ordering Esau to go hunting, the blessing of Jacob, and so forth) have been merged into a single beautifully realized street scene. A perspective grid is employed to suggest depth, the background architecture looks far more convincing than on the north door panels, the figures in the foreground are grouped realistically, and the naturalism and grace of the poses (look at Esau's left leg) have nothing to do with the sacred message being conveyed. Although the religious content remains, man and his place in the natural world are given new prominence and are portrayed with a realism not seen in art since the fall of the Roman Empire, more than a thousand years before.

When Ghiberti was working on these panels, three of his artist friends were bringing the same new humanistic focus to their own very different work. In sculpture, Donato di Niccolò Betto Bardi, known as Donatello, was creating statuary for churches all over town; in painting, Tommaso di Ser Giovanni, known as Masaccio, was executing frescoes at the churches of Santa Maria del Carmine and Santa Maria Novella; in architecture, Filippo Brunelleschi was building the Duomo dome, the Ospedale degli Innocenti, and the church interiors of San Lorenzo and Santo Spirito. They are the fathers of the Renaissance in art and architecture—the four great geniuses who created a new artistic vision—and among them they began a revolution that was to make Florence the artistic capital of Italy for more than a hundred years.

As a footnote to Ghiberti's panels, one small detail of the east doors is worth a special look. Just to the lower left of the Jacob and Esau panel, Ghiberti placed a tiny self-portrait bust. From either side, the portrait is extremely appealing—Ghiberti looks like everyone's favorite uncle—but the bust is carefully placed so that there is a single spot in front of the doors from which you can make direct eye contact with the tiny head. When that contact is made, the impression of intelligent life—of *modern* intelligent life—is astonishing. It is no wonder that when these doors were completed, they received one of the most famous compliments in the history of art, from a competitor known to be notoriously stingy with praise: Michelangelo himself declared them so beautiful that they could serve as the Gates to Paradise.

The immense Duomo—the fourth-largest church in the world—was designed by Arnolfo di Cambio in 1296 but was not consecrated until 1436. The imposing facade dates only from the 19th century; it was built in the neo-Gothic style to complement Giotto's genuine Gothic ❸ (14th-century) **Campanile** (Bell Tower), which stands to the right of the church's facade. The real glory of the Duomo, however, is Filippo Brunelleschi's dome, herald of the new Renaissance in architecture, which hovers over the cathedral (and the entire city when seen from afar) with a dignity and grace that few domes, even to this day, can match. It was the first of its kind in the world, and for many people it is still the best.

Brunelleschi's dome was epoch-making as an engineering feat, as well. The space to be enclosed by the dome was so large and so high above the ground that traditional methods of dome construction—wooden centering and scaffolding—were of no use whatever. So Brunelleschi developed entirely new building methods, which he implemented with equipment of his own devising (including the modern crane). Beginning work in 1420, he built not one dome but two, one inside the other, and connected them with common ribbing that stretched across the intervening empty space, thereby considerably lessening the crushing weight of the structure. He also employed a new method of bricklaying, based on an ancient Roman herringbone pattern, interlocking each new course of bricks with the course below in a way that made the growing structure self-supporting. The result was one of the great engineering breakthroughs of all time: Most of Europe's great domes, including St. Peter's in Rome, were built employing Brunelleschi's methods, and today the Duomo has come to symbolize Florence in the same way that the Eiffel Tower symbolizes Paris. The Florentines are justly proud, and to this day the Florentine phrase for "homesick" is *nostalgia del cupolone* (homesick for the dome).

The interior is a fine example of Italian Gothic, although anyone who has seen the Gothic cathedrals of France will be disappointed by its lack of dramatic verticality. Italian architecture, even at the height of the Gothic era, never broke entirely free of the influence of Classical Rome, and its architects never learned (perhaps never wanted to learn) how to make their interiors soar like the cathedrals in the cities around Paris.

Most of the cathedral's best-known artworks have now been moved to the nearby Cathedral Museum. Notable among the works that remain, however, are two equestrian frescoes honoring famous soldiers: Andrea del Castagno's *Niccolò da Tolentino*, painted in 1456, and Paolo Uccello's *Sir John Hawkwood*, painted 20 years earlier; both are on the left-hand wall of the nave. *Niccolò da Tolentino* is particularly impressive: He rides his fine horse with military pride and wears his even finer hat—surely the best in town—with panache.

If time permits, you may want to explore the upper and lower reaches of the cathedral, as well. Ancient remains have been excavated beneath the nave; the stairway down is near the first pier on the right. The climb to the top of the dome (463 steps) is not for the faint-hearted, but the view is superb; the entrance is on the left wall just before the crossing. *Piazza del Duomo, tel. 055/230-2885. Ex-*

cavation admission: 3,000 lire. Ascent admission: 5,000 lire. Both open Mon.–Sat. 10–5. Duomo open daily 10–5.

Leave the Duomo by the right-aisle exit and turn left; at the east end of the piazza, opposite the rear of the cathedral, is the **Museo dell'Opera del Duomo** (Cathedral Museum). Its major attractions—other than the Ghiberti door panels mentioned earlier and the choir loft (*cantorie*) reliefs by Donatello and Luca della Robbia—are two: Donatello's *Mary Magdalen* and Michelangelo's *Pietà* (not to be confused with the more famous *Pietà* in St. Peter's, in Rome). The High Renaissance in sculpture is in part defined by its revolutionary realism, but Donatello's *Magdalen* goes beyond realism: It is suffering incarnate. Michelangelo's heart-wrenching *Pietà* was unfinished at his death; the female figure supporting the body of Christ on the left was added by one Tiberio Calcagni, and never has the difference between competence and genius been manifested so clearly. *Piazza del Duomo 9, tel. 055/230–2885. Admission: 5,000 lire. Open Mar.–Oct., Mon.–Sat. 9–7:30; Nov.–Feb., Mon.–Sat. 9–5:30.*

Return to the Duomo facade, and turn left onto **Via dei Calzaiuoli.** This unusually wide street dates from the 14th century and probably represents Florence's first effort at modern city planning. The street received special attention because it ran directly from the city's main religious square to its main civic square, Piazza della Signoria, where the medieval city hall was located. Both the axis and the city hall remain intact to this day.

A short detour to the west (down Via degli Speziali) leads to **Piazza della Repubblica.** The piazza's location, if not its architecture, is historically important: The ancient forum that was the core of the original Roman settlement was located here. The street plan in the area around the piazza still reflects the carefully plotted orthogonal grid of the Roman military encampment. The Mercato Vecchio (Old Market), located here since the Middle Ages, was demolished at the end of the last century, and the current piazza was constructed between 1890 and 1917 as a neoclassical showpiece. Nominally the center of town, it has yet to earn the love of most Florentines.

Return to Via dei Calzaiuoli and turn right. Just down the street is the rectangular church of **Orsanmichele,** containing a beautifully detailed 14th-century Gothic tabernacle by Andrea Orcagna. Of particular note here, however, is the exterior. Originally a granary, the building was transformed in 1336 into a church with 14 exterior niches. Each of the major Florentine trade guilds was assigned its own niche and paid for the sculpture the niche contains. All the statues are worth examining, though many are copies. Unfortunately, one that is particularly deserving of scrutiny—Andrea del Verrocchio's *Doubting Thomas* (ca. 1470)—has been removed for restoration (eventually to be put into a museum, perhaps even in Orsanmichele, along with the other originals). Were this niche not empty, you would see Christ, like the building's other figures, entirely framed within the niche, and St. Thomas standing on its bottom ledge, with his right foot outside the niche frame. This one detail, the positioning of a single foot, brings the whole composition to life. It is particularly appropriate that this is the only niche to be topped with a Renaissance pediment, for it is the revolutionary vitality of sculpture like this that gave the Renaissance its name.

From Via dei Calzaiuoli, follow Via dei Tavolini (which turns into Via Dante Alighieri after one block and passes the fraudulently named Casa di Dante on the left) to the intersection of Via del Proconsolo. The church on the southwest corner is the ancient **Badia**

Fiorentina, built in 1285; its graceful bell tower (best seen from the interior courtyard) is one of the most beautiful in Florence. The interior of the church proper was halfheartedly remodeled in the Baroque style during the 17th century; its best-known work of art is Filippino Lippi's delicate *Apparition of the Virgin to St. Bernard* (1486), on the left as you enter. The painting—one of Lippi's finest—is in superb condition and is worth exploring in detail. The Virgin's hands are perhaps the most beautiful in the city. (To illuminate, drop a coin in the box near the floor to the painting's right.)

On the opposite side of Via del Proconsolo from the Badia is the **❻ Bargello.** During the Renaissance the building was used as a prison, and the exterior served as a "most-wanted" billboard: Effigies of notorious criminals and Medici enemies were painted on its walls. Today, the building is the **Museo Nazionale** and houses what is probably the finest collection of Renaissance sculpture in Italy. Michelangelo, Donatello, and Benvenuto Cellini are the preeminent masters here, and the concentration of masterworks is remarkable, though they stand among an eclectic array of arms, ceramics, and enamels. For Renaissance art lovers, the Bargello is to sculpture what the Uffizi is to painting.

One particular display—easily overlooked—should not be missed. In 1402 Filippo Brunelleschi and Lorenzo Ghiberti competed to earn the most prestigious commission of the day: the decoration of the north doors of the baptistery in Piazza del Duomo. For the competition, each designed a bronze bas-relief panel on the theme of the Sacrifice of Isaac; both panels are on display, side by side, in the room devoted to the sculpture of Donatello on the upper floor. The judges chose Ghiberti for the commission; you can decide for yourself whether or not they were right. *Via del Proconsolo 4, tel. 055/238–8606. Admission: 6,000 lire. Open Tues.–Sat. 9–2, Sun. 9–1.*

Leaving the Bargello, continue south along Via del Proconsolo, to the small Piazza San Firenze. The church of San Firenze, on the left, is one of Florence's few Baroque structures; its steps offer a fine view of the Badia bell tower. From the north end of the piazza, go west on Via Condotta, then left onto Via dei Magazzini, which leads into **Piazza della Signoria,** recently excavated and then repaved, the most striking square in Florence. It was here, in 1497, that the famous "bonfire of the vanities" took place, when the fanatical monk Savonarola induced his followers to hurl their worldly goods into the flames; it was also here, a year later, that he was hanged as a heretic and, ironically, burned. A bronze plaque in the piazza pavement marks the exact spot of his execution.

Time Out At the west end of Piazza della Signoria, facing the statuary on the steps of the Palazzo Vecchio, is **Rivoire,** a café famous for its chocolate (both packaged and hot). Its outdoor tables and somewhat less expensive indoor counter are stylish, if pricey, places from which to observe the busy piazza.

❼ The statues in the square and in the 14th-century **Loggia dei Lanzi** on the south side vary in quality. Cellini's famous bronze *Perseus Holding the Head of Medusa* is his masterpiece; even the pedestal is superbly executed (the statuettes in its niches are recent copies of the originals). Other works in the loggia include *The Rape of the Sabine Women* and *Hercules and the Centaur,* both late-16th-century works by Giambologna, and, in the back, a row of sober matrons dating from Roman times. The loggia recently underwent lengthy structural restorations; many of the statues have been replaced by copies.

In the square, Bartolomeo Ammannati's Neptune Fountain, dating from 1565, takes something of a booby prize. Even Ammannati himself considered it a failure, and the Florentines call it *Il Biancone*, which may be translated as "the big white man" or "the big white lump," depending on your point of view. Giambologna's equestrian statue, to the left of the fountain, pays tribute to the Medici Grand Duke Cosimo I. Occupying the steps of the Palazzo Vecchio are a copy of Donatello's proud heraldic lion of Florence, known as the *Marzocco* (the original is now in the Bargello); a copy of Donatello's *Judith and Holofernes* (the original is inside the Palazzo Vecchio); a copy of Michelangelo's *David* (the original is now in the Accademia); and Baccio Bandinelli's *Hercules* (1534).

❽ The **Palazzo Vecchio** itself is far from beautiful, but it possesses a more than acceptable substitute: character. The palazzo was begun in 1299 and designed (probably) by Arnolfo di Cambio, and its massive bulk and towering campanile dominate the piazza masterfully. It was built as a meeting place for the heads of the seven major guilds that governed the city at the time; over the centuries it has served lesser purposes, but today it is once again the City Hall of Florence. The interior courtyard is a good deal less severe, having been remodeled by Michelozzo in 1453; Verrocchio's bronze *puttino*, topping the central fountain, softens the effect considerably.

Although most of the interior public rooms are well worth exploring, the main attraction is on the second floor: two adjoining rooms that supply one of the most startling contrasts in Florence. The first is the vast **Sala dei Cinquecento** (Room of the Five Hundred), named for 500 deputies who debated here from 1865 to 1871, when Florence served as the capital of the Kingdom of Italy. The Sala was decorated by Giorgio Vasari, around 1570, with huge frescoes celebrating Florentine history; depictions of battles with neighboring cities predominate. Continuing the martial theme, the Sala also contains Michelangelo's *Victory* group, intended for the never-completed tomb of Pope Julius II, plus miscellaneous sculptures of decidedly lesser quality.

The second room is the little **Studiolo**, entered to the right of the Sala's entrance. The study of Cosimo de' Medici's son, the melancholy Francesco I, it was designed by Vasari and decorated by Vasari and Agnolo Bronzino. It is intimate, civilized, and filled with complex, questioning, allegorical art. It makes the vainglorious proclamations next door ring more than a little hollow. *Piazza della Signoria, tel. 055/276-8465. Admission: 8,000 lire. Open Mon.–Fri. 9–7, Sun. 8–1.*

❾ Just south of the Palazzo Vecchio is the **Galleria degli Uffizi**, a U-shaped building fronting on the Arno, designed by Vasari in 1559. Built as an office building—"uffizi" means "offices" in Italian—the palazzo today houses the finest collection of paintings in Italy. Hard-core museum goers will want to purchase the English guide sold outside the entrance.

The collection's highlights include Paolo Uccello's *Battle of San Romano* (its brutal chaos of lances is one of the finest visual metaphors for warfare ever committed to paint); Fra Filippo Lippi's *Madonna and Child with Two Angels* (the foreground angel's bold, impudent eye contact would have been unthinkable prior to the Renaissance); Sandro Botticelli's *Primavera* (its nonrealistic fairy-tale charm exhibits the painter's idiosyncratic genius at its zenith); Leonardo da

Vinci's *Adoration of the Magi* (unfinished and perhaps the best opportunity in Europe to investigate the methods of a great artist at work); Raphael's *Madonna of the Goldfinch* (darkened by time, but the tenderness with which the figures in the painting touch each other is undimmed); Michelangelo's *Holy Family* (one of the very few easel works in oil he ever painted, clearly reflecting his stated belief that draftsmanship is a necessary ingredient of great painting); Rembrandt's *Self-Portrait as an Old Man* (which proves that even Michelangelo could, on occasion, be wrong); Titian's *Venus of Urbino* and Caravaggio's *Bacchus* (two very great paintings whose attitudes toward myth and sexuality are—to put it mildly—diametrically opposed); and many, many more. If panic sets in at the prospect of absorbing all this art at one go, bear in mind that the three tours outlined here are structured so as to offer late-afternoon free time, and the Uffizi is, except Sunday, open late. Damage done by the tragic 1993 bombing has been largely erased, and no major works were lost. *Piazzale degli Uffizi 6, tel. 055/23885. Admission: 10,000 lire. Open Tues.–Sat. 9–7, Sun. 9–2.*

Time Out There is a coffee bar inside the Uffizi; its terrace offers a fine close-up view of the Palazzo Vecchio. For something more substantial, try **Cavallino,** the moderately priced restaurant overlooking Piazza della Signoria at Via delle Farine 6/r (closed Wed.).

Leave Piazza della Signoria at the southwest corner and follow Via Vaccchereccia one block west to Via Por Santa Maria. Just north of **⑩** the intersection is an open-air loggia known as the **Mercato Nuovo** (New Market). It was new in 1551. Today it harbors mostly souvenir stands; its main attraction is Pietro Tacca's bronze *Porcellino* (Piglet) fountain on the south side, dating from around 1612 and copied from an earlier Roman work now in the Uffizi. Rubbing its drooling snout is a Florentine tradition—it is said to bring good luck.

Follow Via Por Santa Maria toward the river, and you will arrive at **⑪** the **Ponte Vecchio** (Old Bridge), which is to Florence what Tower Bridge is to London. It was built in 1345 to replace an earlier bridge that was swept away by flood, and its shops housed first butchers, then grocers, blacksmiths, and other merchants. But in 1593 the Medici Grand Duke Ferdinando I, whose private corridor linking the Medici palace (the Palazzo Pitti) with the Medici offices (the Uffizi) crossed the bridge atop the shops, decided that all this plebeian commerce under his feet was unseemly. So he threw out all the butchers and blacksmiths and installed 41 goldsmiths and eight jewelers. The bridge has been devoted solely to these two trades ever since.

In the middle of the bridge, take a moment to study the **Ponte Santa Trinita,** the next bridge downriver. It was designed by Bartolomeo Ammannati in 1567 (possibly from sketches by Michelangelo), blown up by the retreating Germans during World War II, and painstakingly reconstructed after the war ended. Florentines like to claim it is the most beautiful bridge in the world. Given its simplicity, this may sound like idle Tuscan boasting. But if you commit its graceful arc and delicate curves to memory and then begin to compare these characteristics with those of other bridges encountered in your travels, you may well conclude that the boast is justified. The Ponte Santa Trinita is a beautiful piece of architecture.

Once you've crossed the bridge, you are in Florence's Oltrarno—beyond, or across, the Arno—district. A few yards past the south end of the Ponte Vecchio (on the left side of Via dei Guicciardini) is the

⑫ church of **Santa Felicita,** in the tiny piazza of the same name. Rarely visited by sightseers, the church contains one of Florence's finest Mannerist masterpieces: Jacopo da Pontormo's *Deposition*, painted around 1526, above the altar in the Capponi Chapel, just to the right of the entrance. The painting's swirling design and contorted figures are quintessentially Mannerist. The palette, however, transcends Mannerism: Despite being ill-lit (the lights must be turned on by the sacristan), the altarpiece's luminous colors are among the most striking in Florence.

After leaving Santa Felicita, walk along Costa di San Giorgio, which starts as a tiny alley to the left of the church, passes a house once occupied by Galileo (No. 11), and continues on to the Porta San Giorgio entrance in the old city walls. The walk up this narrow street is one of Florence's least-known pleasures. The climb is steep, but just as you begin to wonder when it is going to end, a remarkable transformation takes place: The city falls away, the parked cars disappear, vine-covered walls screening olive trees appear on both sides, birds begin to chirp, and Florence becomes—of all things—tranquil. A narrow Florentine street has suddenly turned into a picturesque Tuscan country lane.

Just before the costa ends at Porta San Giorgio, turn onto the short lane on the right (Via del Forte di San Giorgio), which leads to the
⑬ main entrance of the **Belvedere Fortress** (down the steps and through the arch). The fortress, where temporary art exhibitions are sometimes held, was built in 1429 to help defend the city against siege. But time has effected an ironic transformation, and what was once a first-rate fortification is now a first-rate picnic ground. Buses carry view-seeking tourists farther up the hill to the Piazzale Michelangelo, but, as the natives know, the best views of Florence are right here. To the north, all the city's monuments are spread out in a breathtaking cinemascopic panorama, framed by the rolling Tuscan hills beyond: the squat dome of Santa Maria Novella, Giotto's proud campanile, the soaring dome of the Duomo, the forbidding medieval tower of the Palazzo Vecchio, the delicate Gothic spire of the Badia, and the crenellated tower of the Bargello. It is one of the best cityviews in Italy. To the south the nearby hills furnish a complementary rural view, in its way equally memorable. If time and weather permit, a picnic lunch here on the last day of your stay is the perfect way to review the city's splendors and fix them forever in your memory. *Admission free. Open daily 9–sunset.*

Leave the Belvedere Fortress by the north exit, turn left, and you
⑭ will come to the rear entrance of the **Boboli Gardens,** adjacent to the Pitti Palace. Once inside the entrance, follow the path at the far left. The **Museo delle Porcellane** (Porcelain Museum) here holds the Medici porcelain collections from the palace. The gardens began to take shape in 1549, when the Pitti family sold the palazzo to Eleanor of Toledo, wife of the Medici Grand Duke Cosimo I. The initial landscaping plans were laid out by Niccolò Pericoli Tribolo. After his death in 1550 development was continued by Bernardo Buontalenti, Giulio and Alfonso Parigi, and, over the years, many others, who produced the most spectacular backyard in Florence. The Italian gift for landscaping—less formal than the French but still full of sweeping drama—is displayed here at its best. A description of the gardens' beauties would fill a page but would be self-defeating, for the best way to enjoy a pleasure garden is to wander about, discovering its pleasures for yourself. One small fountain deserves special note, however: the famous *Bacchino*, next to the garden exit at the extreme north end of the palace, nearest the river. It is a copy of the

original, showing Pietro Barbino, Cosimo's favorite dwarf, astride a particularly unhappy tortoise. It seems to be illustrating—very graphically, indeed—the perils of too much pasta. *Admission: 5,000 lire. Open Tues.–Sun. 9–one hour before sunset. Admission to the Porcelain Museum: 6,000 lire; ticket valid also for the Museo degli Argenti in the palace* (see *Pitti Palace,* below). *Open Tues.– Sun. 9–2.*

Tour 2: From the Duomo to the Cascine

Tour 2 also begins at the Duomo. From the north side of the baptistery, walk west along the mostly modern Via dei Cerretani; after three blocks it forks. Take the middle fork (Via dei Banchi), which leads into Piazza Santa Maria Novella, dominated by the church of **Santa Maria Novella** on the north side.

The facade of the church looks distinctly clumsy by later Renaissance standards, and with good reason: It is an architectural hybrid. The lower half of the facade was completed mostly in the 14th century; its pointed-arch niches and decorative marble patterns reflect the Gothic style of the day. About a hundred years later (around 1456), architect Leon Battista Alberti was called in to complete the job. The marble decoration of his upper story clearly defers to the already existing work below, but the architectural features he added evince an entirely different style. The central doorway, the four ground-floor half-columns with Corinthian capitals, the triangular pediment atop the second story, the inscribed frieze immediately below the pediment—these are classical features borrowed from antiquity, and they reflect the new Renaissance era in architecture, born some 35 years earlier at the Ospedale degli Innocenti (*see* Tour 3: From the Duomo to Santa Croce and Beyond, *below*). Alberti's most important addition, however, the S-curve scrolls that surmount the decorative circles on either side of the upper story, had no precedent whatever in antiquity. The problem was to soften the abrupt transition between wide ground floor and narrow upper story. Alberti's solution turned out to be definitive. Once you start to look for them, you will find scrolls such as these (or sculptural variations of them) on churches all over Italy, and every one of them derives from Alberti's example here.

The architecture of the interior is (like the Duomo) a dignified but somber example of Italian Gothic. Exploration is essential, however, because the church's store of art treasures is remarkable. Highlights include the 14th-century stained-glass rose window depicting *The Coronation of the Virgin* (above the central entrance door); the Filippo Strozzi Chapel (to the right of the altar), containing late-15th-century frescoes and stained glass by Filippino Lippi; the chancel (the area around the altar), containing frescoes by Domenico Ghirlandaio (1485); and the Gondi Chapel (to the left of the altar), containing Filippo Brunelleschi's famous wooden crucifix, carved around 1410 and said to have so stunned the great Donatello when he first saw it that he dropped a basket of eggs.

One other work in the church is worth special attention, for it possesses great historical importance as well as beauty. It is Masaccio's *Holy Trinity with Two Donors,* on the left-hand wall, almost halfway down the nave. Painted around 1425 (at the same time Masaccio was working on his frescoes in Santa Maria del Carmine, described later in this tour), it unequivocally announced the arrival of the Renaissance era. The realism of the figure of Christ was revolutionary in itself, but what was probably even more startling to the contemporary Florentines was the coffered ceiling in the background. The mathematical rules for employing perspective in painting had just been discovered (probably by Brunelleschi), and this was one of the first paintings to employ them with utterly convincing success. As art historian E. H. Gombrich expressed it, "We can imagine how amazed the Florentines must have been when this wall-painting was unveiled and seemed to have made a hole in the wall through which they could look into a new burial chapel in Brunelleschi's modern style."

Leave Piazza Santa Maria Novella by Via delle Belle Donne, which angles off to the south where you entered the square from Via dei Banchi and leads to a tiny piazza. In the center is a curious column topped by a roofed crucifix, known as the **Croce al Trebbio.** The cross was erected in 1308 by the Dominican Order (Santa Maria Novella was a Dominican church) to commemorate a famous victory: It was here that the Dominican friars defeated their avowed enemies, the Patarene heretics, in a bloody street brawl.

Beyond the piazza, bear left onto the short Via del Trebbio, then turn right onto Via Tornabuoni. On the left side of the street is the church of **San Gaetano,** with a rather staid Baroque facade (and Albertian scrolls), finished in 1645. Florence never fully embraced the Baroque movement—by the 17th century the city's artistic heyday was long over—but the decorative statuary here does manage to muster some genuine Baroque exuberance. The cherubs on the upper story, setting the coat of arms in place, are a typical (if not very original) Baroque motif.

For those who can afford it, **Via Tornabuoni** is probably Florence's finest shopping street, and it supplies an interesting contrast to the nearby Piazza della Repubblica. There, at the turn of the century, the old was leveled to make way for the new; here, past and present cohabit easily and efficiently, with the oldest buildings housing the newest shops. Ironically, the "modern" Piazza della Repubblica now looks dated and more than a little dowdy, and it is the unrenewed Via Tornabuoni, bustling with activity, that seems up-to-the-minute.

Time Out For a mid-morning pickup, try **Giacosa,** at No. 83 Via Tornabuoni, for excellent coffee, cappuccino, and pastries, or **Procacci,** at No. 64, for finger sandwiches and cold drinks. (Both closed Mon.)

Via Tornabuoni is lined with Renaissance buildings. But its most imposing palazzo is the **Palazzo Strozzi,** a block south, at the intersection of Via Strozzi. Designed (probably) by Giuliano da Sangallo around 1489 and modeled after Michelozzo's earlier Palazzo Medici-Riccardi (*see* Tour 3: From the Duomo to Santa Croce and Beyond, *below*), the exterior of the palazzo is simple and severe; it is not the use of classical detail but the regularity of its features, the stately march of its windows, that marks it as a product of the early Renaissance. The interior courtyard (entered from the rear of the palazzo) is another matter altogether. It is here that the classical vocabulary—columns, capitals, pilasters, arches, and cornices—is given uninhibited and powerful expression. Unfortunately, the courtyard's effectiveness is all but destroyed by its outlandish modern centerpiece: a brutal metal fire escape. Its introduction here is one of the most disgraceful acts of 20th-century vandalism in the entire city.

One block west, down Via della Vigna Nuova, in Piazza Rucellai, is Alberti's **Palazzo Rucellai,** which goes a step further than the Palazzo Strozzi and possesses a more representative Renaissance facade.

A comparison between the two is illuminating. Evident on the facade of the Palazzo Rucellai is the ordered arrangement of windows and rusticated stonework seen on the Palazzo Strozzi, but Alberti's facade is far less forbidding. Alberti devoted a far larger proportion of his wall space to windows, which soften the facade's appearance, and filled in the remainder with rigorously ordered classical elements borrowed from antiquity. The end result, though still severe, is far less fortresslike, and Alberti strove for this effect purposely (he is on record as stating that only tyrants need fortresses). Ironically, the Palazzo Rucellai was built some 30 years *before* the Palazzo Strozzi. Alberti's civilizing ideas here, it turned out, had little influence on the Florentine palazzi that followed. To the Renaissance Florentines, power—in architecture, as in life—was just as impressive as beauty.

If proof of this dictum is needed, it can be found several short blocks away. Follow the narrow street opposite the Palazzo Rucellai (Via del Purgatorio) almost to its end, then zigzag right and left to reach Piazza di Santa Trinita. In the center of the piazza is a column from the Baths of Caracalla, in Rome, given to the Medici Grand Duke Cosimo I by Pope Pius IV in 1560. The column was raised here by Cosimo in 1565, to mark the spot where he heard the news, in 1537, that his exiled Ghibelline enemies had been defeated at Montemurlo, near Prato; the victory made his power in Florence unchallengeable and all but absolute. The column is called, with typical Medici self-assurance, the **Colonna della Giustizia,** the Column of Justice.

⑲ Halfway down the block to the right (toward the Arno) is the church of **Santa Trinita.** Originally built in the Romanesque style, the church underwent a Gothic remodeling during the 14th century (remains of the Romanesque construction are visible on the interior front wall). Its major artistic attraction is the cycle of frescoes and the altarpiece in the Sassetti Chapel, the second to the altar's right, painted by Domenico Ghirlandaio, around 1485. Ghirlandaio was a conservative painter for his day, and generally his paintings exhibit little interest in the investigations into the laws of perspective that had been going on in Florentine painting for more than 50 years. But his work here possesses such graceful decorative appeal that his lack of interest in rigorous perspective hardly seems to matter. The wall frescoes illustrate the life of St. Francis, and the altarpiece, *The Adoration of the Shepherds,* seems to stop just short of glowing.

From Santa Trinita, cross the Arno over the Ponte Santa Trinita and continue down Via Maggio until you reach the crossroads of Sdrucciolo dei Pitti (on the left) and the short Via dei Michelozzi (on the right). Here you have a choice. If the noon hour approaches, you may want to postpone the next stop temporarily in order to see the churches of Santo Spirito and Santa Maria del Carmine before they close for the afternoon. If this is the case, follow the directions given two paragraphs below and return here after seeing the churches. Otherwise, turn left onto the Sdrucciolo dei Pitti.

⑳ As you emerge from the Sdrucciolo into Piazza Pitti, you will see unfold before you one of Florence's largest—if not one of its best—architectural set pieces: the famous **Pitti Palace.** The original palazzo, built for the Pitti family around 1460, comprised only the middle cube (the width of the middle seven windows on the upper floors) of the present building. In 1549 the property was sold to the Medicis, and Bartolomeo Ammannati was called in to make substantial additions. Although he apparently operated on the principle that more is better, he succeeded only in producing proof that enough is enough.

Today the immense building houses four separate museums: the former **Royal Apartments,** containing furnishings from a remodeling done in the 19th century; the **Museo degli Argenti,** containing a vast collection of Medici household treasures; the **Galleria d'Arte Moderna,** containing a collection of 19th- and 20th-century paintings, mostly Tuscan; and, most famous, the **Galleria Palatina,** containing a broad collection of 16th- and 17th-century paintings. The rooms of the latter remain much as the Medici family left them but, as Mary McCarthy pointed out, the Florentines invented modern bad taste, and many art lovers view the floor-to-ceiling painting displays here as Italy's most egregious exercise in conspicuous consumption, aesthetic overkill, and trumpery. Still, the collection possesses high points that are very high indeed, including a number of portraits by Titian and an unparalleled collection of paintings by Raphael, among them the famous *Madonna of the Chair. Piazza Pitti, tel. 055/210323. Admission: Royal Apartments, 8,000 lire; Museo degli Argenti, 6,000 lire; ticket also valid for Museo delle Porcellane* (see *Boboli Gardens,* above); *Galleria d'Arte Moderna, 4,000 lire; Galleria Palatina, 8,000 lire. Open Tues.–Sun. 9–2.*

Return to Via Maggio from the Pitti, take Via dei Michelozzi, a short street that leads into Piazza Santo Spirito; at the north end rises the
㉑ church of **Santo Spirito.** Its unfinished facade gives nothing away, but, in fact, the interior, although appearing chilly (or even cold) compared with later churches, is one of the most important pieces of architecture in all Italy. One of a pair of Florentine church interiors designed by Filippo Brunelleschi in the early 15th century (the other, San Lorenzo, is described in Tour 3: From the Duomo to Santa Croce and Beyond, *below*), it was here that Brunelleschi supplied definitive solutions to the two main problems of interior Renaissance church design: how to build a cross-shaped interior using classical architectural elements borrowed from antiquity and how to reflect in that interior the order and regularity that Renaissance scientists (of which Brunelleschi was one) were at the time discovering in the natural world around them.

Brunelleschi's solution to the first problem was brilliantly simple: Turn a Greek temple inside out. To see this clearly, look at one of the stately arch-topped arcades that separate the side aisles from the central nave. Whereas the ancient Greek temples were walled buildings surrounded by classical colonnades, Brunelleschi's churches were classical arcades surrounded by walled buildings. This was perhaps the single most brilliant architectural idea of the early Renaissance, and its brilliance overthrew the previous era's religious taboo against pagan architecture once and for all, triumphantly reclaiming that architecture for Christian use.

Brunelleschi's solution to the second problem—making the entire interior orderly and regular—was mathematically precise: He designed the ground plan of the church so that all its parts are proportionally related. The transepts and nave have exactly the same width; the side aisles are exactly half as wide as the nave; the little chapels off the side aisles are exactly half as deep as the side aisles; the chancel and transepts are exactly one-eighth the depth of the nave; and so on, with dizzying exactitude. For Brunelleschi, such a design technique would have been far more than a convenience; it would have been a matter of passionate conviction. Like most theoreticians of his day, he believed that mathematical regularity and aesthetic beauty were opposite sides of the same coin, that one was not possible without the other. The conviction stood unchallenged for a hundred years, until Michelangelo turned his hand to architecture and designed the Medici Chapel and the Biblioteca Laurenziana in San Lorenzo across town (*see* Tour 3: From the Duomo to Santa Croce and Beyond, *below*), and thereby unleashed a revolution of his own that spelled the end of the Renaissance in architecture and the beginning of the Baroque.

Leave Piazza Santo Spirito by Via Sant'Agostino, diagonally across the square from the church entrance, and follow it to Via dei Serragli. You are now in the heart of the working-class Oltrarno neighborhood, which is to Florence what Trastevere is to Rome: unpretentious, independent, and proud. Cross Via dei Serragli and follow Via Santa Monaca to Piazza del Carmine. The church of **Santa Maria del Carmine** at the south end contains, in the Brancacci Chapel, at the end of the right transept, a masterpiece of Renaissance painting, a fresco cycle that changed art forever. Fire almost destroyed the church in the 18th century; miraculously, the Brancacci Chapel survived almost intact.

The cycle is the work of three artists: Masaccio and Masolino, who began it in 1423, and Filippino Lippi, who finished it, after a long interruption during which the sponsoring Brancacci family was exiled, some 50 years later. It was Masaccio's work that opened a new frontier for painting; tragically, he did not live to experience the revolution his innovations caused, for he was killed in 1428 at the age of 27.

Masaccio collaborated with Masolino on several of the paintings, but by himself he painted *The Tribute Money* on the upper-left wall; *Peter Baptizing the Neophytes* on the upper altar wall; *The Distribution of the Goods of the Church* on the lower altar wall; and, most famous, *The Expulsion of Adam and Eve* on the chapel's upper-left entrance pier. If you look closely at the latter painting and compare it with some of the chapel's other works, you will see a pronounced difference. The figures of Adam and Eve possess a startling presence, a presence primarily due to the dramatic way in which their bodies seem to reflect light. Masaccio here shaded his figures consistently, so as to suggest emphatically a single, strong source of light within the world of the painting but outside its frame. In so doing, he succeeded in imitating with paint the real-world effect of light on mass, and he thereby imparted to his figures a sculptural reality unprecedented in its day. To contemporary Florentines his Adam and Eve must have seemed surrounded by light and air in a way that was almost magical. All the painters of Florence came to look.

These matters have to do with technique, but with *The Expulsion of Adam and Eve*, his skill went beyond technical innovation, and if you look hard at the faces of Adam and Eve, you will see more than just finely modeled figures. You will see terrible shame and terrible suffering, and you will see them depicted with a humanity rarely achieved in art. *Admission to Brancacci Chapel: 5,000 lire. Open Mon. and Wed.–Sat. 10–5, Sun. 1–5.*

Time Out A popular spot for lunch on Piazza del Carmine is **Carmine,** a moderately priced restaurant with outdoor tables during the warmer months. It is located at the end of the piazza's northern extension. *Closed Sun.*

From Piazza del Carmine, return to Via dei Serragli and walk back across the river over the Ponte alla Carraia (with a fine view of the Ponte Santa Trinita, to the right) to Piazza Carlo Goldoni, named for the 18th-century Italian dramatist. Here you again have a choice:

Turn left to explore the Cascine, a vast (2-mile-long) park laid out in the 18th century on the site of the Medici dairy farms (it begins some 10 blocks downriver, at Piazza Vittorio Veneto), or, if you have not overdosed on art, turn right and return to the Uffizi, which is open all day on most days and which is usually far less crowded in the late afternoon than in the morning.

Tour 3: From the Duomo to Santa Croce and Beyond

Like the other two tours, Tour 3 begins at the Duomo. From the west side of the baptistery, follow Borgo San Lorenzo north one block to Piazza San Lorenzo, in which stands a bustling outdoor clothing market overlooked by the unfinished facade of the church of **㉓ San Lorenzo.** Like Santo Spirito on the other side of the Arno, the interior of San Lorenzo was designed by Filippo Brunelleschi in the early 15th century. The two church interiors are similar in design and effect and proclaim with ringing clarity the beginning of the Renaissance in architecture. (If you have not yet taken Tour 2, you might want to read its entry on Santo Spirito now; it describes the nature of Brunelleschi's architectural breakthrough, and its main points apply equally well here. *See* Tour 2: From the Duomo to the Cascine, *above.*) San Lorenzo possesses one feature that Santo Spirito lacks, however, which considerably heightens the dramatic effect of the interior: the grid of dark, inlaid marble lines on the floor. The grid makes the rigorous regularity with which the interior was designed immediately visible and offers an illuminating lesson on the laws of perspective. If you stand in the middle of the nave at the church entrance, on the line that stretches to the high altar, every element in the church—the grid, the nave columns, the side aisles, the coffered nave ceiling—seems to march inexorably toward a hypothetical vanishing point beyond the high altar, exactly as in a single-point-perspective painting.

The church complex contains two other important interiors, designed by Michelangelo, which contrast markedly with the interior of the church proper and which in their day marked the end of Brunelleschi's powerful influence and the end of the High Renaissance in architecture. The first is the **Biblioteca Laurenziana,** the Laurentian Library and its famous anteroom, entered from the church cloister (exit the church through the door at the left side of the nave just before the crossing, take an immediate right, climb the stairs to the cloister balcony, and enter the first door to the right). Michelangelo the architect was every bit as original as Michelangelo the sculptor. Unlike Brunelleschi, however, he was not interested in expressing the ordered harmony of the spheres in his architecture. He was interested in experimentation and invention and in expressing a personal vision that was at times highly idiosyncratic.

It was never more idiosyncratic than here. This strangely shaped anteroom has had scholars scratching their heads for centuries. In a space more than two stories high, why did Michelangelo limit his use of columns and pilasters to the upper two-thirds of the wall? Why didn't he rest them on strong pedestals instead of on huge, decorative curlicued scrolls, which rob them of all visual support? Why did he recess them into the wall, which makes them look weaker still? The architectural elements here do not stand firm and strong and tall, as inside the church next door; instead, they seem to be pressed into the wall as if into putty, giving the room a soft, rubbery look that is one of the strangest effects ever achieved by Classical architecture. It is almost as if Michelangelo purposely set out to defy his predecessors—intentionally to flout the conventions of the High

Renaissance in order to see what kind of bizarre, mannered effect might result. His innovations were tremendously influential and produced a period of architectural experimentation—the Mannerist era in architecture—that eventually evolved into the Baroque. As his contemporary Giorgio Vasari (the first art historian) put it, "Artisans have been infinitely and perpetually indebted to him because he broke the bonds and chains of a way of working that had become habitual by common usage."

Many critics have thought that the anteroom is a failure and have complained that Michelangelo's experiment here was willful and perverse. But nobody has ever complained about the room's staircase (best viewed head-on), which emerges from the library with the visual force of an unstoppable flow of lava. In its highly sculptural conception and execution, it is quite simply one of the most original and beautiful staircases in the world. *Admission free. Open Mon.–Sat. 10–1.*

The other Michelangelo interior is San Lorenzo's **New Sacristy,** so called to distinguish it from Brunelleschi's **Old Sacristy** (which can be entered from inside the church at the end of the left transept). The New Sacristy is reached from outside the rear of the church, through the imposing **Cappella dei Principi,** the Medici mausoleum that was begun in 1605 and kept marble workers busy for several hundred years.

Michelangelo received the commission for the New Sacristy in 1520 from Cardinal Giulio de' Medici, who later became Pope Clement VII and who wanted a new burial chapel for his father, Giuliano, his uncle Lorenzo the Magnificent, and two recently deceased cousins. The result was a tour de force of architecture and sculpture. Architecturally, Michelangelo was as original and inventive here as ever, but it is—quite properly—the powerful sculptural compositions of the side wall tombs that dominate the room. The scheme is allegorical: On the wall tomb to the right are figures representing day and night, and on the wall tomb to the left are figures representing dawn and dusk; above them are idealized portraits of the two cousins, usually interpreted to represent the active life and the contemplative life. But the allegorical meanings are secondary; what is most important is the intense presence of the sculptural figures, the force with which they hit the viewer. Michelangelo's contemporaries were so awed by the impact of this force (in his sculpture here and elsewhere) that they invented an entirely new word to describe the phenomenon: *terribilità* (dreadfulness). To this day it is used only when describing his work, and it is in evidence here at the peak of its power. *Piazza di Madonna degli Aldobrandini, tel. 055/213206. Admission: 9,000 lire. Open Tues.–Sun. 9–2.*

Just north of the Medici Chapel (a block up Via dell'Ariento) is Florence's busy main food market, the **Mercato Centrale.** If a reminder that Florence is more than just a museum is needed, this is the perfect place for it. There is food everywhere, some of it remarkably exotic, and many of the displays verge on the magnificent. At the Mercato Nuovo, near the Ponte Vecchio, you will see tourists petting the snout of the bronze boar for good luck; here you will see Florentines petting the snout of a real one, very recently deceased and available for tonight's dinner.

Time Out   The **Mercato Centrale** has a number of small coffee bars scattered about; there is even one upstairs among the mountains of vegetables. Have a coffee, watch the activity, and enjoy the fact that for once there is not a painting in sight.

Return to the clothing market in front of San Lorenzo, and from the north end of the piazza follow Via dei Gori east one block, and turn left onto Via Cavour. As you turn the corner, you will pass the **㉔ Palazzo Medici-Riccardi** (entrance on Via Cavour). Begun in 1444 by Michelozzo for Cosimo de' Medici, the main attraction here is the interior chapel on the upper floor. Painted on its walls is Benozzo Gozzoli's famous *Procession of the Magi*, finished in 1460 and celebrating both the birth of Christ and the greatness of the Medici family, whose portraits it contains. Like his contemporary Ghirlandaio, Gozzoli was not a revolutionary painter and is today considered less than first rate because of his technique, old-fashioned even for his day. Gozzoli's gift, however, was for entrancing the eye, not challenging the mind, and on those terms his success here is beyond question. The paintings are full of activity yet somehow frozen in time in a way that fails utterly as realism, but succeeds triumphantly as soon as the demand for realism is set aside. Entering the chapel is like walking into the middle of a magnificently illustrated child's storybook, and the beauty of the illustrations makes this one of the most unpretentiously enjoyable rooms in the entire city. *Via Cavour 11, tel. 055/276-0340. Admission: 6,000 lire. Open Mon., Tues., Thurs.-Sat. 9-1 and 3-6; Sun. 9-1.*

From the Palazzo Medici-Riccardi, follow Via Cavour two blocks north to Piazza San Marco. At the north end of the square is the church of San Marco; attached to the church (entrance just to the right of the church facade) is a former Dominican monastery that **㉕** now houses the **Museo San Marco.** The museum—in fact, the entire monastery—is a memorial to Fra Angelico, the Dominican monk who, when he was alive, was as famous for his piety as for his painting. When the monastery was built in 1437, he decorated it with his frescoes, which were meant to spur religious contemplation; when the building was turned into a museum, other works of his from all over the city were brought here for display. His paintings are simple and direct and furnish a compelling contrast to the Palazzo Medici-Riccardi Chapel (Fra Angelico probably would have considered the glitter of Gozzoli's work there worldly and blasphemous). The entire monastery is worth exploring, for Fra Angelico's paintings are everywhere, including the Chapter House, at the top of the stairs leading to the upper floor (the famous *Annunciation)*, in the upper-floor monks' cells (each monk was given a different religious subject for contemplation), and in the gallery just off the cloister as you enter. The latter room contains, among many other works, his beautiful *Last Judgment;* as usual with Last Judgments, the tortures of the damned are far more inventive than the pleasures of the redeemed. *Piazza San Marco 1, tel. 055/238-8608. Admission: 6,000 lire. Open Tues.-Sun. 9-2.*

From Piazza San Marco, take a short detour a half-block down Via Ricasoli (which runs back toward the Duomo from the square's east **㉖** side) to the **Galleria dell'Accademia.** The museum contains a notable collection of Florentine paintings dating from the 13th to the 18th centuries, but it is most famous for its collection of statues by Michelangelo, including the unfinished *Slaves*—which were meant for the tomb of Michelangelo's patron and nemesis Pope Julius II (and which seem to be fighting their way out of the marble)—and the original *David*, which was moved here from Piazza della Signoria in 1873. The *David* was commissioned in 1501 by the Opera del Duomo (Cathedral Works Committee), which gave the 26-year-old sculptor a leftover block of marble that had been ruined by another artist. Michelangelo's success with the defective block was so dramatic that the city showered him with honors, and the Opera del Duomo voted to build him a house and a studio in which to live and work.

Today the *David* is beset not by Goliath but by tourists, and seeing the statue at all—much less really studying it—can be a trial. After a 1991 attack upon it by a hammer-wielding frustrated artist who, luckily, inflicted only a few minor nicks on the toes, the sculpture is surrounded by a plexiglass barrier. But a close look is worth the effort it takes to combat the crowd. The statue is not quite what it seems. It is so poised and graceful and alert—so miraculously *alive*—that it is often considered the definitive embodiment of the ideals of the High Renaissance in sculpture. But its true place in the history of art is a bit more complicated.

As Michelangelo well knew, the Renaissance painting and sculpture that preceded his work were deeply concerned with ideal form. Perfection of proportion was the ever-sought Holy Grail; during the Renaissance, ideal proportion was equated with ideal beauty, and ideal beauty was equated with spiritual perfection. In painting, Raphael's tender Madonnas are perhaps the preeminent expression of this philosophy: They are meant to embody a perfect beauty that is at once physical and spiritual.

But Michelangelo's *David*, despite its supremely calm and dignified pose, departs from these ideals. As a moment's study will show, Michelangelo did not give the statue ideal proportions. The head is slightly too large for the body, the arms are slightly too large for the torso, and the hands are dramatically too large for the arms. By High Renaissance standards these are defects, but the impact and beauty of the *David* are such that it is the *standards* that must be called into question, not the statue. Michelangelo was a revolutionary artist (and the first Mannerist) because he brought a new expressiveness to art: He created the "defects" of the *David* intentionally. He knew exactly what he was doing, and he did it in order to express and embody, as powerfully as possible in a single figure, an entire biblical story. David's hands *are* too big, but so was Goliath, and these are the hands that slew him. *Via Ricasoli 60, tel. 055/214375. Admission: 10,000 lire. Open Tues.–Sun. 9–2.*

From the Accademia, return to Piazza San Marco and turn right onto Via Battisti, which leads into Piazza della Santissima Annunziata. The building directly across the square as you enter is

㉗ the **Ospedale degli Innocenti,** or Foundling Hospital, built by Brunelleschi in 1419. He designed the building's portico with his usual rigor, building it out of the two shapes he considered mathematically (and therefore philosophically and aesthetically) perfect: the square and the circle. Below the level of the arches, the portico encloses a row of perfect cubes; above the level of the arches, the portico encloses a row of intersecting hemispheres. The whole geometric scheme is articulated with Corinthian columns, capitals, and arches borrowed directly from antiquity. At the time he designed the portico, Brunelleschi was also designing the interior of San Lorenzo, using the same basic ideas. But since the portico was finished before San Lorenzo, the Ospedale degli Innocenti takes the historical prize: It is the very first Renaissance building. The 10 ceramic medallions depicting swaddled infants that decorate the portico are by Andrea della Robbia, done approximately in 1487.

㉘ The church at the north end of the square is **Santissima Annunziata;** it was designed in 1447 by Michelozzo, who gave it an uncommon (and lovely) entrance cloister. The interior is an extreme rarity for Florence: a sumptuous example of the Baroque. But it is not really a fair example, since it is merely 17th-century Baroque decoration applied willy-nilly to an earlier structure—exactly the sort of violent remodeling exercise that has given the Baroque a bad name ever since. The **Tabernacle of the Annunziata**, immediately inside the entrance to the left, illustrates the point. The lower half, with its stately Corinthian columns and carved frieze bearing the Medici arms, was built at the same time as the church; the upper half, with its erupting curves and impish sculpted cherubs was added 200 years later. Each is effective in its own way, but together they serve only to prove that dignity is rarely comfortable wearing a party hat.

One block southeast of the entrance to Santissima Annunziata (on ㉙ the left side of Via della Colonna) is the **Museo Archeologico.** If time and interest permit, a visit here is unquestionably worthwhile. The collection contains Etruscan, Egyptian, and Greco-Roman antiquities; guidebooks in English are available. The Etruscan collection is particularly notable—the largest in northern Italy—and includes the famous bronze *Chimera*, which was discovered (without the tail, which is a reconstruction) in the 16th century. *Via della Colonna 36, tel. 055/247-8641. Admission: 6,000 lire. Open Tues.–Sat. 9–2, Sun. 9–1.*

Follow Via della Colonna east to Borgo Pinti and turn right, following Borgo Pinti through the arch of San Piero to the small Piazza San ㉚ Pier Maggiore. The tower at the south end is the **Torre dei Corbizi,** dating from the Middle Ages. During the Guelph–Ghibelline conflict of the 13th and 14th centuries, Florence was a forest of such towers—more than 200 of them, if the smaller three- and four-story towers are included. Today only a handful survive.

Time Out Have lunch at **I Ghibellini** (closed Wed.), a moderately priced restaurant overlooking Piazza San Pier Maggiore. For dessert, follow Via Palmieri to Via Isola delle Stinche 7/r, and have an ice cream at **Vivoli,** Florence's most famous gelateria.

From Piazza San Pier Maggiore, Via Palmieri (which becomes Via Isola delle Stinche) leads to Via Torta, which curves around to the left—it takes its shape from the outline of a Roman amphitheater once located here—and opens out onto Piazza Santa Croce.

㉛ Like the Duomo, the church of **Santa Croce** is Gothic, but (also like the Duomo) its facade dates only from the 19th century. The interior is most famous for its art and its tombs. As a burial place, the church is a Florentine pantheon and probably contains a larger number of important skeletons than any church in Italy. Among others, the tomb of Michelangelo is immediately to the right as you enter (he is said to have chosen this spot so that the first thing he would see on Judgment Day, when the graves of the dead fly open, would be Brunelleschi's Duomo dome through Santa Croce's open doors); the tomb of Galileo Galilei, who produced evidence that the earth is not the center of the universe (and who was not granted a Christian burial until 100 years after his death because of it), is on the left wall, opposite Michelangelo; the tomb of Niccolò Machiavelli, the Renaissance political theoretician whose brutally pragmatic philosophy so influenced the Medici, is halfway down the nave on the right; the grave of Lorenzo Ghiberti, creator of the Gates of Paradise doors to the Baptistery, is halfway down the nave on the left; the tomb of composer Gioacchino Rossini, of "William Tell Overture" fame, is at the end of the nave on the right. The monument to Dante Alighieri, the greatest Italian poet, is a memorial rather than a tomb (he is actually buried in Ravenna); it is located on the right wall near the tomb of Michelangelo.

The collection of art within the church and church complex is by far the most important of that in any church in Florence. Historically, the most significant works are probably the Giotto frescoes in the two adjacent chapels immediately to the right of the altar. They illustrate scenes from the lives of St. John the Evangelist and St. John the Baptist (in the right-hand chapel) and scenes from the life of St. Francis (in the left-hand chapel). Time has not been kind to them; over the centuries wall tombs were introduced into the middle of them, whitewash and plaster covered them, and in the 19th century they underwent a clumsy restoration. But the reality that Giotto introduced into painting can still be seen. He did not paint beautifully stylized symbols of religion, as the Byzantine style that preceded him prescribed; he instead painted drama—St. Francis surrounded by grieving monks at the very moment of his death. This was a radical shift in emphasis, and it changed the course of art. Before him, the role of painting was to symbolize the attributes of God; after him, it was to imitate life. The style of his work is indeed primitive, compared with later painting, but in the Proto-Renaissance of the early 14th century, it caused a sensation that was not equalled for another 100 years. He was for his time the equal of both Masaccio and Michelangelo.

Among the church's other highlights are Donatello's *Annunciation,* one of the most tender and eloquent expressions of surprise ever sculpted (located on the right wall two-thirds of the way down the nave); Taddeo Gaddi's 14th-century frescoes illustrating the life of the Virgin, clearly showing the influence of Giotto (in the chapel at the end of the right transept); and Donatello's *Crucifix,* criticized by Brunelleschi for making Christ look like a peasant (in the chapel at the end of the left transept). Outside the church proper, in the church museum off the cloister, is Giovanni Cimabue's 13th-century *Triumphal Cross,* badly damaged by the flood of 1966. The **Pazzi Chapel,** yet another of Brunelleschi's crisp exercises in architectural geometry, is at the end of the cloister. *Piazza Santa Croce 16, tel. 055/244619. Church open Apr.–Sept., Mon.–Sat. 8–6:30, Sun. 8– 12:30; Oct.–Mar., Mon.–Sat. 8–12:30 and 3–6:30, Sun. 3–6. Church cloister and museum admission: 4,000 lire. Open Apr.– Sept., Thurs.–Tues. 10–12:30, 2:30–6:30; Oct.–Mar., Thurs.– Tues. 10–12:30, 3–5.*

After leaving Santa Croce, you have a choice. If you have a fair amount of stamina left, cross the river at the Ponte alle Grazie (west of the church complex) and climb the Monte alle Croci above it to investigate the view from **Piazzale Michelangelo** and the church of **San Miniato al Monte;** the latter is a famous example of Romanesque architecture dating from the 11th century and contains a fine 13th-century apse mosaic. If the climb seems too arduous, you can take Bus 12 to Piazzale Michelangelo or you can (as always) return to the Uffizi.

Shopping

Since the days of the medieval guilds, Florence has been synonymous with fine craftsmanship and good business. Such time-honored Florentine specialties as antiques (and reproductions), bookbinding, jewelry, lace, leather goods, silk, and straw attest to that. More recently, the Pitti fashion shows and the burgeoning textile industry in nearby Prato have added fine clothing to the long line of merchandise available in the shops of Florence.

Another medieval feature is the distinct feel of the different shopping areas, a throwback to the days when each district supplied a different product. Florence's most elegant shops are concentrated in the center of town, with Via Tornabuoni and the Galleria Tornabuoni, the world's chic-est shopping mall, leading the list for designer clothing. Borgo Ognissanti and Via Maggio across the river have the city's largest concentration of antiques shops, and the Ponte Vecchio houses the city's jewelers, as it has since the 16th century. Boutiques abound on Via della Vigna Nuova and in the trendy area around the church of Santa Croce. In the less-specialized, more residential areas near the Duomo and in the area south of the Arno, known as the Oltrarno, just about anything goes on sale.

Those with a tight budget or a sense of adventure may want to take a look at the souvenir stands under the loggia of the Mercato Nuovo, the stalls that line the streets between the church of San Lorenzo and the Mercato Centrale, or the open-air market that takes place in the Cascine park every Tuesday morning.

Shops in Florence are generally open from 9 to 1 and 3:30 to 7:30 and closed Sundays and Monday mornings most of the year. During the summer the hours are usually 9 to 1 and 4 to 8, with closings on Saturday afternoons but not Monday mornings. When locating the stores, remember that the addresses with "r" in them, which stands for "rosso," or red, and indicates a commercial address, follow a separate numbering system from the black residential addresses. Most shops take major credit cards and will ship purchases, though it's wiser to take your purchases with you.

Via Tornabuoni

Gucci (Via Tornabuoni 73/r). The Gucci family is practically single-handedly responsible for making designers' initials (in this case the two interlocking "Gs") a status symbol. This Florence store is the one that started it all, and prices on the clothing and leather goods are slightly better here than elsewhere.

Casadei (Via Tornabuoni 33/r). The ultimate fine leathers are crafted into classic shapes here, winding up as women's shoes and bags.

Ugolini (Via Tornabuoni 20/r). This shop once made gloves for the Italian royal family, but now anyone who can afford it can have the luxury of its exotic leathers, as well as silk and cashmere ties and scarves.

Settepassi-Faraone (Via Tornabuoni 25/r). One of Florence's oldest jewelers, Settepassi-Faraone has supplied Italian (and other) royalty with finely crafted gems for centuries. Its selection of antique-looking classics has been updated with a choice of contemporary silver.

Ferragamo (Via Tornabuoni 16/r). Born near Naples, the late Salvatore Ferragamo made his fortune custom-making exotic shoes for famous feet, especially Hollywood stars, and so this establishment knows about less-than-delicate shoe sizes. His palace at the end of the street has since passed on to his wife, Wanda, and displays designer clothing, but the elegant footwear still underlies the Ferragamo success.

Via della Vigna Nuova

Il Bisonte (Via del Parione 31/r). The street address is just off Via della Vigna Nuova; Il Bisonte is known for its natural-look leather goods, all stamped with the store's bison symbol.

Filpucci (Via della Vigna Nuova 14/r). This is Italy's largest manufacturer of yarns. Nearby factories produce skeins of the stuff for

Italy's top designers, and the extensive stock of its retail outlet in Florence encourages the talented to create their own designs.

Laurèl (Via della Vigna Nuova 67/r). An elegant boutique, Laurèl has a reputation for the quality and understatement that is the hallmark of Florentine women's fashions.

Alinari (Via della Vigna Nuova 46/r). This outlet is one of Florence's oldest and most prestigious photographers, and in this store, next to its museum, prints of its historic photographs are sold along with books and posters.

Et Cetera (Via della Vigna Nuova 82/r). In a city of papermakers, this store has some of the most unusual such items, most of which are handmade and some of which have made it into the design collection of New York's Museum of Modern Art.

Antico Setificio Fiorentino (Via della Vigna Nuova 97/r). This fabric outlet really *is* antique, having been producing antique fabrics for over half a millennium. Swaths of handmade material of every style and description are for sale, and the decorative tassels make lovely typically Florentine presents as well.

Borgo Ognissanti

Pratesi (Lungarno Amerigo Vespucci 8/r). The name Pratesi is a byword for luxury, in this case linens that have lined the beds of the rich and famous, with an emphasis on the former.

Giotti (Piazza Ognissanti 3/r). The largest selection of Bottega Veneta's woven-leather bags are stocked at this shop, which carries a full line of the firm's other leather goods, as well as its own leather clothing.

Loretta Caponi (Borgo Ognissanti 12/r). Signora Caponi is synonymous with Florentine embroidery, and her luxury lace, linens, and lingerie have earned her a worldwide reputation.

Fallani Best (Borgo Ognissanti 15/r). The eclectic collection of antiques, while concentrating on 18th- and 19th-century Italian paintings, has enough variety to appeal to an international clientele.

Paolo Ventura (Borgo Ognissanti 16/r). Specialties here are antique ceramics from all periods and places of origin. As with the other shops, the rule of thumb is that the Italian goods are best.

Alberto Pierini (Borgo Ognissanti 22/r). The rustic Tuscan furniture here is all antique, and much of it dates back to the days of the Medici.

Duomo

Bartolini (Via dei Servi 30/r). For housewares, nothing beats this shop, which has a wide selection of well-designed, practical items.

Emilio Pucci (Via dei Pucci 6/r). A member of an aristocratic Italian family, the Marchese di Barsento was a household name in Florence, and until his death in 1992, he presided over the opening of the Renaissance *Calcio in Costume* festivities each year. He became an international name during the early 1960s, when the stretch ski clothes he designed for himself caught on with the dolce vita crowd. His prints and "palazzo pajamas" then became the rage. The shop in the family palazzo still sells the celebrated Pucci prints, along with a line of wines from the family estate in Chianti.

Calamai (Via Cavour 78/r). One of Florence's largest gift shops, Calamai carries everything from inexpensive stationery to housewares in bright, bold colors and designs in its largest of three stores.

Pineider (Piazza della Signoria 14/r and Via Tornabuoni 76/r). Pineider now has shops throughout the world, but it began in Florence and still does all its printing here. Personalized stationery and business cards are its main business, but the stores also sell fine desk accessories.

Casa dello Sport (Via dei Tosinghi 8/r). Here you'll find casual wear for the entire family—sporty clothes by some of Italy's most famous manufacturers.

Santa Croce **Salimbeni** (Via Matteo Palmieri 14/r). Long one of Florence's best art bookshops, Salimbeni specializes in publications on Tuscany; it publishes many itself.

I Maschereri (Borgo Pinti 18/r). Spurred on by the revival of Carnival in recent years, I Maschereri has begun to produce fanciful masks in commedia dell'arte and contemporary styles.

Sbigoli Terrecotte (Via Sant'Egidio 4/r). This crafts shop carries a wide selection of terra-cotta and ceramic vases, pots, cups, and saucers.

Leather Guild (Piazza Santa Croce 20/r). This is one of many such shops throughout the area that produce inexpensive, antique-looking leather goods of mass appeal, but here you can see the craftspersons at work, a reassuring experience.

Ponte Vecchio **Gherardi** (Ponte Vecchio 5). The king of coral in Florence has the city's largest selection of finely crafted and encased specimens, as well as other precious materials such as cultured pearls, jade, and turquoise.

Piccini (Ponte Vecchio 23/r). This venerable shop has literally been crowning the heads of Europe for almost a century, and combines its taste for the antique with contemporary jewelry.

Melli (Ponte Vecchio 44/r). Antique jewelry is the specialty here; it is displayed alongside period porcelains, clocks, and other museum-quality objects.

Della Loggia (Via Por Santa Maria 29/r). For a contemporary look, try this store, which combines precious and semiprecious stones in settings made of precious and nonprecious metals, such as the gold and steel pieces usually on display in its windows.

Oltrarno **Centro Di** (Piazza dei Mozzi 1). Its name stands for Centro di Documentazione Internazionale, and it publishes art books and exhibition catalogues for some of the most important organizations in Europe. Centro Di stocks its own publications along with many others.

Giannini (Piazza Pitti 37/r). One of Florence's oldest paper-goods stores, Giannini is *the* place to buy the marbleized version, which comes in a variety of forms, from flat sheets to boxes and even pencils.

Galleria Luigi Bellini (Lungarno Soderini 5). The Galleria claims to be Italy's oldest antiques dealer, which may be true, since father Mario Bellini was responsible for instituting Florence's international antiques biennial. At any rate, what matters is that the merchandise is genuine.

Via Maggio **Giovanni Pratesi** (Via Maggio 13/r). This shop specializes in Italian antiques, in this case furniture, with some fine paintings, sculpture, and decorative objects turning up from time to time.

Guido Bartolozzi (Via Maggio 18/r). Vying with Luigi Bellini as one of Florence's oldest antiques dealers, Bartolozzi's collection of predominately Florentine objects from all periods is as highly selected as it is priced.

Paolo Paoletti (Via Maggio 30/r). Look for Florentine antiques, with an emphasis on Medici-era objects from the 15th and 16th centuries.

Soluzioni (Via Maggio 82/r). This offbeat store displays some of the most unusual items on this staid street, ranging from clocks to compacts, all selected with an eye for the eccentric.

Sports

Bicycling Bikes are a good way of getting out into the hills, but the scope for biking is limited in the center of town. *See* Getting Around in Essential Information, *above*, for information on where to rent bicycles.

Canoeing Those who get the urge to paddle on the Arno can try **Società Canottieri Firenze** (Lungarno dei Medici 8, tel. 055/282130) near the Uffizi.

Golf **Golf Club Ugolino** (Via Chiantigiana 3, Impruneta, tel. 055/230–1009) is a hilly 18-hole course in the heart of Chianti country just outside town. It is open to the public.

Jogging Don't even think of jogging on city streets, where tour buses and triple-parked Alfa Romeos leave precious little space for pedestrians. Instead, head for the **Cascine**, the park along the Arno at the western end of the city. You can jog to the Cascine along the Lungarno (stay on the sidewalk), or take Bus 17 from the Duomo. A cinder track lies on the hillside just below **Piazzale Michelangelo**, across the Arno from the city center. The views of the Florence skyline are inspirational, but the locker rooms are reserved for members, so come ready to run.

Swimming There are a number of pools open to foreigners who want to beat the Florentine heat, among them **Bellariva** (Lungarno Colombo 6, tel. 055/677521), **Circolo Tennis alle Cascine** (Viale Visarno 1, tel. 055/356651), **Costoli** (Viale Paoli, tel. 055/675744), and **Le Pavoniere** (Viale degli Olmi, tel. 055/367506).

Tennis The best spot for an open court is **Circolo Tennis alle Cascine** (Viale Visarno 1, tel. 055/356651). Other centers include **Tennis Club Rifredi** (Via Facibeni, tel. 055/432552) and **Il Poggetto** (Via Mercati 24/b, tel. 055/460127).

Spectator Sports

Horse Racing You can make your bets at the **Ippodromo Visarno** (Piazzale delle Cascine, tel. 055/360056). Check the local papers to see when they're running.

Soccer *Calcio* (soccer) is a passion with the Italians, and the Florentines are no exception. A medieval version of the game is played in costume each year on or around June 24, feast day of St. John the Baptist, but if you want to see the modern-day equivalent, go and watch the Fiorentina team at the Stadio Comunale (Viale Manfredo Fanti). The big games are played on Sunday afternoon, and the season runs from about late August to May.

Dining

Florentines are justifiably proud of their robust food, claiming that it became the basis for French cuisine when Catherine de' Medici took a battery of Florentine chefs with her when she reluctantly relocated to become Queen of France in the 16th century.

A typical Tuscan repast starts with an antipasto of *crostini* (toasted bread spread with a chicken liver pâté) or cured meats such as *prosciutto crudo* (a salty prosciutto), *finocchiona* (salami seasoned with fennel), and *salsiccia di cinghiale* (sausage made from wild boar). This is the time to start right in on the local wine—Chianti, *naturalmente*. Don't be surprised if the waiter brings an entire flask to the table. Customers are charged only for what they consume (*al consumo*, the arrangement is called), but it's wise to ask for a flask or bottle to be opened then and there, since leftover wines are often mixed together.

Primi piatti (first courses) can consist of excellent local versions of risotto or pasta dishes available throughout Italy. Peculiar to Florence, however, are the vegetable-and-bread soups such as *pappa al pomodoro* (tomatoes, bread, olive oil, onions, and basil), *ribollita* (a thick soup of white beans, bread, cabbage, and onions), or, in the summer, *panzanella* (tomatoes, onions, vinegar, oil, and bread). Before they are eaten, these soups are often christened with *un "C" d'olio*, a generous C-shaped pouring of the excellent local olive oil from the ever-present tabletop cruet.

Second to none among the *secondi piatti* (main courses) is *bistecca alla fiorentina*—a thick slab of local Chianina beef, grilled over charcoal, seasoned with olive oil, salt, and pepper, and served rare. *Trippa alla fiorentina* (tripe stewed with tomatoes in a meat sauce) and *arista* (roast loin of pork seasoned with rosemary) are also regional specialties, as are many other roasted meats that go especially well with the Chianti. These are usually served with a *contorno* (side dish) of white beans, sauteed greens, or artichokes in season, all of which can be drizzled with more of that wonderful olive oil.

Tuscan desserts are typically Spartan. The cheese is the hard pecorino, and locals like to go for the even tougher *biscottini di Prato*, which provide an excuse to dunk them in the potent, sweet dessert wine called *vin santo*, made of dried grapes, which they say will bring the dead back to life!

Remember that dining hours are earlier here than in Rome, starting at 12:30 for the midday meal and from 7:30 on in the evening. Many of Florence's restaurants are small, so reservations are a must. When going to the restaurants, note that the "r" in some of the following addresses indicates the red numbering system used for Florentine businesses, which differs from the black numbers used for residences.

Highly recommended restaurants are indicated by a star ★.

Category	Cost*
$$$$	over 110,000 lire
$$$	70,000–110,000 lire
$$	30,000–70,000 lire
$	under 30,000 lire

**per person, for a three-course meal, including house wine and taxes*

$$$$ **Enoteca Pinchiorri.** A sumptuous Renaissance palace with high,
★ frescoed ceilings and bouquets in silver vases is the setting for this restaurant, considered one of the best in Italy. The "enoteca" part of the name comes from its former incarnation as a wine shop under owner Giorgio Pinchiorri, who still keeps a stock of 70,000 bottles in the cellar. Wife Annie Feolde has added her refined interpretations of Tuscan cuisine—*triglie alla viareggina* (mullet with tomato sauce) and *arrosto di coniglio* (roast rabbit)—to a nouvelle menu that includes *ravioli di melanzane* (ravioli stuffed with eggplant), *petto di piccione* (pigeon breast), and *formaggio alle erbette* (cheese with herbs). *Via Ghibellina 87, tel. 055/242777. Reservations required. Jacket and tie required. AE, MC, V. Closed Sun. and Mon. lunch, Aug., a week in Jan.*

$$$ **La Capannina di Sante.** Florence's best fish restaurant is situated,
★ not surprisingly, along a quiet stretch of the Arno, with indoor tables in an ample, unpretentious trattoria setting and tables out-

doors on the terrace during the warmer months. Risotto and various types of pasta are combined with seafood, and the *grigliata mista di pesce* (mixed grill of fish) is among the standouts. *Piazza Ravenna, tel. 055/688345. Dinner reservations advised. Dress: casual. AE, DC, MC, V. Closed Sun., Mon. lunch, 10 days in Aug., Dec. 23–30.*

$$$ **Il Cestello.** Located across the Arno from the church of San Frediano in Cestello, the restaurant is part of the Excelsior hotel and moves to the roof during the warmer months to enjoy a stupendous view of the city. The Tuscan-based menu features delicious risotto and pasta dishes, including an exemplary *pasta e fagioli* (pasta with beans), a rare selection of seafood, and an ever-changing sampling of whatever is fresh from the market. *Hotel Excelsior, Piazza Ognissanti 3, tel. 055/264201. Reservations advised for nonguests of the hotel. Jacket and tie required. AE, DC, MC, V.*

$$$ **Relais le Jardin.** Another hotel restaurant, this one with a turn-of-the-century, stained-glass-and-wood-paneling setting, stands on its own. Its *crespelle*, or crêpes, come highly recommended in their infinite variety, as do the *medaglioni di vitello al rabarbo* (medallions of veal with rhubarb) and other aromatic meat dishes. *Hotel Regency, Piazza Massimo D'Azeglio 5, tel. 055/245247. Reservations required for nonguests of the hotel. Jacket and tie required. AE, DC, MC, V. Closed Sun.*

$$$ **Terrazza Brunelleschi.** The rooftop restaurant of the Hotel Baglioni
★ has the best view in town. The dining room, decorated in pale blue and creamy tones, has wraparound picture windows framing a close-up of Brunelleschi's dome. The summer terrace outside is charming, with tables placed under arbors and with turrets for guests to climb to get an even better view. The menu offers some traditional Tuscan dishes, such as *minestra di fagioli* (bean soup) and other, more innovative choices, such as vegetable pâté. If you order carefully, your check may be in the $$ category. *Hotel Baglioni, Piazza Unità Italiana 6, tel. 055/215642. Reservations advised, especially in summer. Jacket and tie in evening. AE, DC, MC, V.*

$$$ **Il Verrocchio.** In an elegant 18th-century villa, now a deluxe hotel, the restaurant is about 20 minutes from downtown Florence by car or taxi, and well worth the ride. The dining room has a huge fireplace, columns, and a high, vaulted ceiling. Outdoors you dine on a terrace overlooking the Arno. The menu changes with the seasons but can be described as Tuscan-creative, with such offerings as *agnello con salsa di albicocche* (lamb with apricot sauce) and delicate, fresh pasta dishes. *Villa La Massa, Via La Massa 6, Candeli, tel. 055/666141. Reservations advised. Jacket and tie required. AE, DC, MC, V. Closed Mon. and Tues. lunch Nov.–Mar.*

$$ **Alle Murate.** Situated between the Duomo and Santa Croce, this is a sophisticated but informal restaurant. The menu features creative versions of classic Tuscan dishes—*anatra alle erbe* (boned duck with herb and orange sauce)—but also southern Italian specialties such as *cavatelli con broccoli* (homemade pasta with broccoli and cheese). The main dining room has an elegant, uncluttered look, with warm wood floors and paneling and soft lights. In a smaller adjacent room called the *vineria*, table settings are simpler and the menu more limited. Since the Murate is known for its wine list, this is the place to splurge on a good vintage. *Via Ghibellina 52/r, tel. 055/240618. Reservations advised. Dress: casual. No credit cards. Dinner only. Closed Mon.*

$$ **Angiolino.** This bustling little trattoria in the Oltrarno district is
★ popular with locals and visitors. It has a real charcoal grill and an old woodburning stove to keep customers warm on nippy days. The menu offers Tuscan specialties such as ribollita (thick bread soup)

Dining

Acqua al Due, **25**

Alle Murate, **35**

Angiolino, **6**

Buca
dell'Orafo, **20**

Cantinetta
Antinori, **9**

Enoteca
Pinchiorri, **32**

Harry's Bar, **5**

Il Cestello, **3**

Il Cibreo, **36**

Il Verrocchio, **29**

La Capannina
di Sante, **28**

La Giostra, **33**

La Loggia, **27**

La Maremmana, **31**

Le Fonticine, **12**

Mario, **15**

Mario da Ganino, **21**

Mossacce, **23**

Pallottino, **24**

Relais le Jardin , **42**

Sostanza detto
Il Troia, **4**

Terraza
Brunelleschi, **22**

Toscano, **16**

Za Za, **14**

Lodging

Apollo, **13**

Baglioni, **10**

Beacci Tornabuoni, **7**

Bellettini, **17**

Bencistà, **41**

Brunelleschi, **22**

Excelsior, **3**

Grand Hotel, **2**

Grand Hotel
Villa Cora, **26**

Hermitage, **19**

J+J, **34**

Kraft, **1**

La Residenza, **8**

Liana, **44**

Loggiato dei
Serviti, **39**

Monna Lisa, **37**

Morandi alla
Crocetta, **38**

Nuova Italia, **11**

Pendini, **18**

Plaza Hotel
Lucchesi, **30**

Regency , **43**

Villa San Michele, **40**

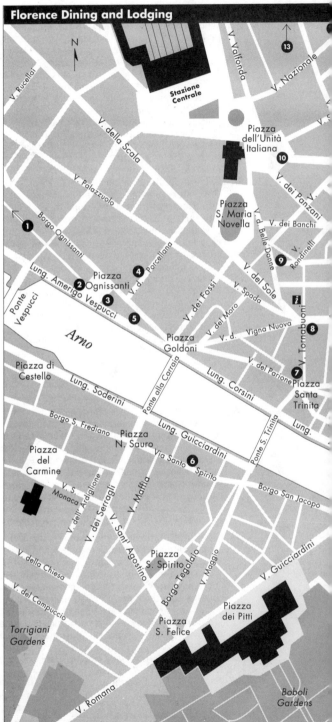

Florence Dining and Lodging

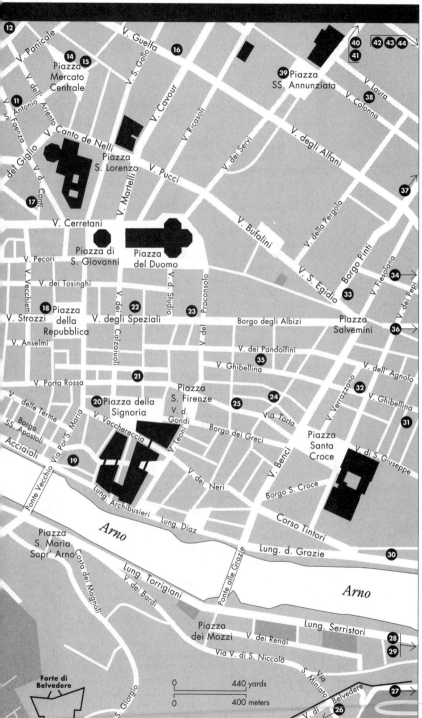

and a classic bistecca alla fiorentina. The bistecca can push the check up, as you pay by weight (order one for two people). *Via Santo Spirito 36/r, tel. 055/239–8976. Dinner reservations advised. Dress: casual. No credit cards. Closed Sun. dinner, Mon., and last 3 weeks in July.*

$$ Buca dell'Orafo. One of the best of the Florentine *buca*, meaning hole, restaurants, Buca dell'Orafo is set in the cellar of a former goldsmith's shop near the Ponte Vecchio. It offers all the Florentine specialties and prides itself on its bistecca. *Via dei Girolami 28, tel. 055/213619. Reservations advised. Dress: casual. Closed Sun., Mon., and Aug.*

$$ Cantinetta Antinori. Set on the ground floor of a Renaissance palace, this is an elegant place for lunch after shopping in nearby Via Tornabuoni. The Antinori family is best known as wine producers, and their wares may be sampled with light salads, bread, sausage, and cheese snacks or more complete meals. *Piazza Antinori 3, tel. 055/292234. Reservations advised. Dress: casual. AE, DC, MC, V. Closed Sat., Sun., and Aug.*

$$ Il Cibreo. ★ Located near the Sant'Ambrogio market, Il Cibreo uses the freshest ingredients to prepare updated versions of Florentine classics, presented in an upscale trattoria-style dining room or in a piazza overlooking the market during the warmer months. The pappa al pomodoro, presented as a thick red dollop on a sparkling white Ginori plate, and inventive dishes such as *anatra farcita di pinoli e uvetta* (duck stuffed with pine nuts and raisins) are two of many specialties. A café annex across the street serves drinks and snacks all day. There is also a small, inconspicuous and inexpensive tavern annex around the corner. *Via dei Macci 118/r, tel. 055/234–1100. Dinner reservations advised. Dress: casual. Closed Sun., Mon., and July 25–Sept. 5, Dec. 31–Jan. 7. AE, DC, MC, V.*

$$ Le Fonticine. ★ Owner Silvano Bruci is from Tuscany, wife Gianna from Emilia-Romagna, and the restaurant combines the best of both worlds in a setting liberally hung with their extensive collection of paintings. Emilia-Romagna specialties such as tortellini ready the taste buds for Tuscan grilled porcini mushrooms so meaty they provide serious competition for the bistecca alla fiorentina. *Via Nazionale 79/r, tel. 055/282106. Reservations advised. Dress: casual. AE, DC, MC, V. Closed Sun., Mon, and July 25–Aug. 25.*

$$ La Giostra. Only about five minutes from the cathedral or from Santa Croce, the Giostra has the typically unpretentious look of a trattoria, but with a difference: the gourmet touch of the courteous owner-chef. Try his ravioli or veal *agli agrumi* (both served with an unusual and delicate citrus sauce) or *spianata di carne* (a skilletful of thinly sliced beef redolent of herbs). Like the menu, the wine list offers good value. Service is informal. *Borgo Pinti 10/r, tel. 055/241341. Reservations advised in evening. AE, MC, V. Check locally for new closing day.*

$$ Harry's Bar. Americans love it, and it *is* the only place in town to get a perfect martini or a hamburger or a club sandwich, but it offers two typical Tuscan dishes every day. The small menu also has well-prepared international offerings, and the bar is open until midnight. *Lungarno Vespucci 22/r, tel. 055/239–6700. Reservations required. Dress: casual. AE, MC, V. Closed Sun. and Dec. 15–Jan. 8.*

$$ La Loggia. Though it may be crowded and somewhat rushed, La Loggia is worth the wait for the view of Florence from atop Piazzale Michelangelo, especially during the summer when there are tables outdoors. The food is almost incidental, but sticking to such Florentine classics as porcini mushrooms and bistecca alla fiorentina makes for a thoroughly memorable evening. *Piazzale Michelangelo 1, tel.*

055/234–2832. Dress: casual. AE, DC, MC, V. Closed Wed. and Aug. 10–25.

$$ Mario da Ganino. On a side street between the Duomo and Palazzo Vecchio, this trattoria is informal, rustic, and cheerful. Your meal might include some of the homemade pasta on the menu. *Gnudoni* (ravioli without the pasta casing) are a specialty, as is cheesecake for dessert. Main courses uphold Florentine tradition, with grilled steak and chops and bean dishes. Get there early; it seats only about 35, and double that number in good weather at outside tables. *Piazza dei Cimatori 4/r, tel. 055/214125. Reservations advised. Dress: casual. AE, DC. Closed Sun. and Aug. 15–25.*

$$ Pallottino. Pallottino has the look of a typical Florentine trattoria, with dark wood tables and benches and copper utensils and old photos on the walls, but here the decor is somehow improved. The menu features traditional fare, from bread or bean soup to *spaghetti alla fiaccheraia* (pasta with piquant tomato sauce). Meat courses are varied; try *involtini alla pallottino* (beef roulades with a creamy sauce). For dessert go down the street for ice cream at Vivoli. *Via Isola delle Stinche 1/r, tel. 055/289573. Reservations advised. Dress: casual. AE, DC, MC, V. Closed Mon.*

$$ Sostanza detto Il Troia. Equally famous for its brusque service as it is for its bistecca alla fiorentina, Il Troia is Florence's oldest restaurant, founded in 1869. Its menu is still strictly Florentine, and all the local classics are served at communal tables, with no frills, to a clientele of out-of-towners and tourists. *Via del Porcellana 25/r, tel. 055/212691. Reservations advised. Dress: casual. No credit cards. Closed Sat. dinner, Sun., and Aug.*

$$ Toscano. A small table attractively set in a show window identifies this restaurant located about five minutes from Palazzo Medici-Riccardi. It lives up to its name in ambience and cuisine. The cold-cuts counter at the entrance, terra-cotta tile floors, and beamed ceilings typify a Tuscan trattoria, but the pink tablecloths, arty photos on the walls, and a touch of creative cuisine take it out of the ordinary. The kitchen prides itself on top-quality meat; this is the place to try *tagliata* (sliced steak) or *spezzatino peposo* (beef stew with lots of black pepper and a wine sauce). The fixed-price menu is good value, at about 28,000 lire. *Via Guelfa 70/r, tel. 055/215475. Reservations not necessary. Dress: casual. AE, DC, MC, V. Closed Tues. and Aug.*

$ Acqua al Due. You'll find this tiny restaurant near the Bargello. It serves an array of Florentine specialties in a lively, very casual setting. Acqua al Due is popular with young Florentines, partly because it's air-conditioned in the summer and always open late. *Via dell'Acqua 2/r, tel. 055/284170. No reservations. Dress: casual. AE, DC, MC, V. Closed Mon. and Aug.*

$ La Maremmana. A display of garden-fresh vegetables and fruit catches your eye as you enter this popular trattoria near Santa Croce. Authentic Tuscan cuisine is offered in the dining room, which has the usual wood paneling and long tables that you will probably be asked to share. The fixed-price menu offers generous servings and good value, and it may include ribollita and *stracotto* (beef stew). *Via dei Macci 77/r, tel. 055/241226. Dress: casual. MC, V. Closed Sun.*

$ Mario. Clean and classic, this family-run trattoria on the corner of Piazza del Mercato near San Lorenzo offers a genuine Florentine atmosphere and cooking, with no frills. Open for lunch only, it's just around the corner from Za-Za (*see below*). *Via Rosina 2/r (Piazza del Mercato Centrale), tel. 055/218550. Dress: casual. No credit cards. Closed dinner and Sun.*

$ Mossacce. You share a heavy wooden trattoria table here and watch the cook in the glassed-in kitchen prepare your order, chosen from a menu of Florentine classics. *Via del Proconsolo 55/r, tel. 055/ 294361. No reservations. Dress: casual. AE, MC, V. Closed weekends and Aug.*

$ Za-Za. Slighty more upscale than neighboring trattorias, Za-Za attracts white-collar workers and theater people. Posters of movie stars hang on wood-paneled walls, and classic Florentine cuisine is served at communal tables. *Piazza Mercato Centrale 16/r, tel. 055/ 215411. Reservations advised. Dress: casual. AE, DC, MC, V. Closed Sun. and Aug.*

Wine Shops In addition, there are many wine shops where you can have a snack or sandwich. Of these, **Le Cantine** (Via dei Pucci) is stylish and popular, as is **Cantinone del Gallo Nero** (Via Santo Spirito 6), which also serves meals in a brick-vaulted wine cellar. More modest are **Borgioli** (Piazza dell'Olio), **Fiaschetteria** (Via dei Neri 2, corner of Via dei Benci), **Fratellini** (Via dei Cimatori), **Nicolino** (Volta dei Mercanti), and **Piccolo Vinaio** (Via Castellani).

Lodging

Florence's importance not only as a tourist city but as a convention center and the site of the Pitti fashion collections throughout the year has guaranteed a variety of accommodations, many in former villas and palazzos. However, these very factors mean that, except during the winter, reservations are a must.

Near the A1 autostrada exits, drivers will find the Sheraton Firenze (tel. 055/64901, fax 055/680747, $$$$), the Holiday Inn (tel. 055/653– 1841, fax 055/653–1806, $$$), and the Forte Agip (tel. 055/421–1881, fax 055/421–9015, $$).

If you do find yourself in Florence with no reservations, go to the **Consorzio ITA** office in the train station. It's open every day from 8:20 AM to 9 PM. If the office is shut, your best bet is to try some of the inexpensive (but clean) accommodations at a one- or two-star hotel; many are located on **Via Nazionale** (which leads east from Piazza Stazione) and on **Via Faenza,** the second left off Via Nazionale.

Highly recommended lodgings are indicated by a star ★.

Category	Cost*
$$$$	over 400,000 lire
$$$	225,000–400,000 lire
$$	150,000–225,000 lire
$	under 150,000 lire

All prices are for a double room for two, including tax and service.

$$$$ **Excelsior.** Traditional Old World charm finds a regal setting at the
★ Excelsior, a neo-Renaissance palace complete with painted wooden ceilings, stained glass, and acres of Oriental carpets strewn over marble floors in the public rooms. The rooms are furnished with the chaises longues, classical decorations, and long mirrors of the Empire style. Plush touches include wall-to-wall carpeting in the rooms and thick terrycloth towels on heated racks in the bathrooms. Its Il Cestello restaurant serves excellent food and in summer moves up to the roof for a wonderful view. *Piazza Ognissanti 3, tel. 055/264201,*

fax 055/210278. 205 rooms with bath. Facilities: restaurant with piano bar. AE, DC, MC, V.

$$$$ **Grand Hotel.** Across the piazza from the Excelsior, this Florentine classic, also owned by the CIGA chain, provides all the luxurious amenities of its sister. Most rooms and public areas are decorated in sumptuous Renaissance style, many with frescoes. Baths are in marble. Some rooms have balconies overlooking the Arno. *Piazza Ognissanti 1, tel. 055/288781, fax 055/217400. 107 rooms with bath. Facilities: restaurant, winter garden, bar, parking. AE, DC, MC, V.*

$$$$ **Grand Hotel Villa Cora.** Built near the Boboli Gardens and Piazzale Michelangelo in the mid-19th century when Florence was briefly the capital of Italy, the Villa Cora retains the opulence of that era. The decor of its remarkable public and private rooms runs the gamut from neoclassical to rococo and even Moorish, and reflects the splendor of such former guests as the Empress Eugénie, wife of Napoléon III, and Madame Von Meck, Tchaikovsky's mysterious benefactress. *Viale Machiavelli 18, tel. 055/2298451, fax 055/229086. 48 rooms with bath. Facilities: restaurant, garden, pool, piano bar, car service. AE, DC, MC, V.*

$$$$ **Regency.** Undisturbed sleep is almost guaranteed at this hotel, which is tucked away in a respectable residential district near the synagogue. The rooms are decorated in richly colored and tasteful fabrics and antique-style furniture faithful to the hotel's 19th-century origins as a private mansion. It has one of Florence's best hotel restaurants. *Piazza Massimo D'Azeglio 3, tel. 055/245247, fax 055/234-2938. 33 rooms with bath. Facilities: restaurant, garden. AE, DC, MC, V.*

$$$$ **Villa San Michele.** The setting for this hideaway is so romantic—nestled in the hills of nearby Fiesole—that it once attracted Brigitte Bardot for her honeymoon. The villa was originally a monastery whose facade and loggia have been attributed to Michelangelo. The rooms now contain sumptuous statuary, paintings, and Jacuzzis. Many have a panoramic view of Florence, while others face an inner courtyard. A luxuriant garden surrounds the whole affair. The restaurant is excellent. *Via Doccia 4, Fiesole, tel. 055/59451, fax 055/598734. 28 rooms with bath. Facilities: restaurant, piano bar, pool, garden, courtesy bus service. AE, DC, MC, V. Open mid-Mar.–mid-Nov.*

$$$ **Baglioni.** This large turn-of-the-century building was conceived in
★ the European tradition of grand hotels; it's located between the train station and the cathedral. The charming roof terrace has the best view in Florence and is home to the Terrazza Brunelleschi restaurant. The hotel has well-proportioned rooms decorated in antique Florentine style, and many have leaded glass windows. Fourth-floor rooms have been done in pastel tones harmonizing with the carpeting or mellow parquet. There is a full range of conference facilities, which makes it a favorite of businesspeople. *Piazza dell'Unità Italiana 6, tel. 055/23580, fax 055/235-8895. 197 rooms with bath. Facilities: roof-garden restaurant. AE, DC, MC, V.*

$$$ **Beacci Tornabuoni.** This is perhaps *the* classic Florentine pensione (although by law all lodgings have been reclassified as hotels of various categories). Set in a 14th-century palazzo, it contains a series of quaint, old-fashioned but modernized rooms, all presided over by a signora full of personality. Half board is required, but the food is good and can also be brought to the rooms, most of which have views of the red-tiled roofs in the neighboring downtown area. *Via Tornabuoni 3, tel. 055/212645, fax 055/283594. 30 rooms with bath. Facilities: restaurant, bar. AE, DC, MC, V.*

\$\$\$ **Brunelleschi.** Architects united a Byzantine tower, a medieval
★ church, and a later building in a stunning structure in the very heart
of Renaissance Florence to make this the city's most unique hotel.
This remarkable place even has its own museum displaying the ancient Roman foundations and pottery shards found during restoration. Medieval stone walls and brick arches contrast pleasingly with
the plush, contemporary decor. The comfortable, soundproof bedrooms, many with good views, are done in coordinated patterns and
soft colors; the ample bathrooms feature beige travertine marble.
Brunelleschi ranks high for atmosphere, interest, and comfort. *Piazza Sant'Elisabetta (Via dei Calzaiuoli), tel. 055/562068, fax 055/
219653. 94 rooms with bath, 7 junior suites. Facilities: restaurant,
bar, conference rooms. AE, DC, MC, V.*

\$\$\$ **J&J.** Away from the crowds, on a quiet street within walking dis-
tance of the sights, this unusual hotel is a converted 16th-century
monastery. Its large, suitelike rooms are ideal for honeymooners,
families, and small groups of friends traveling together. Some
rooms are on two levels, and all are imaginatively arranged around a
central courtyard and decorated with flair. There are also smaller
more intimate rooms, some opening onto their own little courtyard.
The gracious owners chat with guests in the elegant lounge; breakfast is served in a glassed-in Renaissance loggia or in the central
courtyard. *Via di Mezzo 20, tel. 055/240951, fax 055/240282. 20
rooms with bath. Facilities: bar. AE, DC, MC, V.*

\$\$\$ **Kraft.** The efficient and comfortable Kraft is modern, but it has
many period-style rooms, some with balconies looking out toward
the Arno. Its location near the Teatro Comunale (it is also next to the
U.S. consulate) gives it a clientele from the music world. *Via Solferino 2, tel. 055/284273, fax 055/239–8267. 68 rooms with bath. Facilities: rooftop restaurant, pool. AE, DC, MC, V.*

\$\$\$ **Monna Lisa.** Housed in a Renaissance palazzo, the hotel retains its
★ original *pietra serena* staircase, terra-cotta floors, and painted ceilings. Its rooms still have a rather homey quality, and though on the
small side, many have contemplative views of a lovely garden. The
ground-floor lounges give you the feel of living in an aristocratic
town house. *Borgo Pinti 27, tel. 055/247–9751, fax 055/247–9755. 30
rooms with bath. Facilities: garden, bar. AE, DC, MC, V.*

\$\$\$ **Plaza Hotel Lucchesi.** Elegant without being ostentatious, this ho-
tel is right on the Arno near Santa Croce. Front bedrooms have
views of the river and hills beyond; rear rooms on the top floor have
balconies and knockout views of Santa Croce. Spacious, quiet bedrooms (double glazing throughout) are furnished comfortably in ma-
hogany and pastel fabrics, against creamy white walls. The roomy,
welcoming lounges and piano bar are favorite meeting places for
Florentines. *Lungarno della Zecca Vecchia 38, tel. 055/264141, fax
055/248–0921. 100 rooms with bath. Facilities: La Serra restaurant,
bar, garage. AE, DC, MC, V.*

\$\$ **Bencistà.** Below the luxurious Villa San Michele in Fiesole, this hotel has the same tranquil setting and is even two centuries older. The
rooms are furnished with antiques, and half board is required. *Via
Benedetto da Maiano 4, Fiesole, tel. and fax, 055/59163. 40 rooms,
30 with bath. No credit cards.*

\$\$ **Hermitage.** Comfortable and charming are suitable adjectives for
this hotel occupying two floors of a palazzo next to Ponte Vecchio and
the Uffizi. Inviting living rooms overlooking the Arno, bright
breakfast rooms, flowered roof terrace, and well-lighted bedrooms
have the decor and atmosphere of a well-kept Florentine home. Double glazing, air-conditioning, and attentive maintenance sustain the
relaxing ambience. (The hotel has an elevator located at the top of a

short flight of stairs from the street.) _Vicolo Marzio 1 (Piazza del Pesce, Ponte Vecchio), tel. 055/287216, fax 055/212208. 30 rooms with bath. Facilities: roof terrace. AE, MC, V._

$$ Loggiato dei Serviti. A relatively new hotel, the Loggiato dei Serviti
★ is tucked away under a historic loggia in one of the city's quietest and loveliest squares. Vaulted ceilings and tasteful furnishings, some of them antiques, make this a place for those who want to get the feel of Florence in a spare, Renaissance building while enjoying modern creature comforts. The hotel has no restaurant. _Piazza Santissima Annunziata 3, tel. 055/289592, fax 055/289595. 29 rooms with bath. AE, DC, MC, V._

$$ Morandi alla Crocetta. Near Piazza Santissima Annunziata, this is a
★ charming and distinguished residence in which guests are made to feel like privileged friends of the family. It is close to the sights but very quiet, in a former monastery, and is furnished comfortably in the classic style of a gracious Florentine home. The Morandi is not only an exceptional hotel but also a good value. Very small, it is worth booking well in advance. _Via Laura 50, tel. 055/234-4747, fax 055/248-0954. 9 rooms with bath. AE, DC, MC, V._

$$ Pendini. The atmosphere of an old-fashioned Florentine pensione is intact here, though most bedrooms have been freshly renovated. Public rooms are delightful; furnishings throughout are early 19th-century antiques or reproductions. Most bedrooms have brass or walnut beds, pretty floral wallpaper, and pastel carpeting; baths are modern. Many rooms can accommodate extra beds. The location is central, and rates are low for the category. _Via Strozzi 2, tel. 055/ 211170, fax 055/210156. 42 rooms with bath. AE, DC, MC, V._

$$ La Residenza. Located just down the street from the Beacci, on Florence's most elegant shopping street, is La Residenza: The top floor has a charming roof garden and rooms with even better views for fewer lire. The signora here is equally accommodating, the decor equally antique, and the plumbing up to date. _Via Tornabuoni 8, tel. 055/284197. 24 rooms with bath. Facilities: roof garden, garage. AE, DC, V._

$ Apollo. A friendly Italian-Canadian couple owns and manages this conveniently located hotel near the station, offering good value in spacious rooms decorated in Florentine style. The gleaming new bathrooms, though compact, have such amenities as hair dryers. The staff is helpful and attentive to guests' needs. _Via Faenza 77, tel. 055/284119, fax 055/210101. 15 rooms with bath. AE, DC, MC, V._

$ Bellettini. You couldn't ask for anything more central; this small ho-
★ tel is on three floors (the top floor has two nice rooms with a view) of a palazzo near the Duomo. The cordial family management takes good care of guests, providing a relaxed atmosphere and attractive public rooms with a scattering of antiques. Breakfast, with home-made cakes, and air-conditioning are included in the low room rate. The good-size rooms have Venetian or Tuscan provincial decor; bathrooms are bright and modern. _Via dei Conti 7, tel. 055/213561, fax 055/283551. 28 rooms with bath. Facilities: bar, lounge. AE, DC, MC, V._

$ Liana. This small hotel, located near the English Cemetery, is in a quiet 19th-century villa that formerly housed the British Embassy. Its clean and pleasant rooms all face a stately garden. _Via Vittorio Alfieri 18, tel. 055/245303, fax 055/234-4596. 23 rooms with bath or shower. AE, MC, V._

$ Nuova Italia. Near the train station, within walking distance of the sights, this hotel is run by a genial English-speaking family. It has a homey atmosphere; rooms are clean and simply furnished, bright with pictures and posters, and all with private baths. Some rooms can accommodate extra beds. Low, bargain rates include breakfast. *Via Faenza 26, tel. 055/268430, fax 055/210941. 20 rooms with bath. AE, DC, MC, V.*

The Arts and Nightlife

The Arts

Theater **Estate Fiesolana.** From June through August, this festival of theater, music, dance, and film takes place in the churches and the archaeological area of Fiesole (Teatro Romano, Fiesole, tel. 055/599931).

Concerts **Maggio Musicale Fiorentina.** This series of internationally acclaimed concerts and recitals is held in the **Teatro Comunale** (Corso Italia 16, tel. 055/277–9236) from late April through June. From December to early June, there is a concert season of the Orchestra Regionale Toscana in the church of **Santo Stefano al Ponte Vecchio** (tel. 055/210804). Amici della Musica organizes concerts at the **Teatro della Pergola** (box office Via della Pergola 10/r, tel. 055/247–9652).

Opera Operas are performed in the Teatro Comunale from December through February.

Film **Florence Film Festival.** An international panel of judges gathers in late spring at the Forte di Belvedere to preside over a wide selection of new releases.

Festival del Popolo. This festival, held each December, is devoted to documentaries and is held in the Fortezza da Basso.

English-language films are shown at the **Cinema Astro** on Piazza San Simone near Santa Croce. There are two shows every evening, Tuesday through Sunday (closed in July).

Nightlife

Unlike the Romans and Milanese, the frugal and reserved Florentines do not have a reputation for an active nightlife; however, the following places attract a mixed crowd of Florentines and visitors.

Piano Bars Many of the more expensive hotels have their own piano bars, where nonguests are welcome to come for an *aperitivo* or an after-dinner drink. The best view is from the bar at the **Excelsior** (Piazza Ognissanti 3, tel. 055/264201), on a roof garden overlooking the Arno. Music is on tape at the **Champagneria** (Via Lambruschini 15/r, tel. 055/490804, a bistro-type watering hole (closed Sun.). The accent is on Brazil at **Caffè Voltaire** (Via della Scala 9/r, tel. 055/218255), where there's Latin food and music.

Nightclub **The River Club** (Lungarno Corsini 8, tel. 055/282465) has winter-garden decor and a large dance floor (closed Sun.).

Discos The two largest discos, with the youngest crowds, are **Yab** (Via Sassetti 5r, tel. 055/282018) and **Space Electronic** (Via Palazzuolo 37, tel. 055/239–3082). Less frenetic alternatives are **Jackie O'** (Via Erta Canina 24, tel. 055/234–4904) and **Full Up** (Via della Vigna Vecchia 21/r, tel. 055/293006). **Meccanò** (Viale degli Olmi 1, in Cascine Park, tel. 055/331371) is a multimedia experience in a high-tech disco with a late-night restaurant (closed Mon.).

4 Tuscany

*Lucca, Siena, and
the Hill Towns*

Rome may be the capital of Italy, but Tuscany is its heart. Stretching from the Apennines to the sea, midway between Milan and Rome, the region is quintessentially Italian, in both its appearance and its history. Its scenic variety is unmatched in Italy; its past has been ignoble (it produced the Guelph-Ghibelline conflict of the Middle Ages) and glorious (it produced the Renaissance). Its towns are justly famous for their wealth of fine architecture and art, but visitors often come home even more enthusiastic about Tuscany's unspoiled hilly landscapes, about the delicious Chianti wines produced by vineyards on those hills, and about the robust and flavorful Tuscan cooking. Be sure to allot some portion of your time here for leisurely strolls, unhurried meals, and aimless wandering around this peerless countryside, where the true soul of Tuscany is to be found.

Tuscany also produced the Italian language. It was the Tuscan Dialect of Dante, Petrarch , and Boccaccio—all native sons and eminent writers—that became the national tongue, a fact of which the Tuscans are rightly proud. Today the purest Italian is said to be spoken in the area between Siena and Arezzo, and even visitors with limited textbook Italian can often hear the difference. As they enter the region, the language suddenly becomes much easier to understand and takes on a bell-like clarity and mellifluous beauty unequaled throughout the rest of Italy.

It also takes on a notorious wit. As a common proverb has it, "Tuscans have Paradise in their eyes and the Inferno in their mouths" (a wry reference to Dante), and the sting of Tuscan wit is as famous throughout Italy as the beauty of Tuscan speech. Happily, the Tuscans usually reserve their wit for each other and treat visitors with complete and sincere courtesy.

For a long time, the Tuscan hill towns were notorious as well. Even its earliest civilized settlers, the Etruscans, chose their city/sites for defensive purposes (the fortress/town of Fiesole, above Florence, is a fine surviving example). With the end of the Roman Empire, the region fell into disunity, and by the 11th century Tuscany had evolved into a collection of independent city-states, each city seeking to dominate, and sometimes forcibly overpower, its neighbors. The region then became embroiled in an apparently endless international quarrel between a long succession of popes and Holy Roman Emperors. By the 13th century, Tuscany had become a battleground: The infamous conflict between the Guelphs and the Ghibellines had begun.

The Guelphs and the Ghibellines are the bane of Italian schoolchildren; their infinitely complicated, bloody history is to Italy what the Wars of the Roses are to England. To oversimplify grossly, the Ghibellines were mostly allied with both the Holy Roman Emperor (headquartered over the Alps in Germany) and the local aristocracy (dominated by feudal lords); the Guelphs were mostly allied with both the pope (headquartered in Rome) and the emerging middle class (dominated by the new trade guilds). Florence, flourishing as a trade center, was (most of the time) Guelph; its neighboring city-states Pisa and Siena were (most of the time) Ghibelline. But the bitter struggles that resulted were so Byzantine in their complexity, so full of factional disputes and treachery, that a dizzying series of conflicts within conflicts resulted. (Dante, for instance, was banished from Florence not for being a Ghibelline but for being the wrong brand of Guelph.)

Eventually the Florentine Guelphs emerged victorious, and in the 15th century the region was united to become the Grand Duchy of

Tuscany, controlled from Florence by the Medici grand dukes. Today the hill towns are no longer fierce, although they retain a uniquely medieval air, and in most of them the citizens walk the same narrow streets and inhabit the same houses that their ancestors did 600 years ago.

Tuscan art, to most people, means Florence, and understandably so. The city is unique and incomparable, and an astonishing percentage of the great artists of the Renaissance lived and worked there. But there is art elsewhere in Tuscany, and too often it is overlooked in favor of another trip to the Uffizi. Siena, particularly, possesses its own style of architecture and art quite different from the Florentine variety; the contrast is both surprising and illuminating. And even the smallest of the hill towns can possess hidden treasures, for the artists of the Middle Ages and the Renaissance took their work where they could find it. Piero della Francesca's fresco cycle in the church of San Francesco in Arezzo is perhaps the preeminent hidden treasure. Tucked away in a small church in a small town, and, sadly, faded, the frescoes are artistically the equal of almost everything Florence has to offer and are all the more appealing for their uncrowded setting.

Essential Information

Important Addresses and Numbers

Tourist Information **Regional information** on Tuscany is available in **Florence** (Via di Novoli, tel. 055/439311).

Local information is available in the following tourist offices, which are generally open 9–12:30 and 3:30–7:30.

Arezzo (Piazza Risorgimento 116, tel. 0575/23952).
Cortona (Via Nazionale 72, tel. 0575/630557).
Lucca (Piazza Guidiccione 2, tel. 0583/491205).
Pisa (Piazza Duomo 8, tel. 050/560464).
Pistoia (Palazzo dei Vescovi, tel. 0573/21622).
Prato (Via Cairoli 48, tel. 0574/24112).
San Gimignano (Piazza del Duomo, tel. 0577/940008).
Siena (Via di Città 43, tel. 0577/42209; Piazza del Campo 55, tel. 0577/280551).
Volterra (Via Turazza 2, tel. 0588/86150).

Emergencies **Police, ambulance, fire,** tel. 113. This number will also put you in touch with the First Aid Service (Pronto Soccorso).

Travel Agencies **American Express** (Via Guicciardini 49/r, tel. 055/288751), **CIT** (Via Cavour 56, tel. 055/294306), and **Thomas Cook** (c/o World Vision, Via Cavour 154/r, tel. 055/579294), all in Florence.

Car Rentals Cars are for rent at the airports and in the larger cities in Tuscany; Alitalia may offer economical fly/drive packages with discounts on car rentals and hotels.

Arriving and Departing by Plane

The largest airports in the region are Pisa's **Galileo Galilei Airport** and Florence's **Peretola Airport.** There are direct flights from Paris to Pisa or Florence; from London, there are direct flights to Pisa; from the United States, you'll have to get connecting flights from Rome or Milan.

Arriving and Departing by Car and Train

By Car The Autostrada del Sole (A1), connects Florence with Bologna, 105 kilometers (65 miles) north, and Rome, 277 kilometers (172 miles) south, and passes close to Arezzo.

By Train The coastal line from Rome to Genoa passes through Pisa and all the beach resorts. The main line from Rome to Bologna passes through Arezzo, Florence, and Prato.

Getting Around

By Car The best way to see Tuscany, making it possible to explore the tiny towns and country restaurants that are so much a part of the region's charm, is by car. A11 leads west from Florence and meets the coastal A12 between Viareggio and Livorno. The A1 autostrada links Florence with Arezzo and Chiusi (where you turn off for Montepulciano). A toll-free superstrada links Florence with Siena. Drivers should be prepared to navigate through bewildering suburban sprawls around Tuscan cities; to reach the historic sections where most of the sights are located, look for signs to the *Centro Storico*.

By Train The main rail line runs past Chiusi and Cortona through Arezzo and Florence to Prato. Another main line connects Florence with Pisa. A secondary line links Florence, by way of Prato, with Pistoia and Lucca; there are a few other local lines.

By Bus Tuscany is crisscrossed by bus lines that connect the smaller towns and cities on the autostrade and superhighways. They are a good choice for touring the hill towns around Siena, such as San Gimignano; you can then take a Tra-In or Lazzi bus from Siena to Arezzo and get back onto the main Rome-Florence train line. From Chiusi on the main train line you can get a bus to Montepulciano. Buses connect Florence and Siena with Volterra.

By Boat Boat services link the islands of Tuscany's archipelago with the mainland; passenger and car ferries leave from Livorno and Piombino for Elba. The ferry to Giglio leaves from Porto Santo Stefano on the Argentario peninsula.

Guided Tours

From Florence, **American Express** (Via Guicciardini 49/r, tel. 055/288751) is part of a consortium operating one-day excursions to Siena and San Gimignano and can arrange for cars, drivers, and guides for special-interest tours in Tuscany. **CIT** (Via Cavour 56, tel. 055/294306) has a three-day Carosello bus tour from Rome to Florence, Siena, and San Gimignano, as well as a five-day tour that also takes in Venice.

Exploring Tuscany

Since most visitors to Tuscany will also spend some time in Florence (*see* Chapter 3), that city may be considered the starting point for the first two of these excursions. Tour 1 heads west from Florence toward the Tuscan coast, taking in the historic cities of Lucca and Pisa, among others; Tour 2 goes south through lovely inland valleys to several charming hill towns, with special attention given to Siena, Florence's ancient rival for Tuscan supremacy. Tour 3, which leaves the A1 autostrada or the main north–south rail line at a point roughly equidistant from Florence or Rome, explores southern Tuscany and other hill towns, such as unspoiled Montepulciano and the "ideal" Renaissance town of Pienza. No spot on any of these tours is more than a few hours' drive from Florence, but you would be hard pressed to see all the sights in a day trip—better to allow at least two or three days for each itinerary.

Highlights for First-Time Visitors

Lucca (*see* Tour 1: En Route to Pisa).

Piazza del Duomo, in Pisa, including the Leaning Tower (*see* Tour 1: En Route to Pisa).

Piazza del Campo, in Siena (*see* Tour 2: South to Siena).

Duomo, in Siena (*see* Tour 2: South to Siena).

Pinacoteca Nazionale, in Siena (*see* Tour 2: South to Siena).

San Gimignano (*see* Tour 2: South to Siena).

San Francesco, in Arezzo (*see* Tour 2: South to Siena).

Piazza Grande, in Montepulciano (*see* Tour 3: Southern Tuscany).

Tour 1: En Route to Pisa

Numbers in the margin correspond to points of interest on the Tuscany map.

❶ The tour begins at **Prato,** 21 kilometers (13 miles) northwest of Florence. A textile center since its early medieval days, Prato was known for its wool throughout Europe by the 13th century. In the 14th century, a local cloth merchant, Francesco di Marco Datini, who built his business, according to one of his surviving ledgers, "in the name of God and of profit," further stimulated the local industry; the city remains to this day one of the world's largest manufacturers of cloth.

Prato's main attraction is its 11th-century **Duomo.** Romanesque in style, it is famous for its Chapel of the Holy Girdle (to the left of the entrance), which enshrines the sash of the Virgin; it is said that the girdle was given to the apostle Thomas by the Virgin herself, when she miraculously appeared after her Assumption. The Duomo also contains 16th-century frescoes by Prato's most famous son, the libertine monk Fra Filippo Lippi; the best known depict Herod's banquet and Salome's dance. *Piazza del Duomo. Open 7–noon, 4–7.*

Sculpture by Donatello that originally adorned the Duomo's exterior or pulpit is now on display in the **Museo dell'Opera del Duomo.** *Piazza del Duomo 49, tel. 0574/29339. Admission: 5,000 lire (includes Galleria Comunale). Open Mon., Wed.–Sat. 9:30–12:30, 3–6:30; Sun. 9:30–12:30.*

The nearby **Galleria Comunale** contains a good collection of Tuscan and Sienese paintings, mainly from the 14th century. *Palazzo Pretorio, Piazza del Comune, tel. 0574/452302. Admission: 5,000 lire (includes Museo dell'Opera del Duomo). Open Mon., Wed.–Sat. 9:30–12:30, 3–6:30; Sun. 9:30–12:30.*

Prato's **Pecci Center of Contemporary Art** has a burgeoning collection of works by Italian and other artists. *Viale della Repubblica, tel. 0574/570620. Admission: 5,000 lire. Open Wed.–Sun. 10–7.*

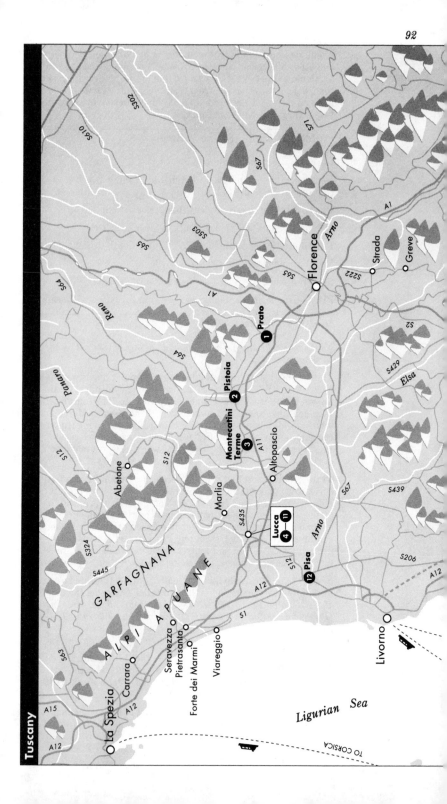

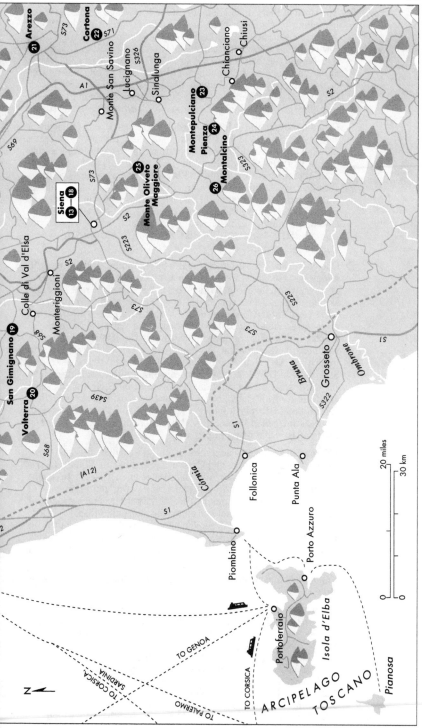

N

Arezzo 21
S73
Cortona 22
S71
Monte San Savino
S326
Lucignano
Sinalunga
A1
Chianciano
Chiusi
S2
Montepulciano 23
Pienza 24
Montalcino 26
S223
Monte Oliveto Maggiore 25
S73
Siena 13—18
S2
S69
S223
Colle di Val d'Elsa
S2
Monteriggioni
S73
San Gimignano 19
S68
Volterra 20
S439
S68
(A12)
S1
Cecina
Bruna
Grosseto
Ombrone
S1
S322
S73
Follonica
Punta Ala
S1
Porto Azzurro
Piombino
Portoferraio
TO GENOA
TO CORSICA/ SARDINIA
TO PALERMO
TO CORSICA
ARCIPELAGO
TOSCANO
Isola d'Elba
Pianosa

0   20 miles
0   30 km

❷ The town of **Pistoia,** 15 kilometers (9 miles) west of Prato, saw the beginning of the bitter Guelph-Ghibelline conflict of the Middle Ages. Reconstructed after heavy bombing during World War II, the town contains some fine Romanesque architecture. Its **Cathedral of San Zeno** in the main square (Piazza del Duomo) houses the **Dossale di San Jacopo,** a magnificent silver altarpiece. The two half-figures on its left side are by Filippo Brunelleschi (1377–1446), better known as the first Renaissance architect (and designer of Florence's magnificent Duomo dome). *Illumination of altarpiece: 2,000 lire.*

Other attractions include the **Ospedale del Ceppo** (Piazza Ospedale, a short way down Via Pacini from Piazza del Duomo), a hospital founded during the 14th century, with a superb early 16th-century terra-cotta frieze by Giovanni della Robbia; the church of **Sant'Andrea** (down Via Pappe to Via Sant'Andrea), with a fine early 14th-century pulpit by Giovanni Pisano that depicts the life of Christ; and, back in Piazza del Duomo, an unusual Gothic baptistery and the 14th-century **Palazzo del Comune,** which houses the **Museo Civico,** containing medieval art. *Palazzo del Comune, Piazza del Duomo, tel. 0573/371275. Admission: 5,000 lire. Open Tues.–Sat. 9–1 and 3–7, Sun. 9–1.*

❸ One of Europe's most famous health spas, **Montecatini Terme** is 16 kilometers (10 miles) west of Pistoia. It is renowned for its mineral springs, which flow from five sources and are used to treat liver and skin disorders. Those "taking the cure" report each morning to one of the town's *stabilimenti termali* (thermal establishments) to drink their prescribed cupful of water. The curative effects of Montecatini's water became known only in the 1800s, and the town was heavily developed at the beginning of this century, leaving a wealth of Art Nouveau buildings. The most attractive is the **Stabilimento Tettuccio,** a neoclassical edifice with colonnades. Here the water spouts from fountains set up on marble counters, the walls are decorated with bucolic scenes depicted on painted ceramic tiles, and an orchestra plays under a frescoed dome. An older town of Montecatini, called **Montecatini Alto,** sits on top of a hill near the spa town and is reached by a funicular.

❹ The town of **Lucca,** 27 kilometers (17 miles) west of Montecatini, was where Caesar, Pompey, and Crassus agreed to rule Rome as a triumvirate in 56 BC; it was later the first town in Tuscany to accept Christianity. Today it still has a mind of its own, and when most of Tuscany was voting communist recently, its citizens rarely followed suit. Lucca is more elegant and enjoyable than duller Pisa, so consider making it your base for exploring northwest Tuscany (but book ahead, as hotels are scarce). For a fine overview of the town, take a walk or a drive along its 16th-century ramparts, which are shaded by stately trees.

Numbers in the margin correspond to points of interest on the Lucca map.

Lucca is one of the most picturesque fortress towns in Tuscany and is worth exploring at length on foot. As usual, the main attraction is
❺ the **Duomo** (Piazza del Duomo, on the southern side of town). Its round-arched facade is a fine example of the rigorously ordered Pisan Romanesque style, in this case happily enlivened by an extremely disordered collection of carved columns. The decoration of the facade and of the porch below are worth a close look; they make this one of the most entertaining church fronts in Tuscany. The Gothic interior contains a moving Byzantine crucifix (called the **Volto Santo,** or Holy Face), brought here in the 8th century, and the

95

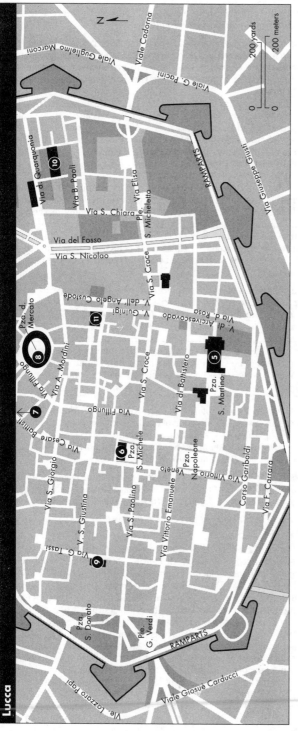

Lucca

Duomo, **5**
Museo Nazionale, **10**
Palazzo Guinigi, **11**
Piazza del Mercato, **8**
Pinacoteca
Nazionale, **9**
San Frediano, **7**
San Michele, **6**

masterpiece of the Sienese sculptor Jacopo della Quercia, the marble *Tomb of Ilaria del Caretto* (1406).

6 Slightly west of the center of town is the church of **San Michele** (Piazza San Michele), with a facade even more fanciful than the Duomo; it was heavily restored in the 19th century, however, and somewhat jarringly displays busts of modern Italian patriots such as Garibaldi and Cavour.

Time Out For dessert, try the local sweet cake, *buccellato*, available at **Pasticceria Taddeucci** (Piazza San Michele 34), or a coffee or ice cream at the venerable **Caffè di Simo** (Via Fillungo), a favorite of Lucca's famous son Giacomo Puccini, composer of some of the world's best-loved operas.

7 The church of **San Frediano** (Piazza San Frediano) is just inside the middle of the north town wall; it contains more works by Jacopo della Quercia, and, bizarrely, the lace-clad mummy of the patron saint of domestic servants, Santa Zita. Near it, to the southeast, is **8** **Piazza del Mercato,** where the **Anfiteatro Romano,** or Roman Amphitheater, once stood. The piazza takes its oval shape from the theater, but the seats disappeared when medieval houses were built on top of them.

9 Near the west walls of the old city, the **Pinacoteca Nazionale** is worth a visit to see the Mannerist, Baroque, and Rococo art on display. *Palazzo Mansi, Via Galli Tassi 43, tel. 0583/55570. Admission: 6,000 lire. Open Tues.–Sat. 9–7, Sun. 9–2.*

Time Out For an inexpensive lunch in pleasant surroundings, try **Trattoria da Giulio** (Via delle Conce 47, near Porta San Donato), which serves orzo and *porri* (leek) soups, roasted meats, and other simple Lucchese specialties. Closed Sun. and Mon.

10 On the eastern end of the historic center, the **Museo Nazionale** houses an extensive collection of local Romanesque and Renaissance art. *Villa Guinigi, Via della Quarquonia, tel. 0583/46033. Admission: 5,000 lire. Open May–Sept., Tues.–Sat. 9–7, Sun. 9–1; Oct.–Apr., Tues.–Sat. 9–4:30, Sun. 9–1.*

Finally, for a fine view of the surrounding countryside, climb the
11 tree-topped tower of the medieval **Palazzo Guinigi,** near the center of town. *Admission: 3,000 lire. Open 10–4 (9–7 in summer).*

Numbers in the margin correspond to points of interest on the Tuscany map.

12 The town of **Pisa,** southwest of Lucca, reached its glory as a maritime republic during the 12th century; its architects and artists strongly influenced the development of the Romanesque and Gothic styles in Tuscany. Defeated by its arch rival, Genoa (also a seaport trading center), in 1284, Pisa went into a gradual decline, its harbor filling with silt from the Arno; in the 15th century it became a satellite to Florence, when the Medici gained full control of Tuscany. During World War II, the city was virtually destroyed by Axis and Allied bombing, which miraculously spared its main attraction, **Piazza del Duomo.** Situated at the northwestern edge of town, it is also known, appropriately, as the **Campo dei Miracoli** (Field of Miracles). On it stand the **Duomo,** the **baptistery,** and the famous **Leaning Tower.** The Leaning Tower was begun in 1174, the last of the three structures to be built, and the lopsided settling began when construction reached the third story. The tower's architects attempted to compensate by making the remaining floors slightly taller on the leaning side, but the extra weight only made the problem worse. The settling continues to this day, as do efforts to prop the structure up. Legend holds that Galileo conducted an experiment on the nature of gravity by dropping metal balls from the top of the 187-foot-high tower; historians say this legend has no basis in fact (which is not quite to say that it is false). The tower is closed (it is undergoing structural reinforcement) and it will probably remain so permanently, but this hardly detracts from its allure. Just the sight of it, and of the resplendent marble monuments on the bright green lawn, is a delight.

The **Duomo** was the first building to use the horizontal marble striping pattern (borrowed from Moorish architecture in the 11th century) so common to Tuscan cathedrals. It is famous for the Romanesque panels on the transept door facing the tower, which depict the life of Christ, and for its beautifully carved 13th-century pulpit, by Giovanni Pisano. The lovely Gothic **baptistery,** which stands across from the Duomo's facade, is best known for the pulpit carved by Giovanni's father, Nicola, in 1260. *Duomo open Apr.– Sept., daily 7:45–1, 3–7; Oct.–Mar., daily 7:45–1, 3–5. Admission to baptistery: 5,000 lire. Open Apr.–Sept., daily 9–7; Oct.–Mar., daily 9–5.*

The walled area on the northern side of the Campo dei Miracoli is the **Camposanto** (Cemetery), which is filled, according to legend, with earth brought back from the Holy Land during the Crusades. Its galleries contain numerous frescoes, notably *The Drunkenness of Noah,* by Renaissance artist Benozzo Gozzoli, and the disturbing *Triumph of Death* (14th century), whose authorship is disputed, but whose subject matter shows what was on people's minds in a century that saw the ravages of the Black Death. At the southeast corner of the Campo dei Miracoli, the **Museo dell'Opera del Duomo** holds a wealth of medieval sculptures and the ancient Roman sarcophagi that inspired Nicola Pisano's figures. The well-arranged **Museo delle Sinopie** across the street, on the south side of the square, holds the *sinopie,* or preparatory drawings, for the Camposanto frescoes and is of limited interest to most tourists. *Camposanto, tel. 050/ 560547. Admission: 5,000 lire. Open Apr.–Sept., daily 8–7; Oct.– Mar., daily 9–5. Museo dell'Opera del Duomo, Via Arcivescovado, tel. 050/560547. Admission: 5,000 lire. Open Apr.–Sept., daily 9–7; Oct.–Mar., daily 9–5. Museo delle Sinopie, Piazza del Duomo, tel. 050/560547. Admission: 5,000 lire. Open daily 9–1, 3–5. Combined admission to baptistery, Camposanto, and museums: 12,000 lire.*

In the center of town, **Piazza dei Cavalieri** possesses some fine Renaissance buildings: the **Palazzo dei Cavalieri,** the **Palazzo dell'Orologio,** and the church of **Santo Stefano dei Cavalieri.** The square was laid out around 1560 by Giorgio Vasari, better known for his chronicles of the lives of Renaissance artists that made him the first art historian. Along the Arno, the tiny Gothic church of **Santa Maria della Spina** (Lungarno Sonnino, south of the river) merits a visit, and the **Museo di San Matteo,** on the northern side, contains some touching examples of local Romanesque and Gothic art. *Lungarno Mediceo, tel. 050/541865. Admission: 6,000 lire. Open Tues.–Sat. 9–7, Sun. 9–1.*

Tour 2: South to Siena

Depending on how much time you have, choose between two roads leading south from Florence to Siena: the speedy modern highway

S2 if you're trying to fit Siena into a day trip from Florence, or the narrower and more meandering S222 if you really want to see the countryside. The S222 is also known as the **Strada Chiantigiana** because it runs through the heart of the Chianti wine-producing country. The most scenic section runs between **Strada in Chianti,** 16 kilometers (10 miles) south of Florence, to **Greve in Chianti,** 11 kilometers (7 miles) farther south, where rolling hillsides are planted with vineyards and olive groves. Greve is a busy provincial town that was once a medieval marketplace, and its triangular central piazza is surrounded by restaurants and vintners offering wine tastings (*degustazioni*). Many British and northern Europeans have relocated to the Chianti countryside, drawn by the unhurried life, a balmy climate, and picturesque villages. There are so many northerners, in fact, that the area is widely known as Chiantishire. Still, it remains strongly Tuscan in character and is sparsely populated. Although it is possible to visit towns in Chianti by bus from Florence or Siena, the way to get to know the district is by car. This allows you to turn off the main road to visit vineyards and perhaps stay at a "rustic-chic" country estate.

⓭ Florence's great historical rival, **Siena,** is located 68 kilometers (42 miles) south of Florence. The town was founded by Augustus around the time of the birth of Christ, although legend holds that it was founded much earlier by Remus, brother of Romulus, the legendary founder of Rome. During the late Middle Ages, the city was both wealthy and powerful (it saw the birth of the world's oldest bank, the Monte dei Paschi, still very much in business). It was bitterly envied by Florence, which in 1254 sent forces that besieged the city for over a year, reducing its population by half and laying waste to the countryside. The city was finally absorbed by the Grand Duchy of Tuscany, ruled by Florence, in 1559.

Unlike Renaissance Florence, Siena is a Gothic city, laid out over the slopes of three steep hills and practically unchanged since medieval times. Its main square, the **Piazza del Campo,** is one of the finest in Italy. Fan shaped, its nine sections of paving represent the 13th-century government of Nine Good Men, and, at the top, like an ornament, is the Fonte Gaia, so called because it was inaugurated to great jubilation. The bas-reliefs on it are reproductions of the originals by Jacopo della Quercia. Twice a year, on July 2 and August 16, the square is the site of the famous **Palio,** a horse race in which the city's 17 neighborhoods compete to possess the cloth banner that gives the contest its name. Unlike many other such in Italy, the Palio is deeply revered by the townspeople, and the rivalries it generates are taken very seriously.

Numbers in the margin correspond to points of interest on the Siena map.

⓮ Dominating the piazza is the **Palazzo Pubblico,** which has served as Siena's Town Hall since the 1300s. It now also contains the **Museo Civico,** its walls covered with pre-Renaissance frescoes, including Simone Martini's early 14th-century *Maestà* and *Portrait of Guidoriccio da Fogliano,* and Ambrogio Lorenzetti's famous *Allegory of Good and Bad Government,* painted from 1327 to 1329 to demonstrate the dangers of tyranny. The original bas-reliefs of the Jacopo della Quercia fountain, moved under cover to protect them from the elements, are also on display. The climb up the palazzo's bell tower is long and steep, but the superb view makes it worth every step. *Piazza del Campo, tel. 0577/292263. Bell tower admission: 4,000 lire. Open Mar. 15–Nov. 15, daily 10–one hour before sunset; Nov. 16–Mar. 14, daily 10–1:30. Palazzo Pubblico (Museo Civico)*

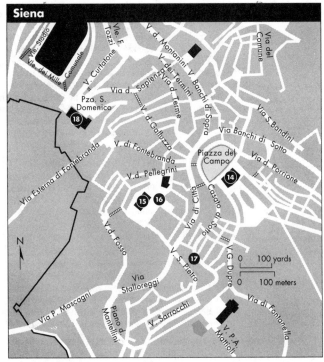

admission: 5,500 lire. Open Mar. 15–Nov. 15, Mon.–Sat 9:30–7:30, Sun. 9:30–1:30; Nov. 16–Mar. 14, daily 9:30–1:30.

Time Out There are several **gelaterie** on Piazza del Campo, excellent for surveying the piazza while enjoying a refreshing ice cream. More substantial sustenance may be found nearby at **Ristorante Il Verrocchio** (Logge del Papa 2, closed Wed.), which serves inexpensive Sienese specialties and is located a block east of the northern side of the campo.

---

15 Siena's **Duomo,** several blocks west of Piazza del Campo, is beyond question one of the finest Gothic cathedrals in Italy. Its facade, with its multicolored marbles and painted decoration, is typical of the Italian approach to Gothic architecture, lighter and much less austere than the French. The cathedral, as it now stands, was completed in the 14th century, but at the time the Sienese had even bigger plans. They decided to enlarge the building, using the current church as the transepts of the new church, which would have a new nave running toward the southeast. The beginnings of construction of this new nave still stand and may be seen from the steps outside the Duomo's right transept. But in 1348 the Black Death decimated Siena's population, the city fell into decline, funds dried up, and the plans were never carried out.

The Duomo's interior is one of the most striking in Italy and possesses a fine coffered and gilded dome. It is most famous for its unique and magnificent marble floors, which took almost 200 years to complete (beginning around 1370); more than 40 artists contributed to the work, made up of 56 separate compositions depicting biblical scenes, allegories, religious symbols, and civic emblems. The Duomo's carousel pulpit, which is almost as famous as the floors, was carved by Nicola Pisano around 1265 and depicts the life of Christ on its rostrum frieze (the staircase is a later addition). Finally, a door in the left-hand aisle just before the crossing leads into the **Biblioteca Piccolomini,** a room painted by Pinturicchio in 1509; its frescoes depict events from the life of native son Aeneas Sylvius Piccolomini, who became Pope Pius II in 1458. The frescoes are in fine repair and have a freshness rarely seen in work so old. *Biblioteca Piccolomini, tel. 0577/283048. Admission: 2,000 lire. Open mid-Mar.–Sept. 30, daily 9–7:30; Oct. 1–Nov. 3, daily 9–6:30; Nov. 4–Mar. 13, daily 10–1, 2:30–5.*

⑯ Next to the Duomo is its museum, the **Museo dell'Opera del Duomo,** occupying part of the unfinished new cathedral's nave and containing a small collection of Sienese art and the cathedral treasury. Its masterpiece is unquestionably Duccio's *Maestà,* painted around 1310 and magnificently displayed in a room devoted entirely to Duccio's work. *Piazza del Duomo, tel. 0577/283048. Admission: 5,000 lire. Open Mar. 14–Sept. 30, daily 9–7:30; Oct. 1–Nov. 3, daily 9–6:30; Nov. 4–Dec. 31, daily 9–1:30; Jan. 2–Mar. 13, daily 9–1.*

Steps between the cathedral and its museum lead to the **Battistero** (Baptistery), with its 15th-century frescoes. Its large bronze baptismal font (also 15th century) was designed by Jacopo della Quercia and is adorned with bas-reliefs by various artists, including two by Renaissance masters: Lorenzo Ghiberti *(The Baptism of Christ)* and Donatello *(Herod Presented with the Head of St. John).*

⑰ Chief among Siena's other attractions is the **Pinacoteca Nazionale,** several blocks southeast of the entrance to the Duomo; it contains a superb collection of Sienese art, including Ambrogio Lorenzetti's 14th-century depiction of a castle that is generally considered the first nonreligious painting—the first pure landscape—of the Christian era. *Via San Pietro 29, tel. 0577/281161. Admission: 8,000 lire. Open Apr.–Sept., Tues.–Sat. 8:30–7; Oct.–Mar., Tues.–Sat. 8:30–2, Sun. 8:30–1.*

⑱ If time permits, a visit to the church of **San Domenico,** northwest of the Duomo, is also worthwhile; its **Cappella di Santa Caterina** displays frescoes by Il Sodoma portraying scenes from the life of Saint Catherine and houses a reliquary containing her head.

Time Out Not far from the church of San Domenico, the **Enoteca Italica** is a fantastically stocked wine cellar in the bastions of the Medici fortress. Here you can taste wines from all over Italy and have a snack, too (Fortezza Medicea, Viale Maccari, tel. 0577/288497. Open 3 PM–midnight).

Numbers in the margin correspond to points of interest on the Tuscany map.

On your way north from Siena toward Colle Val d'Elsa, San Gimignano, and Volterra, be sure to visit Monteriggioni, a tiny hamlet sitting on a rise within a circle of formidable 13th-century walls. Its 14 square towers, which Dante likened to giants, were Siena's northernmost defense against Florence. And take time to make the lengthy detour around Colle Val d'Elsa's workaday lower town up to the ridge, where the medieval center remains practically intact.

⑲ The picturesque town of **San Gimignano** is 31 kilometers (20 miles) northwest of Siena. San Gimignano's high walls and narrow streets are typical of Tuscan hill towns, but it is the surviving medieval towers that set the town apart from its neighbors. Today 14 towers remain, but at the height of the Guelph–Ghibelline conflict, a forest of more than 70 such towers dominated the city. The towers were built partly for defensive purposes—they were a safe refuge and useful for pouring boiling oil on attacking enemies—and partly to bolster the egos of their owners, who competed with deadly seriousness to build the highest tower in town.

Many of the town's most important medieval buildings are clustered around the central Piazza del Duomo. They include the **Palazzo del Podestà,** with its imposing tower; the **Palazzo del Popolo,** now the municipal museum, displaying Sienese and Renaissance paintings; and the Romanesque **Collegiata,** containing fine 15th-century frescoes by Domenico Ghirlandaio in the Chapel of Santa Fina. *Admission to palazzo and chapel: 5,000 lire. Open 9:30–12:30, 2:30–5:30, summer to 7:30.*

Before leaving San Gimignano, be sure to see its most famous work of art, at the northern end of town, in the church of **Sant' Agostino:** Benozzo Gozzoli's beautiful 15th-century fresco cycle depicting the life of St. Augustine. Also try a taste of Vernaccia, the local dry white wine.

⍟ Continue on to **Volterra,** 29 kilometers (18 miles) southwest of San Gimignano. D. H. Lawrence, in his *Etruscan Places,* sang the praises of Volterra, "standing somber and chilly alone on her rock." The town has long been known for its alabaster, which has been mined since Etruscan times; today the Volterrans use it to make ornaments and souvenirs sold all over town. A magnificent collection of small alabaster funerary urns that once held the ashes of deceased Etruscans (along with many other Etruscan artifacts) may be seen at the **Museo Etrusco Guarnacci** (Via Don Minzoni). Later art can be found in the **Duomo,** at the **Pinacoteca** (Palazzo Minucci-Solaini, Via dei Sarti 1), and at the **Museo di Arte Sacra** (Via Roma), though at press time the Museo di Arte Sacra was closed for renovations. It was scheduled to reopen in late 1995. The town's best-known Renaissance works are the 15th-century frescoes in the Duomo by Benozzo Gozzoli and the 16th-century *Deposition* by Rosso Fiorentino in the Pinacoteca. *Combined admission to Museo Etrusco Guarnacci and Pinacoteca: 6,000 lire. Open Mar. 16–Oct. 14, daily 9:30–1, 3:30–6; Oct. 15–Mar. 15, daily 10–2.*

The walls of Volterra also harbor one of the few pieces of Etruscan architecture that escaped Roman destruction: the **Arco Etrusco,** with its weather-worn Etruscan heads, at the Porta all'Arco.

㉑ On the other side of Siena, a major point of interest is **Arezzo,** 88 kilometers (55 miles) northeast of Siena. (You may want to break the drive halfway with a rest stop at **Monte San Savino,** a prosperous-looking small town, with the tiny nearby fortified village of **Gargonza** that has been carefully restored into a vacation resort; *see* Dining and Lodging, *below.*) Arezzo was the birthplace of the poet Petrarch; the Renaissance artist and art historian Giorgio Vasari; and Guido d'Arezzo, the inventor of musical notation. Today the town is best known for the magnificent, but very faint, Piero della Francesca frescoes in the church of **San Francesco,** on Via Cavour in the center of town. Painted between 1452 and 1466, they depict *The Legend of the True Cross* on three walls of the choir. What Sir Kenneth Clark called "the most perfect morning light in all Renaissance painting" may be seen in the lowest section of the right wall, where the troops of the Emperor Maxentius flee before the sign of the cross. Unfortunately, part of the frescoes may be hidden from view while restoration work takes place.

With its irregular shape and sloping brick pavement, framed by buildings of assorted centuries, Arezzo's **Piazza Grande** echoes Siena's Piazza del Campo. Though not so grand, it is lively enough during the outdoor antiques fair every first Sunday of the month and when the Joust of the Saracen, featuring medieval costumes and competition, is held there on the first Sunday of September. The curving, tiered apse on Piazza Grande belongs to Santa Maria della Pieve, one of Tuscany's finest Romanesque churches. And Arezzo's medieval cathedral at the top of the hill harbors an eye-level fresco of a tender Magdalen by Piero della Francesca; look for it next to the large marble tomb near the organ.

Other attractions in Arezzo include the church of **San Domenico,** which houses a 13th-century crucifix by Cimabue, located north of Piazza Grande at Piazza Fossombroni (just inside the walls); the **house** that Giorgio Vasari designed and decorated for himself in 1540, just west of San Domenico; and the **Museo Archeologico,** with a fine collection of Etruscan bronzes. *Vasari house: Via XX Settembre 55, tel. 0575/300301. Admission free. Open Tues.–Sat. 9–7, Sun. 9–1. Museo Archeologico: Via Margaritone 10, tel. 0575/20882. Admission: 6,000 lire. Open Tues.–Sat. 9–2, Sun. 9–1.*

About 30 kilometers (18 miles) south of Arezzo on S71, the medieval town of **Cortona** is known for its excellent small art gallery and a number of fine antiques shops, as well as for its colony of foreign residents. Cortona has the advantage of being on the main train network, though you will have to take a local bus from the station up into the town, passing the Renaissance church of **Santa Maria del Calcinaio** on the way.

The heart of Cortona is formed by **Piazza della Repubblica** and the adjacent **Piazza Signorelli.** Wander into the courtyard of the picturesque **Palazzo Pretorio,** and, if you want to see a representative collection of Etruscan bronzes, climb its centuries-old stone staircase to the **Museo dell'Accademia Etrusca** (Gallery of Etruscan Art). *Piazza Signorelli 9, tel. 0575/630415. Admission: 5,000 lire. Open Apr.–Sept., Tues.–Sun. 10–1, 4–7; Oct.–Mar., Tues.–Sun. 9–1, 3–5.*

The nearby **Museo Diocesano** (Diocesan Museum) houses an impressive number of large and splendid paintings by native son Luca Signorelli, as well as a beautiful *Annunciation* by Fra Angelico, a delightful surprise to find in this small, eclectic town. *Piazza del Duomo 1, tel. 0575/62830. Admission: 5,000 lire. Open Apr.–Sept., Tues.–Sun. 9–1, 3–6:30; Oct.–Mar., Tues.–Sun. 9–1, 3–5.*

Tour 3: Southern Tuscany

The rolling green countryside of southern Tuscany is blanketed with woods; vines grow in rich, reddish-brown earth, and cypresses stand in ranks along roads leading to isolated stone farmhouses, unspoiled hill towns, and medieval abbeys.

This tour begins at **Chiusi,** known for the frescoed tombs dating from the 5th century BC in its necropolis. One of the most powerful of the 12 ancient cities in the Etruscan federation, Chiusi is a transportation hub accessible from either the main north–south rail line or by car or bus from the A1 autostrada. From here, head 12 kilometers (7½ miles) west to **Chianciano,** a modern spa with neat parks and a host of hotels clustered around the medieval walls of the old town.

Billboards here proclaim that Chianciano's restorative waters are indispensable for a *fegato sano*, a healthy liver.

The road north from Chianciano climbs and dips, winding through woods of evergreens and oaks and affording glimpses of the vineyards that are the pride of this part of Tuscany. Two of Italy's best wines—Brunello di Montalcino and Vino Nobile di Montepulciano—originate here and bear the names of the towns where they are made. About 20 kilometers (12 miles) northwest of Chiusi, **Montepulciano** sits high on a hilltop, a pyramid of redbrick buildings set within a circle of cypress trees. At an altitude of almost 2,000 feet, it is cool in summer and chilled in winter by biting winds that sweep its spiraling streets. The town has an unusually harmonious look, the result of the work of three architects, Sangallo il Vecchio, Vignola, and Michelozzo, who endowed it with fine palaces and churches. Their work began under the aegis of Cosimo I de' Medici, who financed the rebuilding of Montepulciano after the town opted for an alliance with Florence in the early 1500s. The 16th-century Renaissance buildings blend in well with earlier medieval edifices lining the stone streets that curve upward to **Piazza Grande**. Montepulciano's many wine cellars and antiques dealers and a few trendy shops and cafés hint that this otherwise sleepy town gets its share of tourists, especially during an international arts festival in July and August. On the hillside below the town walls is the church of **San Biagio**, designed by Sangallo, a paragon of Renaissance architectural perfection that is considered his masterpiece.

Another Florentine architect, Bernardo Rossellino, had his turn at achieving perfection when he was commissioned by vainglorious Pope Pius II, subject of Pinturicchio's frescoes in the Piccolomini Library in Siena, to design an entire town. A year after his election, the pope decided to transform his native village of Corsignano into a monument to himself. **Pienza,** 12 kilometers (7 miles) west of Montepulciano, is not only a curiosity—an imperious pope's personal utopia—it is also an exquisite example of the architectural canons formulated in the early Renaissance by Leon Battista Alberti and utilized by later architects, including Brunelleschi and Michelangelo, in designing many of Italy's finest buildings and piazzas. Today the cool grandeur of Pienza's center seems almost surreal in this otherwise unpretentious village, known locally for *pienzino*, also called *cacio*, a smooth goat cheese.

About 33 kilometers (20 miles) northwest of Pienza, accessible by car but not easily by bus, is the Benedictine **Abbey of Monte Oliveto Maggiore.** The abbey is an oasis of olive and cypress trees amid the harsh landscape of a zone known as the *crete*, where erosion has sculpted the hills starkly, laying open gashes of barren rock in lush farmland. Weather and time have taken their toll on the abbey itself; in 1993 the roof of the library, long closed while awaiting overdue repairs, simply collapsed. In the main cloister of the abbey, the frescoes by Luca Signorelli and Il Sodoma on the walls of the portico relate the life of St. Benedict with earthy realism, a quality that came naturally to Il Sodoma, described by Vasari as "a merry and licentious man . . . of scant chastity." True to his nickname, Il Sodoma delighted in painting handsome young men; he also included a rendering of his pet badger and raven with a robed, black-haired figure that is a self-portrait. *Admission free. Open daily 9–12:30, 1:30–6.*

Montalcino, about 25 kilometers (15 miles) west of Pienza, is another medieval hill town with a special claim to fame. It is home of Brunello di Montalcino, one of Italy's best red wines. You can sample it in wine cellars in town or visit a nearby winery for a free guided tour and tasting. One such winery is the Fattoria dei Barbi (*see* Taverna dei Barbi in Dining and Lodging, *below*).

The **Abbey of Sant'Antimo,** about 10 kilometers (6 miles) southeast of Montalcino, below the town of Castelnuovo dell'Abbate, is worth a visit; it is a medieval gem of pale stone set in the silvery green of an olive grove. To end this itinerary, you could return by way of San Quirico d'Orcia to Pienza and then head northeast for 20 kilometers (12 miles) to **Sinalunga,** a town on the main train line and close to the A1 autostrada. Only 8 kilometers (5 miles) north of Sinalunga, **Lucignano** is another charming old hill town. Like Cortona, Lucignano has a small foreign colony of artists and writers who live on the outskirts in converted farmhouses.

What to See and Do with Children

Just outside Pistoia is the **Giardino Zoologico,** especially laid out to accommodate the wiles of both animals and children. *Via Pieve a Celle 160, Pistoia, tel. 0573/939219. Admission: 10,000 lire adults and children over 9, 7,500 lire children 3–9. Open Apr.–Sept., daily 9–7; Oct.–Mar., daily 9–5.*

Pinocchio aficionados will be delighted by the **Parco di Pinocchio** in Collodi, near Pescia. A statue of the long-nosed puppet is the center-piece of a garden containing sculptural groups that depict scenes from Carlo Lorenzini's children's classic, *The Adventures of Pinocchio.* Close by is the beautifully kept Italian garden of Villa Garzoni. *Parco di Pinocchio, Collodi, tel. 0572/429642. Admission: 8,000 lire adults, 4,000 lire children under 12. Open May–Sept., daily 8–9; Oct.–Apr., daily 8:30–6. Villa Garzoni, tel. 0572/428400. Admission: 8,000 lire. Open daily 8–one hour before sunset.*

Walking, hiking, and **picnicking** in the inviting, hilly Tuscan coun-tryside are natural attractions for children. In the hills of Garfagnana, above Lucca, is a tennis camp, **Il Ciocco,** especially de-signed for children; there are horseback riding, swimming, and health facilities, and adults can participate as well. *Centro Turistico Internazionale, Barga, Lucca, tel. 0583/710021.*

Off the Beaten Track

Elba. The largest island in the Tuscan archipelago, Elba is an hour by ferry or a half hour by Hovercraft from Piombino or a short hop by air from Pisa. Its main port is **Portoferraio,** fortified in the 16th century by the Medici Grand Duke Cosimo I. Victor Hugo spent his boyhood here, and Napoléon his famous exile in 1814–15, when he built (out of two windmills) the **Palazzina Napoleonica dei Mulini** and (a few miles outside town) the **Villa San Martino.** *Palazzina Napoleonica and Villa San Martino, tel. 0565/915846. Admission: 5,000 lire for both if visiting on the same day. Open Tues.–Sat. 9–1:30, Sun. 9–1.*

The island's main attractions, however, are its rough landscape and pristine beaches offering a full array of sports. Portoferraio, the liveliest town and a transportation hub, is the best base for explor-ing the island. Good beaches can be found at Biodola, Procchio, and Marina di Campo. From Elba, private visits can be arranged to the other islands in the archipelago, including **Montecristo,** which in-spired Alexander Dumas's 19th-century best-seller *The Count of Monte Cristo* and is now a wildlife refuge. Elba's restaurants offer excellent seafood, to be sampled with the local Moscato and Aleatico wines.

Forte dei Marmi. Tuscany's most exclusive beach resort, a favorite of moneyed Tuscans and Milanese, whose villas are neatly laid out in an extensive pine wood, is 65 kilometers (30 miles) northwest of Florence by car. It is near the marble-producing towns of **Carrara** (where Michelangelo quarried his stone), **Seravezza,** and **Pietrasanta.**

Marlia. Eight kilometers (5 miles) north of Lucca is the handsome Villa Reale, once owned by Napólean's sister. Its superb gardens, laid out in the second half of the 17th century and surrounded by a park, are a fine place for a break and a stroll. *Villa Reale, tel. 0583/ 30108. Admission: 6,000 lire. Guided tours July–Sept., Tues.– Thurs., Sun. 10, 11, 4, 5, 6; Oct., Mar.–June, Tues.–Sun. 10, 11, 3, 4, 5.*

Shopping

Specialty Items   **Arezzo** is known for its production of gold, as well as a burgeoning cottage knitwear industry. (For sweaters, try Maglierie, Piazza Grande.) The olive oil of **Lucca** is exported throughout the world. **Prato** makes hard almond cookies called *biscottini,* ideal for dunking in the beverage of one's choice. **Siena** is known for a variety of medieval desserts—*cavallucci, panforti,* and *ricciarelli*—as well as for ceramics. **Volterra** has a number of shops selling boxes, jewelry, and other objects made of alabaster. For information and directions, contact Cooperativa Artieri Alabastro (Piazza dei Priori 2, tel. 0588/ 87590).

Flea Markets   The first Sunday of each month, a colorful flea market selling antiques and not-so-antiques takes place in Piazza Grande in **Arezzo.** On the second Sunday of the month, another market goes to Piazza San Martino in **Lucca.** In summer, a beachcomber's bonanza takes place Wednesday mornings in **Forte dei Marmi,** near Lucca, when everything from fake designer sunglasses to plastic sandals and terrycloth towels goes on sale.

Sports

Fishing   For a license, contact the **Federazione Italiana della Pesca Sportiva** (Via dei Neri 6, Firenze). The spot for tuna fishing in Tuscany is **Punta Ala,** from September to October. Fishing trips and charters may be arranged through **Renato Lessi** (Località Porto, Punta Ala, Grosseto, tel. 0564/920710).

Golf   Punta Ala is also the site of the **Golf Club Punta Ala,** an 18-hole course on the sea opposite the island of Elba (Via del Golf 1, Punta Ala, Grosseto, tel. 0564/922121).

Horseback Riding   Some popular riding sites are **Rendola Riding** (Rendola Valdarno, Arezzo, tel. 0575/987045), **Rifugio Prategiano** (Montieri, Grosseto, tel. 0566/997703), **Le Cannelle** (Parco dell'Uccellina, Talamone, Grosseto, tel. 0564/887020). For more information, contact the **Federazione Italiana Sport Equestre** (Via Paoletti 54, Firenze, tel. 055/480039).

Sailing   Charters in Tuscany are available through the **Centro Nautico Italiano** (Piazza della Signoria 31/r, Firenze, tel. 055/287045); **Mario Lorenzoni** (Via degli Alfani 105/r, Firenze, tel. 055/284790); and **Renato Lessi** (Località Porto, Castiglione della Pescaia, Grosseto, tel. 0564/922793). For more information, contact the **Federazione Italiana Vela** (CP 49, Marina di Carrara, tel. 0585/57323) or the

Federazione Italiana Motonautica (Via Goldora 16, 55044 Marina di Pietrasanta, tel. 0584/20963).

Skiing The best spot for skiing in Tuscany is **Abetone.** For information, contact the **Federazione Italiana Sport Invernali** (Viale Matteotti 15, Firenze, tel. 055/576987).

Spectator Sports

Horse Racing Besides the racecourses in the **Cascine** in Florence, horse racing takes place in **Montecatini** and **Punta Ala,** as well as **San Rossore** and **Follonica.**

Dining and Lodging

Dining Though Florentine cuisine now predominates throughout Tuscany, the Etruscan influence on regional food still persists after more than three millennia. Just as the ancient Etruscans were responsible for the introduction of the cypress to the Tuscan landscape, so they are also credited with the use of herbs in cooking. Basic ingredients such as tarragon, sage, rosemary, and thyme appear frequently, happily coupled with game, Chianina beef, or even seafood. Each region has its own specialties, usually based on simple ingredients, and Tuscans are disparagingly called *mangiafagioli,* or bean eaters, by other Italians. However, Tuscan chefs have recently discovered the rest of the world, and for better or worse, an "international cuisine" has been gradually making its appearance throughout the region.

Fortunately, Tuscany's wines remain unaltered. Grapes have been cultivated here since Etruscan times, and Chianti still rules the roost (almost literally when selected by the *Gallo Nero,* Black Rooster, label, a symbol of one of the region's most powerful wine-growing consortiums; the other is a *putto,* or cherub). The robust red wine is still a staple on most tables, and the discerning can select from a multitude of other varieties, including such reds as Brunello di Montalcino and Vino Nobile di Montepulciano, and whites such as Valdinievole and Vergine della Valdichiana. The dessert wine *vin santo* is produced throughout the region and is often enjoyed with biscottini di Prato, which are perfect for dunking.

Highly recommended restaurants are indicated by a star ★.

Category	Cost*
$$$$	over 110,000 lire
$$$	60,000–110,000 lire
$$	35,000–60,000 lire
$	under 35,000 lire

per person, for a three-course meal, including house wine and taxes

Lodging Highly recommended lodgings are indicated by a star ★.

Category	Cost*
$$$$	over 300,000 lire
$$$	220,000–300,000 lire
$$	100,000–220,000 lire
$	under 100,000 lire

*All prices are for a double room for two, including tax and service.

Arezzo   **Buca di San Francesco.** A frescoed cellar restaurant in a historic
Dining   building next to the church of San Francesco, this "buca" (literally
"hole," figuratively "cellar") has a medieval atmosphere and serves
straightforward local specialties. Vegetarians will like the *ribollita*
(vegetable soup thickened with bread) and the *sformato di verdure*
(spinach or chard pie), though it may be served *con cibreo* (with a
giblet sauce). Meat eaters will find the lean Chianina beef a succu-
lent treat. *Piazza San Francesco 1, tel. 0575/23271. Reservations
advised. Dress: casual. AE, DC, MC, V. Closed Mon. dinner,
Tues., and July. $$*

Tastevin. Close to San Francesco and to the central Piazza Guido
Monaco, Tastevin has introduced creative cooking styles in Arezzo
but serves traditional dishes as well, in three attractive dining
rooms, two in warm Tuscan provincial style, one in more sophisti-
cated bistro style. At the small bar the talented owner plays and
sings show tunes and Sinatra songs in the evening; there is a 15%
cover charge for music. The restaurant's specialties are risotto
tastevin (with cream of truffles) and seafood or meat *carpaccio*
(sliced raw). *Via dei Cenci 9, tel. 0575/28304. Dinner reservations
advised. Dress: casual. AE, DC, MC, V. Closed Mon. (Sun. in sum-
mer). $$*

Spiedo d'Oro. Cheery red-and-white tablecloths add a bright note to
this large, reliable trattoria near the archeological museum. This is
your chance to try authentic Tuscan home-style specialties, such as
zuppa di pane (bread soup), *pappardelle all'ocio* (noodles with duck
sauce), and *osso buco all'aretina* (sautéed veal shank). *Via Crispi
12, tel. 0575/22873. No reservations. Dress: casual. V. Closed
Thurs. and July 1–18. $*

Lodging   **Continental.** Centrally located near the train station and within
walking distance of all major sights, the Continental has been a reliable and convenient place to stay since it opened in the 1950s. Recently refurbished, it now has bright white furnishings with yellow
accents, gleaming new bathrooms complete with hair dryers, and a
pleasant roof garden. Rates are at the low end of the $$ category.
*Piazza Guido Monaco 7, tel. 0575/20251, fax 0575/340485. 74 rooms
with bath or shower. Facilities: roof garden, restaurant (closed Sun.
dinner, Mon.). AE, DC, MC, V. $$*

Casola d'Elsa/   **La Suvera.** This luxurious estate in the lovely valley of the river
Pievescola   Elsa, 28 kilometers (17 miles) west of Siena and 56 kilometers (35
Dining and   miles) south of Florence, was once owned by Pope Julius II. The pa-
Lodging   pal villa and adjacent buildings have been restored to accommodate
guests in rooms and suites that are magnificently furnished with antiques and appointed with the latest comforts. With drawing rooms,
a library, Italian garden, park, pool, and the Oliviera restaurant
(serving estate wines) to enjoy, guests find it hard to tear themselves away, though there is plenty to see in the vicinity. *Pievescola
(Casola d'Elsa), off S541, tel. 0577/960300, fax 0577/960220. 25
rooms and 10 suites with bath. Facilities: park, heated pool, sauna,*

tennis, riding, restaurant, bar, heliport, conference rooms. AE, DC, MC, V. Open Mar. 15–Nov. 15. $$$–$$$$

Colle Val **Villa Belvedere.** This stately villa was the residence of Ferdinand
d'Elsa III, archduke of Austria and grand duke of Tuscany in 1820. Set in a
Dining and large park, the entire villa, including the quiet bedrooms overlook-
Lodging ing the park, is furnished in 19th-century (or even earlier) antiques.
The location within 12 kilometers (about 8 miles) of both Siena and
San Gimignano makes it a good choice for anyone touring by car.
Località Belvedere (Colle Val d'Elsa Sud exit on superstrada), tel.
0577/920966. 15 rooms with bath. Facilities: restaurant (closed
Wed.), bar, garden, pool. AE, DC, MC, V. $$

Cortona **La Loggetta.** Located above Cortona's main medieval square, this
Dining attractive restaurant occupies a 16th-century wine cellar; its four
ample dining rooms have a relaxing atmosphere and tasteful decor
in keeping with the setting. In fair weather you can eat outdoors,
overlooking the 13th-century town hall, dining on regional dishes
and such specialties as cannelloni (crepes filled with spinach and ricotta) and *lombatine al cartoccio* (veal chops with porcini mushrooms). The owners pride themselves on their selection of Tuscan
wines. *Piazza Pescheria 3, tel. 0575/630575. No reservations. Dress:*
casual. AC, DC, MC, V. Closed Sun. dinner (except summer),
Mon., Jan. 5–Feb. 10, 2 weeks in July. $$

Tonino. Deservedly well known and popular with locals and visitors
alike, this large modern establishment can be noisy and crowded on
holiday weekends. But it is very satisfactory indeed at all other
times, when you can enjoy the view of the Chiana valley and feast on
host Tonino's own *antipastissimo*, an incredible variety of
delectables. This is the place to taste Chiana beefsteak. *Piazza Gar-*
ibaldi, tel. 0575/630500. Reservations advised, especially weekends.
Dress: casual. AE, DC, MC, V. Closed Mon. dinner, Tues. $$

Gargonza **Castello di Gargonza.** A tiny 13th-century hill town with a castle,
Dining and church, and cobbled streets offers something unusual as hostelries
Lodging go. All its houses—cottages, really—are for rent by the week, and
rooms can be had by the night. This enchanting spot in the countryside between Siena and Arezzo, part of the fiefdom of the aristocratic Florentine Guicciardini family, was restored by the modern Count
Roberto Guicciardini as a way to rescue a dying village. The houses
have one to six rooms each, sleep two to seven people, and have as
many as four baths. La Torre restaurant serves local specialties.
52048 Monte San Savino, tel. 0575/847021, fax 0575/847054. 18
houses with bath. Facilities: restaurant (closed Tues.), parking.
AE, MC, V. Closed Jan. 10–Feb. 10. $$ weekly; inquire about daily
rate.

Lucca **Solferino.** About 6 kilometers (4 miles) outside town, on the road to
Dining Viareggio, this pleasant restaurant serves exquisite variations of
regional favorites, such as *anatra ripiena in crema di funghi*
(stuffed duck with mushroom sauce), made with ingredients from
the family farm. Ask for a piece of buccellato, a sweet, anise-fla-
vored bread with raisins that is a specialty of Lucca. *San Macario in*
Piano, tel. 0583/59118. Reservations required. Dress: casual. AE,
DC, MC, V. Closed Wed., Thurs. lunch, 2 weeks in mid-Aug., Jan.
7–15. $$$

★ **La Mora.** Some 9 kilometers (6 miles) outside Lucca, this former
country inn and coach station is worth going out of your way. The
menu offers a range of local specialties, from *minestra di farro*
(wheat soup) with beans to *tacconi* (homemade pasta) with rabbit
sauce and lamb from the nearby Garfagnana hills. You'll be tempted
by the variety of *crostini* (toast with liver pâté) and delicious des-

serts as well. *Via Sesto di Ponte a Moriano 1748, tel. 0583/406402. Reservations advised. Dress: casual. AE, DC, MC, V. Closed Wed. dinner, Thurs. and June 25–July 8, Oct. 10–30. $$–$$$*

Buca di Sant'Antonio. Near the church of San Michele, this was once a rustic inn. The specialties here are local dishes, some unfamiliar but well worth trying, such as *ravioli di ricotta alle zucchine* (cheese ravioli with zucchini) and roast *capretto* (kid) or *agnello* (lamb) with savory herb seasoning. *Via della Cervia 3, tel. 0583/55881. Dinner reservations advised. Dress: casual. AE, DC, MC, V. Closed Sun. dinner and Mon.; July 9–29. $$*

Il Giglio. Located just off Piazza Napoleone and close to the Hotel Universo, this restaurant has quiet, turn-of-the-century charm and classic cuisine. Seafood is a specialty, but it can be expensive. You may prefer to order crostini and *stracotto* (braised beef with mushrooms). *Piazza del Giglio 3, tel. 0583/494508. Dinner reservations advised. Dress: casual. AE, DC, MC, V. Closed Tues. dinner, Wed. $$*

Lodging **Villa La Principessa.** Just outside Lucca, only 3 kilometers (2 miles) from town, this is an exquisitely decorated 19th-century country mansion that has been converted into an exclusive hotel. Some rooms have beamed ceilings, and doors are individually decorated; antique furniture and portraits give an aura of gracious living. The restaurant is known for its creative cuisine. A well-manicured park and large swimming pool lure guests outdoors in fair weather. *Massa Pisana, tel. 0583/370037, fax 0583/379136. 44 rooms and suites with bath. Facilities: restaurant (closed Sun.), park, pool. AE, DC, MC, V. Closed Nov. 5–Mar. 31. $$$*

La Luna. There's an aura of Old World charm in this family-run hotel on one of Lucca's most central and historic streets. Recent extensive renovations have endowed the establishment with sparkling modern bathrooms while leaving the atmosphere intact. A plus for anyone touring by car is the hotel's own garage and parking area. *Corte Compagni 12 (corner of Via Fillungo), tel. 0583/493634, fax 0583/490021. 30 rooms with bath. AE, DC, MC, V. Closed Dec. 24–Jan. 6. $$*

Ilaria. A family-run hotel beside a minuscule canal within easy walking distance of the main sights, it has rooms that are small but fresh and functional. *Via del Fosso 20, tel. 0583/47558. 17 rooms, 12 with bath. AE, DC, MC, V. $*

Montalcino **La Cucina di Edgardo.** This tiny restaurant on Montalcino's main *Dining* street seats 30 in two charming dining rooms done in off-white and beige with dark wooden beams, a fireplace, and terra-cotta floors. It offers a complete menu, including everything from antipasto to after-dinner sweets, wine, and mineral water, for about 60,000 lire. The specialties of the house are *crema contadina* (bean soup garnished with onion) and *brasato al Brunello* (beef braised in the local Brunello wine). *Via Soccorsi Saloni 33, tel. 0577/848232. Reservations advised, especially weekends and summer. Dress: casual. AE, DC, MC, V. Closed Wed. and Jan. 10–30. $$*

★ **Taverna dei Barbi.** A meal at this delightful tavern, set among vineyards and mellow brick buildings on a wine-producing country estate (Fattoria dei Barbi), may well be a highlight of your journey through this part of Tuscany. The rustic dining room features a beamed ceiling, huge stone fireplace, and arched windows. The estate farm produces practically all the ingredients used in such traditional specialties as *zuppa di fagioli* (country-style bean soup with chard) and *scottiglia di pollo* (browned chicken served with garlic bread). The estate-produced Brunello is excellent, and other wines with the Barbi label are available. *Fattoria dei Barbi, tel. 0577/*

849357. Reservations required. Dress: casual. No credit cards. Closed Tues. dinner Oct.–May, Wed., Jan. 15–31, and July 1–15. $$

Montepulciano **Il Marzocco.** A 16th-century building within the town walls, it is fur-
Dining and nished in 19th-century style, complete with dignified, old-fashioned
Lodging parlors and a billiard room. Many bedrooms have large terraces
overlooking the countryside, and many rooms are large enough to
accommodate extra beds; they are furnished in heavy turn-of-the-
century style or in spindly white wood. *Piazza Savonarola 18, tel.
0578/757262. 18 rooms, 13 with bath or shower. Facilities: restau-
rant (closed Wed.). AE, DC, MC, V. $$*

Monteriggioni **Il Pozzo.** On the village square, this rustic tavern serves hearty Tus-
Dining can country cooking, including *maltagliati al sugo di agnello* (fresh
pasta in a tomato sauce made with lamb) and *cinghiale in dolce forte*
(boar with a tangy sauce). The desserts are homemade. *Piazza
Roma 2, tel. 0577/304127. Reservations advised. Dress: casual. AE,
DC, MC, V. Closed Sun. dinner, Mon., Jan., and July 31–Aug. 10.
$$*

Pisa **Bruno.** A pleasant restaurant, with beamed ceilings and the look of a
Dining country inn, Bruno is located just outside the old city walls, a short
walk from the bell tower and cathedral. Dine on classic Tuscan
dishes, from *zuppa alla pisana* (thick vegetable soup) to *baccalà con
porri* (cod with leeks). *Via Luigi Bianchi 12, tel. 050/560818. Dinner
reservations advised. Dress: casual. AE, DC, MC, V. Closed Mon.
dinner, Tues., and Aug. 5–15. $$*
Osteria dei Cavalieri. Just off the beautiful old Piazza dei Cavalieri,
this popular tavern has a one-course lunch menu and offers vegetari-
an dishes, too. The cordial owner also proposes a range of meat and
fish choices, including *faraone al forno* (roast guinea hen with
mushrooms). *Via San Frediano 16, tel. 050/580858. Reservations
advised in the evening. Dress: casual. MC, V. Closed Sat. lunch,
Sun. and Aug. $$*
La Pergoletta. In a medieval tower in the heart of the old town, La
Pergoletta is on a street named for its "beautiful towers." The res-
taurant is small and simple and has a shady garden for outdoor din-
ing. The signora who is the owner-cook offers traditional Tuscan
minestra di farro and *grigliata* (grilled beef, veal, or lamb). *Via
delle Belle Torri 36, tel. 050/542458. Reservations advised. MC, V.
Closed Tues. and Aug. $$*

Lodging **Cavalieri.** Opposite the railway station, in an unremarkable 1950s
building, this hotel offers functional, modern comforts in completely
soundproof and air-conditioned rooms, all with color TV and
minibar. The restaurant specializes in homemade pasta and seafood
and is open every day. *Piazza della Stazione 2, tel. 050/43290, fax
050/502242. 100 rooms with bath or shower. Facilities: bar, garage.
AE, DC, MC, V. $$$*
Royal Victoria. In a pleasant palazzo facing the Arno, a 10-minute
walk from the Campo dei Miracoli, this hotel is about as close as Pisa
comes to Old World ambience. It's comfortably furnished, featuring
antiques and reproductions in the lobby and in some rooms, in which
the decor varies from functional modern to turn-of-the-century.
There's a large restaurant open every day for hotel guests.
*Lungarno Pacinotti 12, tel. 050/940111. 67 rooms, 46 with bath. AE,
DC, MC, V. $$*

Pistoia **La Casa degli Amici.** The name means "the house of friends," and
Dining that's the atmosphere that the two industrious ladies who own it
succeed in creating in this restaurant located outside Pistoia's old

walls, on the road toward the exit of the A11 autostrada. They offer homey specialties such as ribollita and pasta e fagioli, and some creative dishes, too. There's a terrace for outdoor dining in the summer. *Via Bonellina 111, tel. 0573/380305. Reservations advised. Dress: casual. AE, DC, MC, V. Closed Sun. dinner, Tues., and Aug. $$*

Leon Rosso. From the center of town take Via Roma, off the beautiful Piazza del Duomo, and walk straight ahead to find this small and usually crowded restaurant. It serves Tuscan cuisine, starting with appetizing crostini and *fusilli all'orto* (corkscrew pasta with seasonal vegetables). For dessert try *panna cotta* (milk custard) with caramel sauce. *Via Panciatichi 4, tel. 0573/29230. Reservations advised. Dress: casual. AE, DC, MC, V. Closed Sun., Aug. $$*

Rafanelli. *Maccheroni all'anatra* (pasta with duck sauce) and other game dishes are the specialties, served with careful attention to tradition and quality for more than half a century by the same family. The restaurant is located just outside the old city walls; prices are in the low range of this category. *Via Sant'Agostino 47, tel. 0573/ 532046. No reservations. Dress: casual. AE, DC, MC, V. Closed Sun. dinner, Mon., and Aug. $$*

Prato
Dining

Piraña. Oddly named for the cannibalistic fish swimming in an aquarium in full view of diners, this sophisticated restaurant, decorated in shades of blue with steely accents, is a favorite in Prato. Seafood is the specialty and may take the form of *ravioli di pesce* (seafood ravioli with cream of scampi sauce) or *rombo* al forno (baked turbot). It's a bit out of the way for sightseers but handy if you have a car, for it's near the Prato Est autostrada exit. *Via G. Valentini 110, tel. 0574/25746. Reservations advised. Dress: casual. AE, DC, MC, V. Closed Sat. lunch, Mon. lunch, Sun., and Aug. $$$*

La Veranda. A large antipasto buffet greets you just inside the door of this restaurant near Prato's 13th-century Castello dell'Imperatore. The decor is elegant, with pale pink walls, terra-cotta tiled floors, and Venetian glass chandeliers, but the atmosphere is friendly and family oriented. Although the large menu has several international dishes, including Spanish paella, it does not ignore Tuscan specialties: *agnello alla cacciatora* (lamb with a tangy wine-vinegar sauce) or *tagliata* (sliced beef) with rucola and truffle are two good choices. *Via dell'Arco 10, tel. 0574/38235. Dress: casual. AE, DC, MC, V. Closed Sat. lunch, Sun., and Aug. $$*

San
Gimignano
Dining

Bel Soggiorno. On the top floor of a 100-year-old inn, this rustic restaurant has a wall of windows from which to view the landscape. Tuscan specialties include *pappardelle alla lepre* (noodles with hare sauce) and risotto *del Bel Soggiorno* (with saffron and nutmeg). *Via San Giovanni 91, tel. 0577/940375. Reservations advised. Dress: casual. AE, DC, MC, V. Closed Mon. and Jan. 7–Feb. 7. $$*

Stella. At this rustic, upscale trattoria, located between the main church and that of Sant'Agostino, prices are more moderate than at places with a view. The owner prides himself on farm-fresh vegetables and his own olive oil. The specialty of the house is grilled meat, including beef, lamb, and pork. *Via San Matteo 77, tel. 0577/940444. Reservations not required. Dress: casual. AE, DC, MC, V. Closed Wed. and Jan. 6–Feb. 15. $$*

Le Terrazze. This restaurant in a time-honored inn in the heart of San Gimignano has a charming view of rooftops and countryside and an ample menu featuring Tuscan dishes in seasonal variations. The specialties are served *alla sangimignanese* (finished off in the oven). *Piazza della Cisterna 23, tel. 0577/940328. Reservations advised. Dress: casual. AE, DC, MC, V. Closed Tues. and Wed. lunch and Nov. 10–Mar. 10. $$*

Lodging **Pescille.** This is a rambling farmhouse situated 8 kilometers (5 miles)
★ outside San Gimignano that has been converted into a handsome hotel, in which restrained contemporary and country classic decors
blend well. It also houses the fine Cinque Gigli restaurant. *Località
Pescille, Strada Castel San Gimignano, tel. 0577/940186, fax 0577/
940186. 33 rooms with bath. Facilities: outdoor pool, tennis, park,
restaurant (closed Wed.). AE, DC, MC, V. Closed Jan.–Feb. $$*

Siena **Al Marsili.** Located between Piazza del Campo and the cathedral,
Dining this 900-year-old wine cellar is an elegant place to dine, under broad,
★ brick-vaulted ceilings. The menu offers Tuscan and Italian special-
ties, among them homemade pastas such as *pici* and *tortelloni burro
e salvia* (large cheese-filled ravioli with butter and sage). Various
meat dishes are cooked in wine, and the wine list features the finest
Tuscan and Italian labels, including many from the nearby Chianti
country. *Via del Castoro 3, tel. 0577/47154. Reservations advised.
Dress: casual. AE, DC, MC, V. Closed Mon. $$*

★ **Le Logge.** Near Piazza del Campo, this typically Sienese trattoria
has rustic dining rooms on two levels and tables outdoors from June
to October. The menu features Tuscan dishes, such as *pennette
all'osteria* (pasta with creamy herbed sauce) and *coniglio con
pignoli* (rabbit with pine nuts). *Via del Porrione 33, tel. 0577/48013.
Reservations advised. Dress: casual. MC, V. Closed Sun. and June
1–15, Nov. 1–15. $$*

Tullio Tre Cristi. This is a typical and historic neighborhood
trattoria, long ago discovered by tourists and still reliable. The
paintings on the walls are by famous local artists of the 1920s, but
the culinary tradition here goes back even further. Try spaghetti
alle briciole, a poor-man's dish of pasta with bread-crumbs, tomato,
and garlic, or veal escalopes subtly flavored with *dragoncello* (tarra-
gon). You can eat outdoors in summer. To find the restaurant, take
Via dei Rossi from Via Banchi di Sopra. *Vicolo di Provenzano 1, tel.
0577/280608. Reservations advised. Dress: casual. MC, V. Closed
Sun. dinner, Mon., and mid-Jan–mid-Feb. $$*

Lodging **Certosa di Maggiano.** A former 14th-century monastery converted
★ into an exquisite country hotel, this haven of gracious living is little
more than a mile from the center of Siena. The atmosphere is that of
an exclusive retreat in which a select number of guests enjoy the
style and comfort of an aristocratic villa. *Via Certosa 82, tel. 0577/
288180, fax 0577/288189. 18 rooms with bath. Facilities: outdoor
pool, tennis, gardens, restaurant (closed Tues. $$$). AE, DC, MC,
V. $$$$*

Park. Set among olive groves and gardens on a hillside just outside
the city walls, this hotel offers solid comfort and spacious rooms
with views of the grounds and countryside. A historic 16th-century
villa, it has the restful atmosphere and antique charm of Tuscan
country life. The Olivo restaurant is known for fine regional cuisine.
*Via Marciano 18, tel. 0577/44803, fax 0577/49020. 68 double rooms
with bath or shower. Facilities: pool, 2 tennis courts, riding, park,
minibus service to town, 2 restaurants, poolside service, Caminetto
bar. AE, DC, MC, V. $$$$*

Antica Torre. A restored 17th-century tower within the town walls
in the southeast corner of Siena, Antica Torre is a 10-minute walk
from Piazza del Campo. It is the work of a cordial couple who have
created the atmosphere of a private home, furnished simply but in
good taste and with only eight guest rooms. The old stone staircase
and brick-vaulted ceilings here and there are reminders of the build-
ing's august age. *Via Fieravecchia 7, tel. and fax 0577/222255. 8
rooms with bath. MC, V. $–$$*

Chiusarelli. A handy location—near the long-distance bus terminal and a parking area and only a 10-minute walk from the main sights—makes this hotel a good choice. In a well-kept neoclassic villa, built in the early 1900s complete with caryatids, it has functional rooms that are airy and reasonably quiet. There is a small garden and a downstairs restaurant that caters to tour groups. *Viale Curtatone 9, tel. 0577/280562, fax 0577/271177. 50 rooms with bath. MC, V. $-$$*

Duomo. Occupying the top floor of a 300-year-old building in the center of Siena, near Piazza del Campo, the hotel is quiet and is furnished in a neat contemporary style, with traces of the past showing in the artfully exposed brickwork in the breakfast room. Many bedrooms have superb views of the city's towers and the hilly countryside. Two rooms are endowed with balconies. *Via Stalloreggi 38, tel. 0577/289088, fax 0577/43043. 23 rooms with bath. AE, MC, V. $-$$*

Sinalunga
Dining and Lodging
★

Locanda dell'Amorosa. A medieval hamlet set in Tuscan farmland has become a rustic retreat for jaded city folk, who reserve ahead for a meal or weekend in the country only a half-hour by car from Siena or Arezzo and even less from Montepulciano, Cortona, and Monte Oliveto Maggiore. The stone and brick buildings have been tastefully adapted to their current use, and the restaurant serves regional dishes that seem to taste even better in such apt surroundings. You can take home estate-produced wines and preserves as a souvenir of your stay. *Località Amorosa, Sinalunga, 10 km (6 mi) from the Valdichiana exit of A1, tel. 0577/679497, fax 0577/678216. 15 rooms with bath. Facilities: pool, restaurant (reservations required; dress: casual). AE, DC, MC, V. Closed Mon. and Tues. lunch and Jan. 15–Feb. 28). $$$$*

La Bandita. This attractive old farmhouse has been converted into a hotel by the Fiorini family. It has great charm, with terra-cotta floors throughout, lace curtains and antique pieces in the bedrooms, and a fireplace and grandfather's 19th-century Tuscan provincial furniture in a large, brick-vaulted living room. Some rooms can accommodate an extra bed, there is a garden, and meals are available. *Via Bandita 72, Bettolle (1 km, [.6 mi], from the Valdichiana exit of the A1 autostrada), tel. and fax 0577/624649. 8 rooms, 4 with bath. AE, DC, MC, V. $*

Volterra
Dining

Etruria. This restaurant on the town's main square, serves an excellent minestra di farro, an array of local game, and its own version of *panforte,* the dark, hard dessert cake that dates from medieval times. *Piazza dei Priori 8, tel. 0588/86064. No reservations. Dress: casual. AE, DC, MC, V. Closed Thurs. and Nov. 10–30, Jan. $$*

Lodging

San Lino. Located in a former convent, this hotel has modern comforts, a swimming pool, and its own regional restaurant. On top of that, it's located within the town walls, 10 minutes' walk from the main piazza. *Via San Lino 26, tel. 0588/85250, fax 0588/85250. 43 rooms with bath. Facilities: pool, restaurant (closed lunch and Wed.). AE, DC, MC, V. $$*

The Arts

Theater The seasons at the **Teatro Metastasio** (which include performances at a converted factory space called the **Capannone**), in Prato, run from January to May and October to December.

Music The Tuscan hills ring with music from July to September, when music festivals abound. These include the **Estate Musicale Lucchese,** in Lucca; the **Festival di Marlia;** and other festivals in Barga and Torre del Lago. In late July and August Siena hosts the **Settimane**

Musicali Senesi. The **Cantiere Internazionale d'Arte,** held in July and August in Montepulciano, is a multifaceted festival of figurative art, music, and theater, ending with a major theatrical production in Piazza Grande.

5 Umbria and the Marches

Perugia, Assisi, Urbino, Spoleto, and Orvieto

Umbria is the green heart of Italy. Blessed with steep, austere hills, deep valleys, and fast-flowing rivers, the region has not yet been swamped by tourism and has escaped the unplanned industrial expansion that afflicts much of central Italy. No town in Umbria boasts the extravagant wealth of art and architecture of Florence, Rome, or Venice, but this lack works in your favor. Cities can be experienced whole, rather than as a series of museums and churches, forced marches through 2,000 years of Western culture; in Umbria the visitor comes to know the towns as people live in them today.

This is not to suggest that the cultural cupboard is bare—far from it. Perugia, the capital of the region, and Assisi, Umbria's most famous city, are rich in art and architecture, as are Orvieto, Todi, and Spoleto. Virtually all the small towns in the region boast a castle, church, or museum worth a stop.

The earliest inhabitants of Umbria, the Umbri, were thought by the Romans to be the most ancient inhabitants of Italy. Little is known about them, since with the coming of Etruscan culture, the tribe fled into the mountains in the eastern portion of the region. The Etruscans, who founded some of the great cities of Umbria, were in turn supplanted by the Romans. Unlike Tuscany and other regions of central Italy, Umbria had few powerful medieval families to exert control over the cities in the Middle Ages—proximity to Rome ensured that Umbria would always be more or less under papal domination.

The relative political stability of the region did not mean that Umbria was left in peace. Located in the center of the country, it has for much of its history been a battlefield where armies from north and south clashed. Hannibal destroyed a Roman army on the shores of Lake Trasimeno, and the full and bloody course of the interminable Guelph-Ghibelline conflict of the Middle Ages was played out in Umbria. Dante considered it the most violent place in Italy. Trophies of war still decorate the facade of the Palazzo dei Priori in Perugia, and the little town of Gubbio continues a warlike rivalry begun in the Middle Ages—every year it challeges the Tuscan town of Sansepolcro to a crossbow tournament. Today, of course, the bowmen shoot at targets, but neither side has forgotten that 500 years ago its ancestors shot at each other.

In spite of—or perhaps because of—this bloodshed, Umbria has produced more than its share of Christian saints. The most famous is St. Francis, the decidedly unmartial saint whose life shaped the Church and the history of his time. His great shrine at Assisi is visited by hundreds of thousands of pilgrims each year. St. Clare, his devoted follower, was Umbria born, as were St. Benedict, St. Rita of Cascia, and, ironically, the shadowy patron saint of lovers, St. Valentine.

East of Umbria, the Marches—or Marche, in Italian—stretch between the hills of the southern Apennines down to the Adriatic sea. It is a scenic region of mountains and valleys, with great turreted castles standing on high peaks defending passes and roads—silent testament to the region's warlike past. The Marches have passed through numerous hands. First the Romans supplanted the native civilizations; then Charlemagne supplanted the Romans (and gave the region its name: It was divided into "Marks," or provinces, under the rule of the Holy Roman Emperor); then began the seemingly never-ending struggle between popes and local lords. Cesare Borgia succeeded in wresting control of the Marches from the local suzerains, annexing the region to the papacy of his father, Alexander VI.

Despite all this martial tussling, it was in the lonely mountain town of Urbino that the Renaissance came to its fullest flower; that small town became a haven of culture and learning that rivaled the greater, richer, and more powerful city of Florence, and even Rome itself.

Essential Information

Important Addresses and Numbers

Tourist Information

Ancona (Via Thaon de Revel 4, tel. 071/33249; railway station, Piazza Fratelli Rosselli, tel. 071/41703).
Ascoli Piceno (Piazza del Popolo, tel. 0736/255250).
Assisi (Piazza del Comune 12, tel. 075/812534).
Gubbio (Piazza Oderisi 6, tel. 075/922–0693).
Loreto (Via Solari 3, tel. 071/977139).
Orvieto (Piazza del Duomo, tel. 0763/41772).
Perugia: Umbria's provincial tourist office (Via Mazzini 21, tel. 075/25341); Perugia's city tourist office (Piazza IV Novembre 3, tel. 075/572–3327).
Spoleto (Piazza della Libertà 7, tel. 0743/49890 or 220311).
Urbino (Piazza Duca Federico 35, tel. 0722/2441).

Emergencies

Police: Perugia (Piazza dei Partigiani, tel. 113), **Assisi** (Piazza Matteotti 3, tel. 075/812239), **Spoleto** (Via Cerquiglia 36, tel. 0743/49044), **Orvieto** (Piazza Cahen, tel. 0763/42476).

Arriving and Departing

By Car

On the western edge of the region is the Umbrian section of the Autostrada del Sole (A1), the principal north–south highway in Italy. It links Florence and Rome with the important Umbrian town of Orvieto and passes near Todi and Terni. The S3 intersects with A1 and leads on to Assisi and Urbino. The Adriatica superhighway (A14) runs north–south along the coast, linking the Marches to Bologna and Venice.

By Train

The main rail line from Rome to Ancona passes through Narni, Terni, Spoleto, and Foligno. Travel time from Rome to Spoleto is a little less than 90 minutes on Intercity trains. The main Rome–Florence line stops at Orvieto, and, with a change of trains at the small town of Terontola, one can travel by rail from Rome or Florence to Perugia and Assisi.

By Bus

Perugia and Orvieto are served by private bus services, leaving from Rome and Florence.

Getting Around

By Car

Umbria has an excellent and modern road network. Central Umbria is served by a major highway, S75bis, which passes along the shore of Lake Trasimeno and ends in Perugia, the principal city of the region. Assisi, the most visited town in the region, is well served by the modern highway S75, which connects to S3 and 3bis, which cover the heart of the region. Major inland routes connect coastal A14 to large towns in the Marches, including Urbino, Jesi, Macerata, and Ascoli Piceno, but inland secondary roads in mountain areas can be tortuous and narrow.

By Train Branch lines link the central rail hub, Ancona, with the inland towns of Fabriano and Ascoli Piceno. In Umbria, a small, privately owned railway runs from Città di Castello in the north to Terni in the south.

By Bus There is good local bus service between all the major and minor towns of Umbria. Some of the routes in rural areas, especially in the Marches, are designed to serve as many destinations as possible and are, therefore, quite roundabout and slow. Schedules often change, so consult with local tourist offices before setting out.

Exploring Umbria and the Marches

The steep hills and deep valleys that make Umbria and the Marches so picturesque also make them difficult to explore. Driving routes must be chosen carefully to avoid tortuous mountain roads; major towns are not necessarily linked to each other by train, bus, or highway. A convenient base for exploring the region might be Perugia, the largest city in Umbria and the hub of Tour 1, but to see the region properly you would still need to stay overnight in other towns along the way. Tour 2 heads east across the Apennines to the Marches region; we begin exploring it in the hilltop city of Urbino, travel down to the Adriatic coast to visit Ancona, then climb back west into the hills to Loreto and Ascoli Piceno. Back in Umbria, Tour 3 concentrates on two memorable towns: Spoleto, site of the famous arts festival, south of Perugia, and Assisi, St. Francis's hometown, just east of Perugia. The final tour centers on Orvieto, built on a huge rock outcropping in western Umbria, southwest of Perugia.

Highlights for First-Time Visitors

Palazzo dei Priori, and **Fontana Maggiore** Perugia (*see* Tour 1: Perugia to Gubbio).

Collegio del Cambio, Perugia (*see* Tour 1: Perugia to Gubbio).

Palazzo dei Consoli, Gubbio (*see* Tour 1: Perugia to Gubbio).

Ducal Palace, Urbino (*see* Tour 2: The Marches).

House of the Virgin Mary, Loreto (*see* Tour 2: The Marches).

Piazza del Popolo, Ascoli Piceno (*see* Tour 2: The Marches).

Duomo, Spoleto (*see* Tour 3: Spoleto and Assisi).

Basilica of San Francesco, Assisi (*see* Tour 3: Spoleto and Assisi).

Duomo, Orvieto (*see* Tour 4: Orvieto and Environs).

Tour 1: Perugia to Gubbio

Numbers in the margin correspond to points of interest on the Umbria and the Marches and Perugia maps.

❶ **Perugia,** the largest and richest of Umbria's cities, is an old and elegant place of great charm. Despite a rather grim crust of modern suburbs, Perugia's location on a series of hills high above the suburban plain has ensured that the medieval city remains almost completely intact. Perugia is the best-preserved hill town of its size, and few other places in Italy illustrate better the concept of the self-contained city-state that so shaped the course of Italian history.

The best approach to the city is by train—the station is located in the unlovely suburbs, but there are frequent buses running directly to Piazza d'Italia, the heart of the old town. If you are driving to Perugia, it is best to leave your car in one of the parking lots near the station and then take the bus or the escalator (which passes through fascinating subterranean excavations of the Roman foundations of the city) to the center of town.

The nerve center of the city is the broad, stately **Corso Vannucci,** a pedestrian street that runs from Piazza d'Italia to Piazza IV Novembre. As evening falls, Corso Vannucci is filled with Perugians out for their evening *passeggiata*, a pleasant predinner stroll that may include a pause for an aperitif at one of the many bars that line the street.

Time Out   You can enjoy the lively comings and goings on Corso Vannucci from the vantage point of the **Bar Sandri** (Corso Vannucci 32). This fine old bar is a 19th-century relic with wood-paneled walls and an elaborately frescoed ceiling.

Corso Vannucci runs into Piazza IV Novembre, a pretty, sunny square dominated by the **Duomo** (Cathedral of San Lorenzo), the medieval **Palazzo dei Priori,** or seat of government, and the **Fontana Maggiore,** a fountain by Giovanni and Nicola Pisano that dates from the 13th century.

❷ The **Duomo** is a large and rather plain building dating from the Middle Ages but with many additions from the 15th and 16th centuries. The interior is vast and echoing, with little in the way of decoration. There are some elaborately carved choir stalls, executed by Giovanni Battista Bastone in 1520. The great relic of the church—the wedding ring of the Virgin Mary that the Perugians stole from the nearby town of Chiusi—is kept in a chapel in the left aisle. The ring is the size of a large bangle and is kept under lock (15 locks, actually) and key every day of the year except July 30, when it is exposed to view. *Open daily 8–12, 4–7:30.*

In the adjoining **Museum of the Duomo** there is a large array of precious objects associated with the cathedral, including vestments, vessels, manuscripts, and gold work, as well as one outstanding piece of artwork, an early masterpiece by Luca Signorelli, the altarpiece showing the Madonna with St. John the Baptist, St. Onophrius, and St. Lawrence (1484). *Admission: 2,000 lire. Open Wed.–Fri. 9–noon, Sat. 9–noon, 3:30–5:30, Sun. 3:30–5:30.*

❸ The **Palazzo dei Priori** faces the Duomo across the piazza. It is an imposing building, begun in the 13th century, with an unusual staircase that fans out into the square. The facade is decorated with symbols of Perugia's pride and past power: The griffin is the symbol of the city; the lion denotes Perugia's allegiance to the Guelph (or papal) cause; and both figures support the heavy chains of the gates of Siena, which fell to Perugian forces in 1358.

❹ Attached to the Palazzo dei Priori, but entered from Corso Vannucci, is the **Collegio del Cambio,** a series of elaborate rooms that housed the meeting hall and chapel of the guild of bankers and money changers. The walls were frescoed from 1496 to 1500 by the most important Perugian painter of the Renaissance, Pietro Vannucci, better known as Perugino. The decorative program in the Collegio includes common religious themes, like the Nativity and the Transfiguration (on the end walls), but also figures intended to inspire the businessmen who congregated here. On the left wall are female fig-

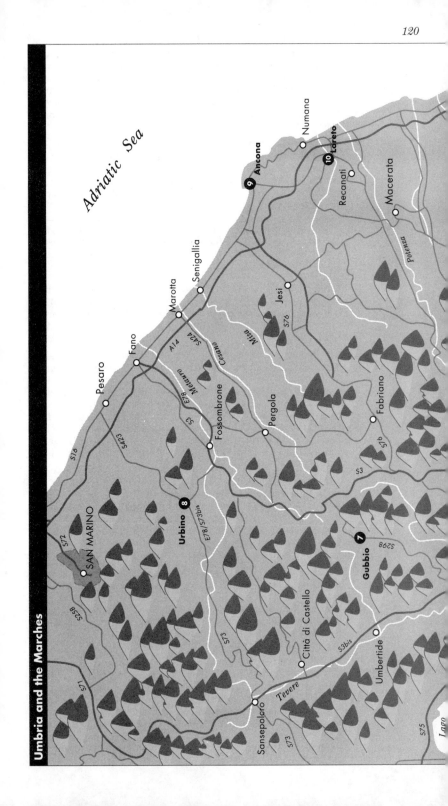

Umbria and the Marches

Adriatic Sea

Numana

9 Ancona

10 Loreto

Recanati

Macerata

Senigallia

Marotta

Jesi

S76

Misa

Fano

A14

S424

Pesaro

Metauro

Cesano

E78

S3

Fossombrone

Pergola

Fabriano

S76

S423

S16

S3

Urbino 8

E78/S73bis

SAN MARINO

S72

7 Gubbio

S298

S258

Città di Castello

S73

S3bis

Umbertide

S71

S73

Sansepolcro

Tevere

S75

Lago

Polenza

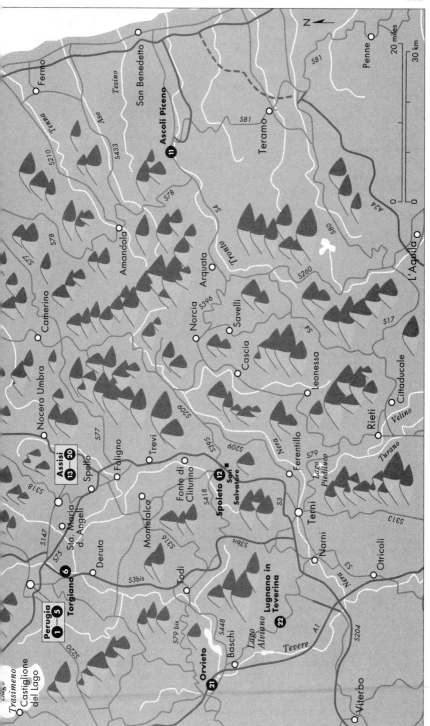

Archaeological
Museum of
Umbria, **5**

Collegio del
Cambio, **4**

Duomo, **2**

Palazzo dei
Priori, **3**

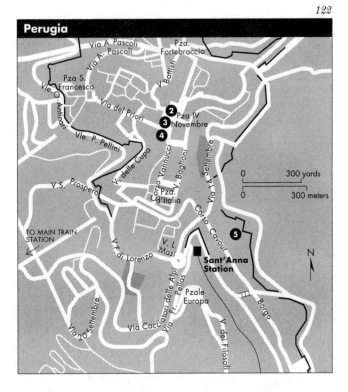

ures representing the virtues, and beneath them the heroes and
sages of antiquity. On the right wall are the Prophets and Sibyls—
said to have been painted in part by Perugino's most famous pupil,
Raphael, whose hand, the experts say, is most apparent in the figure of Fortitude. On one of the pilasters is a remarkably honest self-
portrait of Perugino surmounted by a Latin inscription and contained in a faux frame. *Admission: 3,000 lire. Open Nov.–Feb.,
Tues.–Sat. 8–2, Sun. 9–12:30; Mar.–Oct., Tues.–Sat. 9–12:30,
2:30–5:30, Sun. 9–12:30.*

⑤ About a 10-minute walk south of the center along Corso Cavour
leads to the **Archaeological Museum of Umbria,** which contains an
excellent collection of Etruscan artifacts from throughout the region. Perugia was a flourishing Etruscan site long before it fell under Roman domination in 310 BC. (Other than this collection, little
remains of Perugia's mysterious ancestors, although the Gate of Augustus, in Piazza Fortebraccio, the northern entrance to the city, is
of Etruscan origin.) *Piazza Giordano Bruno. Admission: 4,000 lire.
Open summer, Mon.–Sat. 9–1:30, 3–7, Sun. 9–1; winter, Mon.–
Sat. 9–1:30, 2:30–6, Sun. 9–1.*

⑥ Wine lovers are certain to want to visit **Torgiano,** 15 kilometers (9
miles) southeast of Perugia. It is home to the famous Lungarotti
winery, best known for delicious Rubesco Lungarotti, San Giorgio,
and chardonnay. The town is also home to a fascinating wine museum, which has a large collection of ancient wine vessels, presses,
documents, and tools that tell the story of viticulture in Umbria and
beyond. The museum traces the history of wine in all its uses—for
drinking at the table, as medicine, and in mythology. *Corso Vittorio*

Emanuele 11. Admission: 3,000 lire. Open Apr.–Sept., daily 9–noon, 3–8; Oct.–Mar., daily 9–1, 3–6.

❼ The 40-kilometer (25-mile) trip from Perugia northeast to **Gubbio** follows S298 through rugged, mountainous terrain. There is something otherworldly about Gubbio, a small jewel of a medieval town tucked away in this mountainous corner of Umbria. Even at the height of summer, the cool serenity and silence of Gubbio's streets remain intact. The town is perched on the slopes of Mount Ingino, and the streets are dramatically steep.

Gubbio's relatively isolated position has kept it free of hordes of high-season visitors, but even during the busiest times of year the city lives up to its Italian nickname, the City of Silence. Parking in the central Piazza dei Quaranta Martiri (named for 40 hostages murdered by the Nazis in 1944) is easy and secure, and it is wise to leave your car there and explore the narrow streets on foot.

Walk up the main street of the town, Via della Repubblica (a steep climb), to Piazza della Signoria. This square is dominated by the magnificent **Palazzo dei Consoli,** a medieval building designed and built by a local architect known as Gattapone—a man still much admired by today's residents (every other hotel, restaurant, and bar has been named after him).

While the Palazzo dei Consoli is impressive, it is the piazza itself that is most striking. When approached from the thicket of medieval streets, the wide and majestic square is an eye-opener. The piazza juts out from the hillside like an enormous terrace, giving wonderful views of the town and surrounding countryside.

The Palazzo dei Consoli houses a small museum, famous chiefly for the Tavole Eugubine, bronze tablets written in an ancient Umbrian language. Also in the museum are the *ceri,* three 16-foot-high poles crowned with statues of Saints Ubaldo, George, and Anthony. These heavy pillars are the focal point of the best-known event in Gubbio, the Festival of the Candles ("Ceri"), held every May 15. On that day, teams of Gubbio's young men, dressed in medieval costumes and carrying the ceri, race up the steep slopes of Mount Ingino to the Monastery of St. Ubaldo, high above the town. This festival, enacted faithfully every year since 1151, is a picturesque, if strenuous, way of thanking the patron saints of the town for their assistance in a miraculous Gubbian victory over a league of 11 other towns. *Admission: 4,000 lire. Open mid-Mar.–Sept., daily 9–12:30, 3:30–6; Oct.–mid-Mar., daily 9–1, 3–5.*

The **Duomo** and the **Palazzo Ducale** face each other across a narrow street on the highest tier of the town. The Duomo dates from the 13th century, with some Baroque additions—in particular, a lavishly decorated bishop's chapel. *Duomo. Open daily 9–12:30, 3–5.*

The Palazzo Ducale is a scaled-down copy of the Palazzo Ducale in Urbino (Gubbio was once the possession of that city's ruling family, the Montefeltro). Gubbio's palazzo contains a small museum and a fine courtyard. There are magnificent views from some of the public rooms. *Admission: 4,000 lire. Open daily 9–1:30.*

Time Out Under the arches that support the Palazzo Ducale is the **Bar del Giardino Pubblico** (open May–Sept., daily 9–7), a bar set in the tiny public gardens, which seem to hang off the side of the mountain. It is a charming place for a cold drink and a rest after a tiring climb up to the Duomo and Palace.

Tour 2: The Marches

An excursion from Umbria into the region of the Marches is recommended for those who want to get off the beaten track and see a part of Italy rarely visited by foreigners. It must be admitted that traveling in the Marches is not as easy as in Umbria or Tuscany. Beyond the narrow coastal plain and away from major towns, the roads are steep and twisting. Train travel in the region is slow, and destinations are limited, although one can reach Ascoli Piceno by rail, and there's an efficient bus service from the coastal town of Pesaro to Urbino, the other principal tourist city of the region.

8 **Urbino** is a majestic city, sitting atop a steep hill, with a skyline of towers and domes. It is something of a surprise to come upon it—the location is remote—and it is even stranger to reflect that this quiet country town was once a center of learning and culture almost without rival in western Europe. The town looks much as it did in the glory days of the 15th century, a cluster of warm brick and pale stone buildings, all topped with russet-colored tiled roofs. The focal point is the immense and beautiful Ducal Palace.

The tradition of learning in Urbino continues to this day. The city is the home of a small but prestigious Italian state university—one of the oldest in the world—and during term time the streets are filled with hordes of noisy students. It is very much a college town, with the usual array of bookshops, record stores, bars, and coffeehouses. During the summer, the Italian student population is replaced by foreigners who come to study Italian language and arts at several prestigious, private fine-arts academies.

Urbino's fame rests on the reputation of three of its native sons: Duke Federico da Montefeltro, the enlightened warrior-patron who built the Ducal Palace; Raphael, one of the most influential painters in history and an embodiment of the spirit of the Renaissance; and the architect Donato Bramante, who translated the philosophy of the Renaissance into buildings of grace and beauty. Why three of the greatest men of the age should have been born within a generation of one another in this remote town has never been explained. Oddly enough, there is little work by either Bramante or Raphael in the city, but the duke's influence can still be felt strongly, even now, some 500 years after his death.

The **Ducal Palace** holds the place of honor in the city, and in no other palace of its era are the principles of the Renaissance stated quite so clearly. If the Renaissance was, in ideal form, a celebration of the nobility of man and his works, of the light and purity of the soul, then there is no place in Italy, the birthplace of the Renaissance, where these tenets are better illustrated. From the moment you enter the peaceful courtyard, you know that you are in a place of grace and beauty, the harmony of the building reflecting the high ideals of the men who built it.

Today the palace houses the **National Museum of the Marches,** with a superb collection of paintings, sculpture, and other objets d'art, well arranged and properly lit. It would be hard to mention all the great works in this collection—some originally the possessions of the Montefeltro family, others brought to the museum from churches and palaces throughout the region—but there are a few that must be singled out. Of these, perhaps the most famous is Piero della Francesca's enigmatic work *The Flagellation of Christ.* Much has been written about this painting, and few experts agree on its meaning. Legend has it that the three figures in the foreground represent a murdered member of the Montefeltro family (the barefoot young man) and his two murderers. Others claim the painting is a heavily veiled criticism of certain parts of Christian Europe—the iconography is obscure and the history extremely complicated. All the experts agree, though, that the painting is one of Piero della Francesca's masterpieces. Piero himself thought so. It is one of the few works he signed (on the lowest step supporting Pilate's throne).

Other masterworks in the collection are Paolo Uccello's *Profanation of the Host,* Piero della Francesca's *Madonna of Senigallia,* and Titian's *Resurrection* and *Last Supper.* Duke Federico's study is an astonishingly elaborate, but tiny, room decorated with inlaid wood, said to be the work of Botticelli. *Piazza Duca Federico, tel. 0722/ 2760. Admission: 8,000 lire. Open Apr.–Sept., Mon.–Sat. 9–7, Sun. 9–1; Oct.–Mar., Mon.–Sat. 9–2, Sun. 9–1.*

The **house of the painter Raphael** really is the house in which he was born and in which he took his first steps in painting (under the direction of his artist father). There is some debate about the fresco of the Madonna that adorns the house. Some say it is by Raphael, others attribute it to the father—with Raphael's mother and the young painter himself standing in as models for the Madonna and Child. Either way, it's an interesting picture. *Via Raffaello. Admission: 5,000 lire. Open Apr.–Sept., Mon, Tues., Thurs.–Sat. 9–7, Sun. 9–1; Oct.–Mar., Mon., Tues., Thurs.–Sat. 9–2, Sun. 9–1.*

❾ To reach **Ancona,** on the Adriatic coast, from Urbino, a distance of approximately 87 kilometers (54 miles), take the E78 or S3 to the superhighway A14, which runs along the coast but inland by a mile or so. The coast road, S16, is a congested two-lane highway with little to recommend it.

Ancona was probably once a lovely city. It is set on an elbow-shaped bluff (hence its name; ankon is Greek for "elbow") that juts out into the Adriatic. But Ancona was the object of serious aerial bombing during World War II—it was, and is, an important port city—and was reduced to rubble. The city has been rebuilt in the unfortunate postwar poured-concrete style, practical and inexpensive but certainly not pleasing. Unless you are taking a ferry to Venice, there is little reason to visit the city—with a few exceptions. Once in a while there are glimpses of the old architecture, as in the Duomo San Ciriaco and the Loggia dei Mercanti. In addition, Ancona can be the base for an excursion to Loreto or to Ascoli Piceno, farther down the Adriatic coast.

❿ **Loreto** is an easy excursion from Ancona. To reach this small inland hill town, take A14 to the Loreto turnoff, a 24-kilometer (15-mile) drive south.

Loreto is famous for one of the best-loved shrines in the world, that of the **house of the Virgin Mary.** The legend is that angels moved the house from Nazareth, where the Virgin was living at the time of the Annunciation, to this hilltop in 1295. The reason for this sudden and divinely inspired move was that Nazareth had fallen into the hands of Muslim invaders, not suitable landlords, the angelic hosts felt. More recently, following archaeological excavations made at the behest of the Church, evidence has come to light proving that the house did once stand elsewhere and was brought to the hilltop by human means around the time the angels are said to have done the job.

The house itself consists of three rough stone walls contained within an elaborate marble tabernacle; built around this centerpiece is the giant basilica of the Holy House, which dominates the town. Millions of visitors come to the site every year (particularly at Easter and on the Feast of the Holy House, December 10), and the little town of Loreto can become uncomfortably crowded with pilgrims. Many great Italian architects, including Bramante, Sangallo, and Sansovino, contributed to the design of the basilica. Inside are a great many mediocre 19th- and 20th-century paintings but also some fine works by Renaissance masters such as Luca Signorelli and Melozzo da Forlì.

Nervous air travelers may take comfort in the fact that the Holy Virgin of Loreto is the patroness of air travelers and that Pope John Paul II has composed a prayer for a safe flight—available in the church in a half-dozen languages.

⑪ Ascoli Piceno, 105 kilometers (65 miles) from Ancona, is not a hill town. Rather, it sits in a valley, ringed by steep hills and cut by the fast-racing Tronto River. The town is almost unique in Italy, in that it seems to have its traffic problems—in the historic center, at any rate—pretty much under control; you can drive *around* the picturesque part of the city, but driving *through* it is most difficult. This feature makes Ascoli Piceno one of the most pleasant large towns in the country for exploring on foot. True, there is traffic, but you are not constantly assaulted by jams, noise, and exhaust fumes the way you are in other Italian cities.

The heart of the town is the majestic **Piazza del Popolo,** dominated by the Gothic church of San Francesco and the Palazzo del Popolo, a 13th-century town hall that contains a graceful Renaissance courtyard. The square itself functions as the living room of the entire city. At dusk each evening the piazza is packed with people standing in small groups, exchanging news and gossip as if at a cocktail party.

Time Out Ascoli Piceno is indelibly associated with the Meletti distillery situated on the outskirts of town. You can sample the aniseedlike spirit at the wood-paneled **Bar Centrale,** a small and cozy establishment that dates from the turn of the century, at Piazza del Popolo No. 9. For a light lunch or snack, pick up some delicious sandwiches and homemade pastries across the square at the **Pasticceria Angelini.**

The 175-kilometer (108-mile) drive to Spoleto takes you out of the Marches and back into Umbria. The route, S4 southwest to Rieti, then S79 north to Terni, then S3 into Spoleto, is roundabout but vastly preferable to a series of winding mountain roads that connect Ascoli Piceno with Umbria.

Tour 3: Spoleto and Assisi

⑫ Spoleto is an enchanting town perfectly situated in wooded countryside. "A little bit of heaven fallen to earth" it was once called, and it is not hard to understand the sentiment. "Quaint" may be an overused term, but it is the most appropriate word to describe this city still enclosed by stout medieval walls. The chief pleasure of Spoleto is that the city itself is the sight. There is no long tramp through museums and churches in store for you here; rather, you can enjoy the simple treat of walking through the maze of twisting streets and up and down cobbled stairways, enjoying the beauty of the town and its wonderful peace and quiet.

Quiet, that is, except when Spoleto is hosting the Festival of Two Worlds, an arts festival, held every year from mid-June to mid-July. During those two months the sleepy town is swamped with visitors who come to see world-class plays and operas, to hear concerts, and to see extensive exhibitions of paintings and sculpture. Hotels in the city and countryside are filled to overflowing, and the streets are packed with visitors. It is unwise to arrive in Spoleto during this period without confirmed hotel reservations. Furthermore, experiencing the town itself, rather than the festival, is very difficult during these months. Those who don't care for crowds are advised to stay away during the festival.

Even in the off-season, parking in the Old City is difficult. If you are traveling by car, it is best to park outside the walls. There is usually ample parking available near Piazza della Vittoria.

Spoleto is dominated by a huge castle that was built in 1359–63 by the Gubbio-born architect Gattapone. It was until recently a high-security prison, but is now undergoing restoration and is shortly due to open to the public. The castle was built to protect the town's most famous monument, the massive bridge known as the **Ponte delle Torri** (Bridge of the Towers), built by Gattapone on Roman foundations. This massive structure stands 262 feet above the gorge it spans and was built originally as an aqueduct. The bridge is open to pedestrians, and a walk over it affords marvelous views—looking down to the river below is the best way to appreciate the colossal dimensions of the bridge. The central span is actually higher than that of the dome of St. Peter's in Rome.

The bridge and castle stand at the highest point in the town. From there you can head downhill to the **Duomo,** set in a lovely square. The church facade is dourly Romanesque but with the pleasant light addition of a Renaissance loggia. The contrast between the heavy medieval work and the graceful later embellishment graphically demonstrates the difference, not only in style, but in philosophy, of the two eras. The earlier was strong but ungiving; the later, human and open-minded.

From Piazza del Duomo make your way to Piazza del Mercato, site of the old Roman forum and today the main square of the Old Town.

Time Out The square is lined with bars and delicatessens that serve good pastries and coffee. Parked in the square every day except Sunday is the van of a *porchetta* seller. These mobile snack bars are common to all central and northern Italy, and they serve only one product—roast pork. The whole pig is roasted on a spit, and slices are carved off to make delicious sandwiches on crusty rolls called *rosette*. The porchetta seller in Piazza del Mercato is particularly cheerful, and his portions are generous.

The **Arch of Drusus,** off the southern end of the square, was built by the Senate of Spoleto to honor the Roman general Drusus, son of the Emperor Tiberius.

North of Piazza del Mercato, past the picturesque Via Fontesecca, with its tempting shops selling local pottery and other handicrafts, is the church of **Sant'Eufemia** (in the courtyard of the archbishop's palace), an ancient, austere church built in the 11th century. Its most interesting feature is the gallery above the nave where female worshippers were required to sit—a holdover from the Eastern Church—one of the few such galleries in this part of Italy. *Open daily summer, 8–1, 4–8; winter, 8–1, 4–6.*

At the southern end of Corso Mazzini is a small but well-preserved **Roman theater,** used in summer for performances of Spoleto's arts festival. The theater was the site of one of the town's most macabre incidents. During the Middle Ages, Spoleto took the side of the Holy

Roman Emperor in the interminable struggle between Guelph (papal) and Ghibelline (imperial) factions over the question of who would control central and northern Italy. Four hundred of the pope's supporters were massacred in the theater, and their bodies were burned in an enormous pyre. It is not an episode of which Spoleto is proud, and, furthermore, the Guelphs were triumphant in the end. Spoleto was incorporated into the states of the Church in 1354. *Open Tues.–Sun. summer, 9–1:30, 3–6; winter, 9–1, 2:30–6. Closed holidays.*

On the outskirts of the city, just off Via Flaminia (S3), is the lovely church of **San Salvatore**. You may already have seen a lot of old churches in Italy, but few are as old as this one. It needed *renovation* in the 9th century—by that time it was already 600 years old. It is nestled under cypresses and surrounded by Spoleto's cemetery and is quiet, cool, and peaceful. The church was built by Eastern monks in the 4th century, and little has been added (or removed) since its renovation. San Salvatore has an air of timelessness and antiquity rarely found in churches so close to major towns. *Open daily 8–1, 4–6.*

Assisi is a total of 47 kilometers (30 miles) north and west of Spoleto on S3 and S75.

⓭ The first sight of **Assisi** is memorable. The hill on which Assisi sits rises dramatically from the flat plain, and the town is dominated at the top of the mount by a medieval castle; on the lower slopes of the hill is the massive basilica of San Francesco, rising majestically on graceful arched supports.

Except in the depths of the off-season, Assisi, the most famous and most visited city in Umbria, is always thronged with sightseers and pilgrims. Somehow, though, despite the press of visitors, there is an unspoiled quality to the city—although that charm can be taxed to the limit during major feasts of the church, like Christmas or Easter, or on the feast of the patron saint himself (October 4). But if you come to Assisi on a weekday or in the low season, you are sure to see this charming rose-colored town at its best.

St. Francis was born here in 1181, the son of a well-to-do merchant. He had, by his own account, a riotous youth, but forsook the pleasures of the flesh quite early in life, adopting a life of austerity. His mystical approach to poverty, asceticism, and the beauty of man and nature struck a responsive chord in the medieval mind, and he quickly attracted a vast number of followers. He was a humble and unassuming man, and his compassion and humility brought him great love and veneration in his own lifetime. Without actively seeking power, as did many clerics of his day, he amassed great influence and political power, changing the history of the Catholic church. He was the first person to receive the stigmata (wounds in his hands, feet, and side corresponding to the torments of Christ on the cross), injuries that caused him great pain and suffering, which he bore with characteristic patience. Nonetheless, St. Francis welcomed the coming of "Sister Death," in 1226. Today the Franciscans are the largest of all the Catholic orders. And among the mass of clergy at Assisi, you can identify the saint's followers by their simple, coarse brown habits bound by belts of knotted rope.

Numbers in the margin correspond to points of interest on the Assisi map.

⓮ The **Basilica of San Francesco** is one of Italy's foremost monuments and was begun shortly after the saint's death. What St. Francis

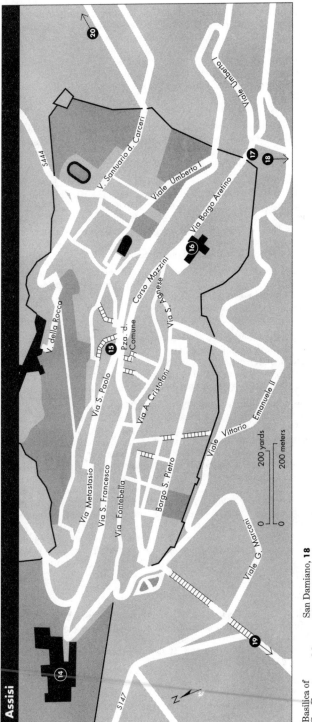

Assisi

Basilica of
San Francesco, **14**
Hermitage of the
Carceri, **20**
Porta Nuova, **17**

San Damiano, **18**
Santa Chiara, **16**
Santa Maria degli
Angeli, **19**
Temple of Minerva, **15**

would have made of a church of such size, wealth, and grandeur—the opposite of all he preached and believed—is hard to imagine. His coffin, unearthed from its secret hiding place in 1818, is on display in the crypt below the lower church and is a place of piety. The basilica is not one church, but two huge structures built one over the other. The lower church is dim and full of candlelit shadows, while the upper is a bright and airy place. Both are magnificently decorated artistic treasure houses, however, especially the upper church, where a fresco cycle by Giotto is a milestone in the history of Western art.

Visit the lower church first. The first chapel on the left of the nave was decorated by the Sienese master Simone Martini. Frescoed in 1322–26, the paintings show the life of St. Martin—the sharing of his cloak with the poor man, the saint's knighthood, and his death.

There is some dispute about the paintings in the third chapel on the right. Experts have argued for years as to their authorship, with many saying that they were done by Giotto. The paintings depict the life of St. Mary Magdalen. There is a similar dispute about the works above the high altar—some say they are by Giotto; others claim them for an anonymous pupil. They depict the marriage of St. Francis to poverty, chastity, and obedience.

In the right transept are frescoes by Cimabue, a Madonna and Saints, one of them St. Francis himself. In the left transept are some of the best-known works of the Sienese painter Pietro Lorenzetti. They depict the Madonna with Saints John and Francis, a Crucifixion, and a Descent from the Cross.

It is quite a contrast to climb the steps next to the altar and emerge into the bright sunlight and airy grace of the double-arched Renaissance cloister called the Cloister of the Dead. A door to the right leads to the treasury of the church and contains relics of St. Francis and other holy objects associated with the order.

The upper church is dominated by Giotto's 28 frescoes, each portraying incidents in the life of St. Francis. Although the artist was only in his twenties when he painted this cycle, the frescoes show that Giotto was the pivotal artist in the development of Western painting, breaking away from the stiff, unnatural styles of earlier generations and moving toward a realism and grace that reached its peak in the Renaissance. The paintings are viewed left to right, starting in the transept. The most beloved of all the scenes is probably that of *St. Francis Preaching to the Birds*, a touching painting that seems to sum up the gentle spirit of the saint. It stands in marked contrast to the scene of the dream of Innocent III. The pope dreams of a humble monk who will steady the church. Sure enough, in the panel next to the sleeping pope, you see a strong Francis supporting a church that seems to be on the verge of tumbling down. *Upper and lower churches. Open summer, Mon.–Sat. 6 AM–7 PM, Sun. 6 AM–7:30 PM; winter, Mon.–Sat. 6:30–noon, 2–6, Sun. 6:30 AM–7 PM.*

15 Follow Via San Francesco from the Basilica up the hill to the central square of the town, Piazza del Comune. The **Temple of Minerva,** on the left, is made up of bits and pieces of a Roman temple that dates from the time of Augustus. It has been converted into a church. *Open daily 7–noon, 4–7.*

 Follow Corso Mazzini out of the square, heading toward the church of **Santa Chiara.** This 13th-century church is dedicated to St. Clare, one of the earliest and most fervent of St. Francis's followers and the founder of the order of the Poor Ladies, or Poor Clares, in imitation of the Franciscans. The church contains the body of the saint, and in the chapel of the Crucifix (on the right) is the cross that spoke to St. Francis and led him to a life of piety. A member of St. Clare's order is stationed before the cross and is heavily veiled in perpetual adoration of the image. *Open daily 8–1, 4–7.*

Walk past the church of Santa Chiara, along Via Borgo Aretino and ❶⑦ out through the walls of the gate called the **Porta Nuova.** From there, approximately 1 kilometer (.6 mile) farther on, you reach the ⑱ church of **San Damiano.** It was here that the crucifix spoke to St. Francis, saying "Vade, Francisce, et repara domum meam" ("Go, Francis, and repair my house"). It was also in this church, pleasantly situated in an olive grove, that St. Francis brought St. Clare into the religious life. The church became the first home of her order, and it, and its convent, simple and austere, give a far better idea of St. Francis and his movement than the great basilica. *Open daily 8–12:30, 2–6.*

⑲ Also on the outskirts of the town, on the plain near the train station, is the church of **Santa Maria degli Angeli.** It is a Baroque building constructed over the **Porziuncola,** a little chapel restored by St. Francis. The shrine is much venerated because it was here, in the Transito chapel, then a humble cell, that St. Francis died. *Open daily 9–1, 4–7.*

⑳ Four kilometers (2½ miles) east of Assisi is the **Hermitage of the Carceri,** a monastery set in dense woodlands on the side of Mount Subasio. In the caves on the slope of the mountain, Francis and his followers established their first home, to which he returned often during his lifetime to pray and meditate. The church and monastery retain the tranquil contemplative air St. Francis so prized. *Open daily 8 AM–sunset.*

Tour 4: Orvieto and Environs

Numbers in the margin correspond to points of interest on the Umbria and the Marches map.

Orvieto, on the western edge of Umbria, is 112 kilometers (70 miles) from Assisi and 86 kilometers (53 miles) from Perugia. The drive to Orvieto (on S3bis) is a pleasant one that cuts south through the center of the region and takes you through Todi, a lovely hill town. Todi has an extraordinary grouping of Gothic palaces and a medieval cathedral in its central Piazza del Popolo. At Todi, change to S448, which connects with the main north–south autostrada (A1).

㉑ **Orvieto,** 37 kilometers (23 miles) west of Todi, off A1, is one of Umbria's greatest cities. Its commanding, dramatic position on a great square rock is an amazing sight, dominating the countryside for miles in every direction. This natural fort was first settled by the Etruscans, but not even Orvieto's defenses could withstand the might of the Romans, who attacked, sacked, and destroyed the city in 283 BC. From that time, Orvieto has had close ties with Rome. It was solidly Guelph in the Middle Ages, and for several hundred years popes sought refuge in the city, at some times seeking protection from their enemies, at other times fleeing from the summer heat of Rome.

Orvieto's position on its rock has meant that little new building has ever been done here, giving the town an almost perfect medieval character. The jewel, the centerpiece of Orvieto, is its **Duomo,** set in the wide and airy Piazza del Duomo. The church, built to commemorate the Miracle of Bolsena, was started in 1290 and received the attention of some of the greatest architects and sculptors of the time. It was further embellished inside by great Renaissance artists. The facade is a prodigious work, covered with carvings and mosaics, the latter intricately ornamenting practically every pillar and post and also used in large representations of religious scenes (many of these were restored or redone in the 18th and 19th centuries). The bas-reliefs on the lower parts of the pillars were carved by Maitani, one of the original architects of the building, and show scenes from the Old Testament and some particularly gruesome renderings of the Last Judgment and Hell, as well as a more tranquil Paradise. (They have been covered with Plexiglas following some vandalizing in the 1960s.)

The vast interior of the cathedral is famous chiefly for the frescoes in the Cappella Nuova (the last chapel on the right, nearest the high altar). The earliest works here are above the altar and are by Fra Angelico. They show Christ in Glory and the Prophets. The major works in the chapel, however, are by Luca Signorelli and show a very graphic Last Judgment. The walls seem to be filled with muscular, writhing figures, and most critics draw a direct connection between these figures and the later Last Judgment of Michelangelo on the wall of the Sistine Chapel. Leonardo da Vinci, however, was less than impressed. He said that the figures, with their rippling muscles, reminded him of sacks "stuffed full of nuts."

Across the nave of the cathedral from the Cappella Nuova is the Cappella del Corporale. It houses the relics of the Miracle of Bolsena, the raison d'être for the Duomo. A priest in the nearby town of Bolsena suddenly found himself assailed by doubts about the transubstantiation—he could not bring himself to believe that the body of Christ was contained in the consecrated communion host. His doubts were put to rest, however, when a wafer he had just blessed suddenly started to drip blood. Drops of blood fell onto the linen covering the altar, and this cloth and the host itself are the principal relics of the miracle. They are contained in a sumptuous gold-and-enamel reliquary on the altar of this chapel and are displayed on the Feast of Corpus Christi and at Easter. *Duomo open daily 7–1, 3–sunset.*

To the right of the Duomo is the medieval **Palazzo dei Papi,** once the summer residence of popes, which contains the Archaeological Museum. *Admission free. Open May–Oct., Mon.–Sat. 9–1:30, 3–7, Sun. 9–1; Nov.–Apr., Mon.–Sat. 9–1:30, 2:30–6, Sun. 9–1.*

Time Out Orvieto is known for its wines, particularly the whites. Some of the finest wines in Umbria are produced here (Signorelli, when painting the Duomo, asked that part of his contract be paid in wine), and the rock on which the town sits is honeycombed with caves used to ferment the Trebbiano grapes that are used in making Orvieto vintages. Taking a glass of wine, therefore, at the **wine cellar** at No. 2, Piazza del Duomo, is as much a cultural experience as a refreshment stop. You'll find a good selection of sandwiches and snacks there as well.

The countryside southeast of Orvieto, heading toward the town of Narni, is rarely included in most travel itineraries—a pity, since the scenery and rustic charm of the small towns on the route make this one of the most pleasant parts of Umbria. It is also a manageable chunk of country that can be seen in a half-day's touring by car.

Drive southeast of Orvieto on S448 for 7.6 kilometers (4½ miles), then turn south onto a narrow country road that leads to the tiny

medieval hamlet of **Baschi.** South of Baschi on S205, after 20 kilome-
㉒ ters (12 miles), you'll come to **Lugnano in Teverina,** another picturesque town crowned with a beautiful Romanesque church, **Santa
Maria Assunta.** *Open daily 9–1.*

What to See and Do with Children

Several of the region's historical pageants, like the **crossbow tournament** in Gubbio (usually the last Sunday in May; contact the Gubbio
tourist agency, Piazza Oderisi 6, tel. 075/922–0693 for details) or the
Torneo della Quintana, a medieval-style joust (the first Sunday in
August) in Ascoli Piceno, are delightful for young and old alike.

The only attraction aimed directly at the younger set is **La Città
della Domenica,** a Disney-style playground in the town of Monte-
pulito, 8 kilometers (4.8 miles) west of Perugia on the secondary
road that leads to Corciano. The 500 acres of parkland contain a variety of buildings based on familiar fairy-tale themes—Snow White's
House, the Witches Wood—as well as a reptile house, a medieval
museum, an exhibit of shells from all over the world, game rooms,
and a choice of restaurants. *Tel. 075/754941. Admission: 16,500 lire
adults, 13,900 lire children 4–10. Open Mar. 21–Sept. 19, daily 9–7;
Sept. 20–Nov. 1, weekends and holidays 9–7; Nov. 2–Mar. 19 (exhibitions only), Sat. 2–7, Sun. 10–7.*

Off the Beaten Track

The area east of Umbria, known as the **Valnerina,** is the most beautiful of central Italy's many well-kept secrets. The roads that serve
the rugged landscape are poor, but a drive through the region, even
with all those time-consuming twists and turns, will be worth it to
see forgotten medieval villages and dramatic mountain scenery. The
first stop should be the **waterfalls at Marmore,** the highest falls in
Europe. You'll find them a few miles east of Terni, on the road to
Lake Piediluco and Rieti. The waters are diverted on weekdays to
provide hydroelectric power for the town of Terni, so check with the
tourist office (Viale C. Battisti 7/a, tel. 0744/43047) in Terni before
heading there. On summer evenings, when the falls are in full spate,
the cascading water is floodlit—and a delightful sight.

Close to the picturesque town of Ferentillo (northeast of Terni on
S209) is the outstanding 8th-century abbey of **San Pietro in Valle.**
There are fine frescoes in the nave of the church, and the cloister is
graceful and peaceful. As a bonus, one of the abbey outbuildings
houses a fine restaurant with moderate prices.

Farther east are the towns of **Norcia** and **Cascia;** Norcia is the most
famous town for Umbrian food specialties. It is also the birthplace of
St. Benedict. Cascia is the birthplace of the uncrowned patron saint
of Italian women, St. Rita.

Shopping

Pottery and wine are the two most famous Umbrian exports, and examples of both commodities are excellent and unique to the region.

Gubbio, Perugia, and **Assisi** all produce ceramics, but those with the
most flair are found in **Deruta,** south of Torgiano on S3bis. The red
glazes of Gubbio pottery have been famous since medieval times.
The secret of the original glaze died with its inventor some 500 years

ago, but there are contemporary potters who produce a fair facsimile.

Perugia is a well-to-do town, and judging by the array of expensive shops on Corso Vannucci, the Perugians are not afraid to part with their money. The main streets of the town are lined with clothing shops selling the best-known Italian designers, either in luxurious boutiques or shops—such as Gucci, Ferragamo, Armani, and Fendi—run by the design firms themselves.

The best and most typical thing to buy in Perugia is, of course, some of the famous and delicious Perugina chocolate. *Cioccolato al latte* (milk chocolate) and *fondente* (dark chocolate) are available in tiny jewellike boxes or in giant gift boxes the size of serving trays. The most famous chocolates made by Perugina are the round chocolate-and-nut-filled candies called Baci (Kisses), which come wrapped in silver paper and, like fortune cookies, contain romantic sentiments or sayings.

Orvieto is a center of woodworking, particularly fine inlays and veneers. The Corso Cavour has a number of artisan shops specializing in woodwork, the best known being the studio of the Michelangeli family, which is crammed with a variety of imaginatively designed objects ranging in size from a giant *armadio* (wardrobe) to a simple wooden spoon.

Minor arts, such as embroidery and lace making, flourish in Orvieto as well. One of the best shops for lace (*merletto*) is Duranti, at Via del Duomo 10.

Excellent Orvieto wines are justly prized throughout Italy and in foreign countries. The whites are fruity, with a tart aftertaste, and are made from the region's Trebbiano grapes. Orvieto also produces its own version of the Tuscan dessert wine *vin santo*. It is darker than its Tuscan cousin and is aged five years before bottling. The Lungarotti cellars at **Torgiano** sell the winery's award-winning reds and whites.

Sports

Hiking   Magnificent scenery makes Umbria fine hiking and mountaineering country. The area around Spoleto is particularly good, and the tourist office for the town (*see* Important Addresses and Numbers in Essential Information, *above*) will supply itineraries of walks and climbs to suit all ages and levels of ability.

Swimming   Lakes Trasimeno and Piediluco offer safe and clean bathing facilities. **Castiglione del Lago,** on Lake Trasimeno, has a public beach, with no strong undercurrents or hidden depths.

Dining and Lodging

Dining   Umbria is mountainous, and the cuisine of the region is typical of mountain people everywhere. The food is hearty and straightforward, with a stick-to-the-ribs quality that sees hardworking farmers and artisans through a long day's work and helps them make the steep climb home at night. Italians are generally thought not to eat much meat, but this is untrue of Italy in general and of Umbria in particular. Novelist Anthony Burgess once observed that a beefsteak in Italy is never *"una bistecca,"* but always *"una bella bistecca"*—a beautiful steak—and a simple steak in Umbria is almost always bella.

The region has made several important contributions to Italian cuisine. Particularly prized are black truffles from the area around Spoleto (signs warning against unlicensed truffle hunting are posted at the base of the grand Ponte delle Torri) and from the hills around the tiny town of Norcia. Norcia, in fact, exports truffles to France and hosts a truffle festival every year in November. Many regional dishes are given a grating of truffle before serving; unless the truffle is a really good one, however, its subtle taste may not come through. The local pasta specialty—thick, handmade spaghetti called *ciriole* or *strengozzi*—is good *al tartufo*, with a dressing of excellent local olive oil and truffles.

In addition, Norcia's pork products—especially sausages, *salami*, and *arista*—are so famous that pork butchers throughout Italy are called *norcini*, no matter where they hail from, and pork butcher shops are called *norcinerie*.

In the Marches, fish in various forms is the thing to look for. One of the characteristic dishes in Ancona is *brodetto*, a rich fish chowder containing as many as nine types of Adriatic saltwater fish. Ascoli Piceno, inland, is famous for two dishes: *olive ascolane* (stuffed olives rolled in batter and deep fried) and *vincisgrassi* (a local version of lasagne, far richer than you're likely to find elsewhere in Italy). Ascoli Piceno is also the home of the licorice-flavored liqueur *anisette*.

Highly recommended restaurants are indicated by a star ★.

Category	Cost*
$$$$	over 85,000 lire
$$$	60,000–85,000 lire
$$	25,000–60,000 lire
$	under 25,000 lire

**per person, including first course, main course, dessert or fruit, and house wine*

Lodging Virtually every historic town in Umbria has some kind of hotel, no matter how small the place may be. In most cases a small city boasts one or two hotels in a high price category and a few smaller, basic hotels in the inexpensive-to-moderate ($–$$) range. The cheaper the hotel, the fewer the services. Most basic hotels offer breakfast, but few have restaurants or bars.

A new and popular trend is the conversion of old villas and monasteries into first-class hotels. These tend to be outside the towns, in the countryside, and the splendor of the settings often outweighs the problem of getting into town. In all cases, these country hotels are comfortable, often luxurious, and offer a mixture of Old World charm and modern convenience.

Reservations at any hotel are recommended, and traveling in high season to Perugia, Assisi, Spoleto, Todi, or Orvieto without advance bookings is a chancy proposition.

Highly recommended hotels are indicated by a star ★ .

Category	Cost*
$$$$	over 300,000 lire
$$$	160,000–300,000 lire
$$	100,000–160,000 lire
$	under 100,000 lire

All prices are for a standard double room for two, including tax, service, and breakfast.

Ancona
Dining

La Moretta. This family-run trattoria is located on the central Piazza del Plebiscito. In summer there is dining outside in the square, which has a fine view of the Baroque church of San Domenico. Among the specialties of La Moretta are *tagliatelle in salsa di ostriche* (pasta in an oyster sauce) and the famous brodetto fish stew. *Piazza del Plebiscito 52, tel. 071/202317. Reservations advised. Dress: casual. AE, DC, MC, V. Closed Sun., and Aug. 10–15, Dec. 26–Jan. 10. $$*

Lodging

Grand Hotel Palace. In the center of town, near the entrance to the port of Ancona, and widely held to be the best in town, this is an old-fashioned place well run by a courteous staff. *Lungomare Vanvitelli 24, tel. 071/201813, fax 071/207–4832. 41 rooms with bath. Facilities: restaurant, bar, garage. AE, DC, MC, V. $$$*

Hotel Roma e Pace. The only two reasons to stay in this hotel are the location and price. The rooms are ugly and cramped, and those facing the street are noisy (choose inward-facing ones). A historical note: In 1907 a Russian named Josef Dzhugashvili applied for a job here and was refused. He later found better-paying employment as supreme head of the Soviet Union under the name Stalin. *Via Leopardi 1, tel. 071/202007, fax 071/207–4736. 73 rooms with bath or shower. Facilities: restaurant, bar. AE, DC, MC, V. $$*

Ascoli Piceno
Dining
★

Ristorante Tornasacco. In this attractive family-run restaurant with rustic decor and vaulted brick ceilings, you can sample Ascoli's specialties, like *vincisgrassi* (pasta al forno in meat sauce) and *olive ascolane* (green olives stuffed with minced meat), as well as *maccheroncini alla contadina* (a homemade pasta in a thick meat sauce). *Piazza del Popolo 36, tel. 0736/254151. Dress: casual. Closed Fri. and June 15–30. AE, DC, MC, V. $$*

Lodging

Cantina dell'Arte. This newly renovated hotel is one of the few lodgings in the center of the Old Town. Although the service can be sloppy, the rooms are clean and well equipped with TV and telephone, representing excellent value for the money. There is a boisterous and inexpensive restaurant run by the same management across the road. *Rua della Lupa 8, tel. 0736/255744. 11 rooms with shower. No credit cards. $*

Assisi
Dining

Buca di San Francesco. This central restaurant is Assisi's busiest and most popular. The setting is lovely no matter what the season. In summer you dine outside in a cool green garden; in winter, in the cozy cellars of the restaurant. The food is first-rate, and the *filetto al rubesco* (fillet steak cooked in a hearty red wine) is the specialty of the house. *Via Brizi 1, tel. 075/812204. Reservations advised in high season (June–Sept.). Dress: casual. AE, DC, MC, V. Closed Mon. and July. $$*

La Fortezza. Parts of the walls of this modern restaurant were built by the Romans. The service is personable, and the kitchen reliable. A particular standout is *coniglio in salsa di asparagi* (rabbit in asparagus sauce). La Fortezza also has seven simple but clean guest rooms available. *Vicolo della Fortezza 19/b, tel. 075/812418. Reservations advised in high season. Dress: casual. AE, DC, MC, V. Closed Thurs. (except Aug.–Sept.), Feb. $$*

La Stalla. Just outside the town proper, this one-time stable has been turned into a simple and rustic restaurant. In summer, lunch and dinner are served outside under a delightful trellis shaded with vines and flowers. In keeping with the decor, the food is hearty country cooking. *Via Eremo delle Carceri 8, tel. 075/812317. Reservations advised in high season. Dress: casual. No credit cards. Closed Mon. $$*

Lodging **Hotel Subasio.** This hotel, close to the basilica of St. Francis, has counted Marlene Dietrich and Charlie Chaplin among its guests. It is housed in a converted monastery and has plenty of atmosphere. Some of the rooms remain a little monastic, but the views, comfortable old-fashioned sitting rooms, flowered terraces, and lovely garden more than make up for the simplicity. Ask for a room with a view of the valley. *Via Frate Elia 2, tel. 075/812206, fax 075/816691. 65 rooms with bath or shower. Facilities: garden, restaurant, bar, conference/reception rooms, baby-sitting, garage. AE, DC, MC, V. $$$*

★ **Hotel Umbra.** A 16th-century town house is home to this hotel, which is located in a tranquil part of the city, an area closed to traffic, near Piazza del Comune. The rooms are arranged as small apartments, with a tiny living room and terrace. *Via degli Archi 6, tel. 075/812240, fax 075/813653. 27 rooms with bath or shower. Facilities: restaurant (closed Tues.), bar. AE, DC, MC, V. Closed mid-Jan.–mid-Mar. $$*

San Francesco. This is a centrally located hotel in a renovated 16th-century building. Some of the rooms have a view of the basilica or the valley. *Via di San Francesco 48, tel. 075/812281, fax 075/816237. 45 rooms with bath or shower. Facilities: restaurant, bar. AE, DC, MC, V. $$*

Gubbio **Fornace di Mastro Giorgio.** This atmospheric restaurant is located in
Dining the medieval workshop of a famous master potter, one of Gubbio's most famous sons. The food is lighter than typical Umbrian fare, with the occasional southern dish, like *tiella barese* (a mixture of rice, mussels, and potatoes), added. *Via Mastro Giorgio 2, tel. 075/927–5740. Reservations advised in summer. Dress: casual. AE, DC, MC, V. Closed Sun. dinner and Mon. $$*

Grotta dell'Angelo. This rustic trattoria is in the lower part of the Old Town, near the main square and tourist information office. The menu features simple local specialties, including *capocollo* (a type of salami), strengozzi pasta, and *lasagna tartufate* (lasagne made with truffles). There are a few tables for outdoor dining. Inexpensive guest rooms are available here as well. *Via Gioia 47, tel. 075/927–3438. Reservations advised. Dress: casual. AE, DC, MC, V. Closed Tues. and Jan. 7–Feb. 7. $$*

Taverna del Lupo. It's one of the best restaurants in the city, as well as one of the largest—it seats 200 people and can get a bit hectic during the high season. Lasagne made in the Gubbian fashion, with ham and truffles, is the best pasta. You'll also find excellent desserts and an extensive wine cellar here. *Via G. Ansidei 21, tel. 075/927–4368. Reservations advised in high season. Dress: casual but neat. AE, DC, MC, V. Closed Mon. (except July–Aug.) and Jan. $$*

Lodging **Hotel Bosone.** Occupying the old central Palazzo Raffaelli, the Hotel Bosone has many rooms decorated with frescoes from the former palace. *Via XX Settembre 22, tel. 075/922–0688, fax 075/922–0552. 30 rooms with bath or shower. Facilities: restaurant, bar. AE, DC, MC, V. $$*

Hotel Gattapone. Right in the center of town is this hotel with wonderful views of the sea of rooftops. It is casual and family run, with good-size, modern, comfortable rooms, some with well-preserved timber-raftered ceilings. *Via Ansidei 6, tel. 075/927–2489, fax 075/ 927–1269. 13 rooms with bath or shower. AE, DC, MC, V. Closed Jan. $*

Orvieto **Le Grotte del Funaro.** This restaurant has an extraordinary location,
Dining deep in a series of caves within the volcanic rock beneath Orvieto.
★ Once you have negotiated the steep steps, typical Umbrian specialties, like tagliatelle *al vino rosso* (with red wine sauce) and grilled beef with truffles, await. Sample the fine Orvieto wines, either the whites or the lesser-known reds. *Via Ripa Serancia 41, tel. 0763/ 43276. Reservations advised. Dress: casual. AE, DC, MC, V. Closed Mon. and 2 weeks in July. $$*

★ **Maurizio.** In the heart of Orvieto, just opposite the cathedral, this warm and welcoming restaurant gets its share of tourists and has a local clientele as well. The decor is unusual, with wood sculptures by Orvieto craftsman Michelangeli. The menu offers hearty soups and homemade pastas such as *tronchetti* (a pasta roll with spinach and ricotta filling). *Via del Duomo 78, tel. 0763/41114. Reservations advised in summer. Dress: casual. AE, MC, V. Closed Tues. and 3 weeks in Jan. $$*

Lodging **Hotel La Badia.** This is one of the best-known country hotels in Umbria. The 700-year-old building, a former monastery, is set in rolling parkland that provides wonderful views of the valley and the town of Orvieto in the distance. Facilities include a swimming pool and several tennis courts. The rooms are well appointed. *Località La Badia 8, 5 km (3½ mi) south of Orvieto, tel. 0763/90359, fax 0763/92796. 26 rooms with bath or shower. Facilities: restaurant, bar, conference rooms, tennis courts, pool, garage. AE, MC, V. Closed Jan.–Feb. $$$*

Hotel Maitani. The most deluxe hotel in the town of Orvieto itself, the Hotel Maitani is also centrally located. It is set in a 17th-century Baroque palazzo with a garden and a panoramic terrace but no restaurant. The rooms are old-fashioned but comfortable. *Via Maitani 5, tel. 0763/42011, fax 0763/42011. 40 rooms with bath or shower. Facilities: air-conditioning, bar, garage, conference rooms. AE, DC, MC, V. $$$*

Villa Bellago. This recently opened hotel outside the village of Baschi, 12 kilometers (7.5 miles) south of Orvieto, is run by a New York restaurateur and his wife. In a tranquil setting on a spit of land overlooking Lake Corbara, three farmhouses have been completely overhauled to include well-lighted and spacious guest rooms, a pool, a fully equipped gym, and a fine restaurant specializing in imaginatively prepared Umbrian and Tuscan dishes, with fresh fish always on the menu. *Baschi, S448, tel. 0744/950521, fax 0744/950524. 12 rooms with bath. Facilities: pool, gym, tennis court, bar, restaurant (closed Tues.). AE, DC, MC, V. $$–$$$*

Grand Hotel Reale. The best feature of this hotel is its location in the center of Orvieto, across a square that hosts a lively market. Facing the impressive Gothic-Romanesque Palazzo del Popolo, rooms are spacious and adequately furnished, if somewhat old-fashioned. *Piazza del Popolo 25, tel. 0763/41247, fax 0763/41247. 32 rooms with bath or shower. Facilities: restaurant, bar, garage. MC, V. $$*

Virgilio. The modest Virgilio is situated right in Piazza del Duomo, and the rooms with views of the cathedral are wonderful. The rooms are small but well furnished. *Piazza del Duomo 5, tel. 0763/41882. 13 rooms with bath or shower. Facilities: bar. No credit cards. $$*

Perugia   **Il Falchetto.** Here you'll find exceptional food at reasonable prices—
Dining   making this Perugia's best restaurant bargain. The service is smart
but relaxed, and the two dining rooms are medieval, with the kitch-
en and chef on view. The house specialty is *falchetti* (homemade
gnocchi with spinach and ricotta cheese). *Via Bartolo 20, tel. 075/
573–1675. Reservations advised. Dress: casual. AE, DC, MC, V.
Closed Mon. $$*

La Rosetta. This restaurant, in the hotel of the same name, is a
peaceful, elegant place. In the winter you dine inside under medi-
eval vaults; in summer, in the cool courtyard. The cuisine is simple
but reliable and flawlessly served. *Piazza d'Italia 19, tel. 075/572–
0841. Reservations advised. Dress: casual. AE, DC, MC, V. Closed
Mon. $$*

La Taverna. Signposted next to the Teatro Pavone, off Corso
Vannucci, medieval steps lead to this rustic restaurant on two levels,
where lots of wine bottles and artful clutter heighten the tavern atmosphere. The menu features regional specialties and better-known
Italian dishes. Good choices include *chitarrini* (pasta), with either
mushrooms (*funghi*) or pricier truffles (*tartufi*), and grilled meats.
*Via delle Streghe 8, tel. 075/572–4128. Dinner reservations advised.
Dress: casual. AE, DC, MC, V. Closed Mon. and 3 weeks in Jan.,
last week in July. $$*

Lodging   **The Brufani Hotel.** The two hotels (this one and the Palace Hotel
Bellavista, below) in this 19th-century palazzo were once one. The
Brufani's public rooms and first-floor guest rooms have high ceilings
and are done in the grand style of the Belle Epoque. The second-
floor rooms are more modern, and many on both floors have a mar-
velous view of the Umbrian countryside or the city. *Piazza d'Italia
12, tel. 075/62541, fax 075/572–0210. 24 rooms with bath. Facilities:
restaurant, bar, air-conditioning, garage, 2 meeting rooms. AE,
DC, MC, V. $$$$*

★ **Locanda della Posta.** This luxuriously decorated small hotel in the
center of Perugia's historic district is a delight to behold, from its
faux-marble moldings, paneled doors, and tile bouquets in the baths
to the suede-upholstered elevator and fabric-covered walls. Archi-
tectural details of the 18th-century palazzo are beautiful, and views
of city rooftops from windows and balconies are soothing. Breakfast
is included here. *Corso Vannucci 97, tel. 075/572–8925, fax 075/572–
2413. 40 rooms with bath or shower. Facilities: breakfast room, sit-
ting room. AE, DC, MC, V. $$$*

Palace Hotel Bellavista. The rooms in this hotel are decorated in
splendid Belle Epoque grandeur, and many have a view over the
hills. The hotel's entrance is unimpressive, but the public rooms are
palatial. Weekly rates are available. *Piazza d'Italia 12, tel. 075/572–
0741, fax 075/572–9092. 81 rooms with bath or shower. Facilities:
conference facilities, bar, breakfast room. AE, DC, MC, V. $$*

Priori. On an alley leading off the main Corso Vannucci, this unpre-
tentious but elegant hotel has spacious and cheerful rooms with
modern furnishings. There is a panoramic terrace where breakfast
(included in the price) is served in summer. The hotel is difficult to
find if you're driving, but a car is an encumbrance wherever you are
in Perugia's historic center. *Via Vermiglioli 3, tel. 075/572–3378,
fax 075/572–3213. 48 rooms with bath or shower. Facilities: bar, ga-
rage. MC, V. $$*

Rosalba. This is a bright and friendly choice on the fringes of
Perugia's historic center. Rooms are scrupulously clean, and the
ones at the back enjoy a view. Although somewhat out of the way,
the hotel is only a matter of minutes from Corso Vannucci by virtue
of the nearby escalator stop, saving a good deal of legwork. Parking

is easy, too. *Via del Circo 7, tel. 075/572–8285. 11 rooms with shower. No credit cards. $*

Spoleto
Dining

Il Pentagramma. Just off the central Piazza della Libertà, this restaurant features such local dishes as *coda di bue alla spoletina* (oxtail) and *bocconcini di agnello tartufati* (lamb in a truffle sauce). *Via Martani 4, tel. 0743/223141. Reservations advised during the festival and on weekends. Dress: casual. AE, DC, MC, V. Closed Mon. $$*

Il Tartufo. Spoleto's most famous restaurant has a smart modern dining room on the second floor and a rustic dining room downstairs—both of which incorporate the ruins of a Roman villa. The traditional cooking is spiced up in summer to appeal to the cosmopolitan crowd who are attending (or performing in) the Festival of Two Worlds. As its name indicates, the restaurant specializes in dishes prepared with truffles, though there is a second menu from which you can choose items not containing this expensive delicacy. *Piazza Garibaldi 24 tel. 0743/40236. Reservations required during the festival and advised on weekends rest of year. Dress: casual but neat. AE, DC, MC, V. Closed Wed. and mid-July–1st week in Aug. $$*

Trattoria Panciolle. In the heart of Spoleto's medieval quarter, this restaurant has one of the most romantic settings you could wish for. Dining outside in summer is a delight in a small piazza filled with lime trees. Specialties include stringozzi with mushroom sauce and *agnello scottadito* (grilled lamb chops). Seven guest rooms are also available here. *Via del Duomo 3, tel. 0743/45598. Reservations advised. Dress: casual but neat. AE, MC, V. Closed Wed. $$*

Lodging

Dei Duchi. This excellent, well-run hotel is in the center of the town, near the Roman amphitheater. It's a favorite with performers in the Festival of Two Worlds. Some rooms have fine views of the city. *Viale Matteotti 4, tel. 0743/44541, fax 0743/44543. 51 rooms with bath or shower. Facilities: restaurant, bar, conference center, parking, garden. AE, DC, MC, V. $$$*

Hotel Gattapone. The tiny four-star Hotel Gattapone is situated at the top of the Old Town, near the Ponte delle Torri, and has wonderful views of the ancient bridge and the wooded slopes of Monteluco. The rooms are well furnished and tastefully decorated. *Via del Ponte 6, tel. 0743/223447, fax 0743/223448. 8 rooms with bath. Facilities: garden, bar. AE, DC, MC, V. $$$*

Nuovo Clitunno. A renovated 18th-century building houses this pleasant hotel, a five-minute walk from the town center. Bedrooms and public rooms, some with lovely timber-beamed ceilings, have a mixture of period as well as less characterful modern furniture. *Piazza Sordini 6, tel. 0743/223340, fax 0743/222663. 40 rooms with bath or shower. Facilities: restaurant, bar. AE, DC, MC, V. $$*

Urbino
Dining

La Vecchia Fornarina. These two small rooms just down from Urbino's central Piazza della Repubblica are often filled to capacity. The trattoria specializes in meaty country fare such as *coniglio in porchetta* (rabbit) and *vitello alle noci* or *ai porcini* (veal cooked with nuts or fresh mushrooms). There is also a good range of pasta dishes. *Via Mazzini 14, tel. 0722/320007. Reservations advised. Dress: casual. DC, MC, V. $$*

Lodging

Hotel San Giovanni. This hotel is located in the Old Town and is housed in a renovated medieval building. The rooms are basic, clean, and comfortable—with a wonderful view from No. 24 and No. 25—and there is a handy restaurant/pizzeria below. *Via Barocci 13, tel. 0722/2827. 33 rooms, 21 with shower. No credit cards. Closed July and Christmas week. $*

The Arts

The Festival of Two Worlds in Spoleto (mid-June–mid-July) features leading names in all branches of the arts—particularly music, opera, and theater—and draws thousands of visitors from all over the world. Tickets for all performances should be ordered in advance from the festival's box office (Via del Duomo 7, tel. 0743/220321). Information is available year-round from the festival's Rome office (Cesare Veccaria 18, tel. 06/321–0288).

There are other music festivals in Umbria throughout the year. The **Jazz Festival of Umbria** (July) and the **Festival of Sacred Music** (September) are both held in Perugia. Event and ticket information for both festivals can be obtained, year-round, from the Perugia Tourist Office (Piazza IV Novembre 3, tel. 075/572–3327).

The **Chamber Music Festival of Umbria** is held every August and September in the town of Città di Castello. For information, contact the tourist office (Via R. di Cesare 2/b, tel. 075/855–4817).

Index